new century

PUBLISHING

Dedication

This book is dedicated to my friend, Linda, who has always made me feel more accomplished and talented than I really am. Her words have lifted me up for more than a decade, helping me see that nothing is impossible. She took me under her wing and showed me how to be a strong woman, caring mother, and true friend. On the morning we left, June 3, 2005, she drove 45 minutes through rush-hour traffic to give me a hug and a funny t-shirt, and to wish me well. Now *that's* a friend.

"My children, we should love people not only with words and talk, but by our actions and true caring."

1 John 3:18

Ron & Cindy,
I hope your trip
out west was as memorable
as ours. Thank you for
your friendship.
Traci

Vicariously Yours,

letters and lessons
from the ultimate road trip

By Traci L Bray

From: Traci Bray [traci@vicariouslyyoursbooks.com]
Sent: Monday, May 30, 2005
Subject: The Beginning of the Story

When I graduated from high school, I wanted to embark on an adventure before committing to four years of college. I was young and free from the responsibilities of adulthood. Besides, I had no idea what I wanted to do with my life. What would be the point of a declared major of "Undecided"? Although I had been accepted at several schools, I was flummoxed. It didn't matter to the registration boards that I had no direction for my future...no passion or drive. Would living on their campuses, attending freshman classes, and socializing with undergrads somehow solidify my life's purpose?

My sister had joined the military when she needed focus. This idea appealed to me, but only because basic training had worked wonders on her body. The twice-daily runs, discipline-building push-ups, and abbreviated chow times would be a trade-off to my chance at becoming a sharpshooter and wearing a size four. I also loved men in uniform. However, I've never done well with authority figures yelling at me and being known as a cry-baby wouldn't inspire me to greatness. Military life wasn't for me.

I read stories of young adults backpacking across Europe and wondered if I could do that. Probably not, I thought. My family usually traveled no further than Arkansas or Illinois and I had only been on a plane once—an experience that didn't need repeating. With that in mind, I considered backpacking the Appalachian Trail...for a couple of days, anyway. Then I remembered that I hate bugs, hiking, and sleeping outside. Surely, there were better ways to find aspirations of significance.

I thought about moving to Florida where I could work as a costumed character for Walt Disney. I had had some experience playing the role of "Grumpy," one of the seven dwarfs, and felt certain that living in the heart of Disney magic would help me discover my dreams. So far, the only thing I knew I wanted was a more realistic version of Cinderella's "happily ever after." I would gladly settle for a home minus the ladies-in-waiting. Heck, I'd even whistle while I worked.

As much as I wanted to have an adventure after high school, it never happened. I accepted a scholarship to a state university and began a long sentence of pursuing a career I had no interest in. At seventeen, I was too young to do anything about it. Before I knew it, several years had passed and all desires to discover my true passion were lost. I had responsibilities now—student loans, car payments, and rent—that necessitated a full-time income. That became my purpose. It was time to grow up and do what other adults do: go to work, earn a paycheck, and pay the bills. Regardless of youthful ambition, my life had been decided for me, I thought, and all I could do was settle in and try to enjoy it.

And I did. I married a great guy, had a beautiful son, and whistled while I cooked and cleaned our suburban Indianapolis home. But after ten years of marriage, my husband, Daniel, and I were in a difficult situation. We had just moved into our dream home when a large corporation obliterated my husband's compensation plan, a dishonest businessman stole money from us, and a frivolous lawsuit meant lawyers became both the bane and salvation of our daily lives. At 34 years of age, I found myself asking, "What did I do to deserve this?" I needed to escape, so in January 2004, I asked Daniel what he thought about taking a year-long journey around the country in a motorhome. He looked at me in astonishment and said, "You'd really walk away from this house and live in a bus for a year?" Thoughts of the past raced around in my head—the adventures I *almost* experienced—but words weren't necessary. The look on my face answered his question.

Within fifteen minutes the decision was made. We still had to convince our eight-year-old son that living in a motorhome with his parents for a year would be fun. We hit the highlights of the trip—beaches, amusement parks, and natural wonders—but it was when we told him that he would be out of school for a year, homeschooled along the way, that he ran upstairs to pack his bags. So, over the course of the next few months, we began making preparations for our departure from normal life. However, one question was left unanswered: How would we buy a motorhome? Cue Oprah Winfrey.

On September 13, 2004, three friends and I sat in Oprah's studio audience, all of us giddy with excitement and anticipation. The show began and we watched in amazement as the benevolent talk show host gave away brand new Pontiac G6 sedans to a select few guests who really needed new cars. And then she did something else: Oprah announced that another car would be given away to someone in the audience and as she said this, a stream of people walked throughout the many aisles, passing out beautiful boxes with bright red bows on top. Like good girls and boys, we waited until the appropriate moment to open our gift and when my friend Kelly pulled a key out of her box, I jumped for joy, thinking she had won the car. However, I soon noticed that several other people held keys in their hands...which meant *what*? Surely they hadn't all won cars, had they? I opened my box and found my key just as Oprah began pointing and shouting, "You get a car and you get a car and you get a car!" I won a car? I've never won anything before in my life and *I won a car?* My head swam and I held onto my chair to keep myself from collapsing. My friends jumped up and down, hugging each other and people they didn't even know. I won a car? I was excited but couldn't figure out what I was going to do with this gift. I didn't need another car. I needed a motorhome or a large amount of money to buy a motorhome.

The aftermath of the *Oprah* show was unlike anything I had ever experienced. Suddenly, I was a local celebrity. Everyone wanted to know about the car. "Have you gotten the car yet?" "What color is it?" "When can I ride in the car?" "What's Oprah really like?" I had few answers to any of the questions. I was still wondering why I had won the car in the first place. I had a perfectly good car. As my husband and I prayed during the many months of planning our RV adventure, it never once occurred to me that God would use Oprah Winfrey and her car giveaway to enable us to buy our motorhome, but that was exactly what happened.

Because my friends invited me to see the *Oprah* show with them, because Oprah had chosen our audience to experience her "Wildest

Dreams" giveaway, and because I was able to use the proceeds from the sale of that car...well, my wildest dream—my dream of buying a motorhome and traveling around the country for a year—was about to come true. Wow, I never saw that one coming!

We received the "Oprah car" in December 2004 and immediately sold it. The new car had suddenly turned into the large sum of money necessary for a down payment on a motorhome. After countless trips to RV dealerships and trade shows, we settled on a new Fleetwood Expedition and, on February 20, 2005 (my 35th birthday), signed the paperwork for our new home on wheels. We couldn't wait to try it out.

Since we weren't leaving on our trip until June, we planned a few trial runs—just a weekend here and there to learn about the bus. We had been out in a rental a couple of times; however, we were still as green as could be. This was evident in our first planned outing in March when we drove to the South Bend, Indiana, KOA campground only to find that there was still snow on the ground and frozen water pipes. We never thought to ask the KOA staff about the weather or the facilities. Mental note for next trial run: ask if the water lines are operating and check to see if the temperature is above freezing. Something else we learned on that trip was that our dog—a Jack Russell/dachshund mix—was a bit high strung for RV life. We discovered this important information when Daniel stopped at Wal-Mart to pick up a couple of flashlights.

As we waited for Daniel in the parking lot, Reesey, our lively pet, noticed a frail little old lady crossing in front of the bus. Our bouncing and misbehaving dog jumped on the steering wheel, blasted the diesel horn, and scared this woman to the point of a near heart attack. When she recovered her composure and looked up into the bus to see who had honked at her, I held up the dog to show her that it wasn't me. I don't think she believed me. My son thought this was hysterical. Daniel thought this was hysterical. I thought it was reason enough to find a semi-permanent pet-sitter for the year we would be gone.

Lesson number three: Arriving at a campground after dark is not an ideal situation for an inexperienced RV driver. Daniel learned this valuable tidbit while attempting to make a right-hand turn inside the South Bend KOA. First, there was a loud crunching noise followed by the sight of a crumbling fence in the sideview mirror. Fortunately, the owners of the campground didn't care much for the fence—at least that's what I think they said in their broken English. Unfortunately, the owners of the bus—which would be us—were beside themselves about the gaping hole in the side of our brand new motorhome.

With freezing temperatures, no running water, and no television, we opted to stay just one night and then head home. "We'll do better next time," we told each other as we drove back to Indianapolis the next day. Our neighbors came over to see how the first trial run had gone and, catching sight of the bus's new exterior feature, recommended that we wait until after the next "new driver" incident to get it fixed. Good idea. My husband and I were both certain that there would be a next time. We were still novices, but we were determined to make this motorhome trip happen.

In April, we left our beloved dog with Grandma and drove to Anderson, Indiana, where we spent our second trial run weekend in the bus. Spring had come, which meant warmer temperatures, running water, and a chance to redeem ourselves as RV'ers. We still hadn't figured out what we were going to do about towing our car behind the bus for the year we would be gone, but there was still time—two months to be exact. In this campground we figured out how to hook everything up—water hose, sewer hose, power cord, cable line or "umbilical cords" as real RV'ers call them. We sure didn't feel like real RV'ers yet, but then we didn't look like them, either. Being in our thirties, we are incredibly young for the RV lifestyle, a fact that apparently signaled an unspoken invitation to the many "old-timers" there to come over and share their experiences, vital information, and sage counsel.

One piece of advice we received was to purchase a dolly in order to tow my husband's car for the entirety of our trip. A dolly? Really? I was lobbying for the ability to tow the car with a tow bar, something RV'ers call "four wheels down." Not that I had any experience with towing anything—I just thought a tow bar would be easier. What would we do with the cart once we got to a campground? How long would it take to get the car off of it and back on again?   How would I ever be able to drive the car up onto the ramps in the first place?   No, the dolly wasn't what I wanted; unfortunately, it was much less expensive than the tow bar, which meant we would be buying the two-wheeled nuisance.

During our stay at the Anderson campground there were still a few glitches and minor annoyances for each of us.   With no hot water yet in the bus, I was forced to shower in the complimentary, and yet entirely creepy, campground facilities where I challenged myself to lather, rinse, and *not* repeat in hopes of finishing in less than 60 seconds.   Our son was upset that we hadn't figured out the satellite dish yet, and he was stuck watching a lineup of only 20 cable channels instead of the usual hundred.   Poor thing.   "Don't make me tell you about the days when we had only four channels to choose from and you had to get up and walk to the television to channel surf," I said as he rolled his eyes at me.   It shouldn't surprise you to learn that a campground with such an abysmal cable lineup also didn't offer wireless internet.   Who knew camping could be so primitive?

Daniel drove his car to a nearby apartment complex where he was able to use an unsecured wireless network to connect to the internet from inside the car.   I'm not sure what vital information hanging in cyberspace couldn't wait until we got home—maybe there was an exciting auction on eBay.   After two nights in Anderson, trial run number two was over and we were only slightly closer to figuring out how to leave home and live in this bus for a year.   Slightly?   Not the best place to be when you are trying to convince yourself and everyone else in your circle of influence that you know what you're doing.   There was time, though, and two more trial runs before we would drive away from Indianapolis on June 3.   Plenty of time.   Besides, now we knew we needed to buy a dolly, right?

We bought the automobile rickshaw and towed it, without the car attached, to our local KOA for trial run number three.   It was the beginning of May—one month until our scheduled departure date from home.   We sold most of our belongings and put the rest in storage.   Our house was going on the market.   We had found a place for my car to spend the year, the dog to spend the year, and yet, we hadn't quite figured out how *we* were going to spend the year. Not only did we still have minor details to contend with, like banking and mail delivery, but we had decided against planning an exact route. Instead, we thought it would be more fun to just drive north until we chose to drive south and then we would head west until we needed to come east. It was a loose plan, one that bewildered all who heard it. But then, the trip wasn't exactly what people thought we should be doing, anyway.

With our lives heading in sort of a topsy-turvy direction, most people thought we were just plain crazy to leave our comfort zones and enter the unknown. We, however, thought it was the perfect time to leave. Not that I didn't have occasional second thoughts—and then third, fourth, and fifth thoughts—but never did I think that the trip was a bad idea. Now, if only I could take a hot shower in my soon-to-be residence on wheels. Yes, there were still "bugs" to work out and things to learn, but Daniel had no ego about picking up the phone and calling whatever "help line" necessary.

We didn't have a lot of fun during our weekend at the Indianapolis KOA because Daniel was on the phone much of the time, but we did take our first hot showers in the bus and fell asleep while watching a movie, courtesy of Direct TV. No, we hadn't traveled far from home, but we had learned much more about what life would be like living in a 38-foot bus...and we had a dolly; unfortunately, we had no idea how to use it. It was just one more minor detail to attend to in the next couple of weeks.

Trial run number four was supposed to begin at 3:00 p.m. on a Friday so we could avoid the rush hour traffic. The bus was packed and Thomas was waiting to hit the road, but we still had no idea how to use the dolly. We dragged it out of the garage and pulled it up behind the motorhome, which was blocking a good part of our street, something very much against neighborhood covenants. Daniel thought it was best for me to drive the car up on the ramps while he watched the wheels closely and yelled when it was time for me to stop. I was completely uncomfortable with this arrangement: I get nervous when I pull into the automatic car wash! I'm afraid I'll hit the person guiding me in or miss the conveyor altogether and flatten my tires on some piece of machinery. I'm not a bad driver, but I had a certain history of weird things happening to me while operating automobiles. How was I supposed to line up the front tires with ramps I couldn't see and accelerate just enough, but not too much? As I sat behind the wheel, the thought crossed my mind that I might accidentally squish my husband…and then who would drive the bus?

Thirty minutes later, Daniel was still alive and the car was in position on the dolly. The problem was that we didn't know how to make it stay there. We had been given tie-downs, but with no instructions or experience, they might as well have been chopsticks. It took more than 90 minutes and several friends and neighbors to assist us in our dilemma. Finally, at 5:30 p.m., we left the neighborhood, bound for Louisville. We didn't get far.

Just as we made it to the south side of Indianapolis, a tire blew out on the low-budget towing wonder. It was the middle of rush hour and we were sitting on the side of the interstate trying to remain optimistic while planning our next move. Daniel called the complimentary roadside assistance that came with the bus, but they were based in India (yes, India, *not* Indiana) and weren't able to find us help for at least an hour.

Thomas started complaining, which didn't help Daniel's blood pressure, so I gathered my courage, pasted a smile on my face and said, "Why don't we just unhook the car, leave the dolly on the side of the road, and I'll follow you all the way to Louisville?" Daniel soon realized it was the quickest solution. He exited the bus, carefully slid between our car and heavy traffic, and slashed the tie-downs (the ones that took a neighborhood huddle to figure out) with a steak knife and backed the car onto the shoulder of the highway.

In minutes, we were on our way. Trial run number four had started out rough, but we made it to Louisville in one piece (well, technically two, since I had to drive separately.) The campground was easy to find, easy to park in, and full of old-timers with lots of advice. Daniel shared the sad tale of our dolly with the campground operators and they chuckled before predicting that by the time we got back to Indy, it would be gone.

Stolen. *Really?* I thought (but didn't dare say), "That hadn't been my plan, but it might be for the best, you know?" Daniel lamented about what he should do; should he drive back to Indianapolis and stay with our crippled contraption? Surely he was kidding. It didn't help when one of the old-timers again said, "Oh, that dolly will be gone tonight, rest assured." Daniel was on his way out the door when the old guy added, "And, by the way, you don't want that thing anyway. What you need is a tow bar."

And do you know what? Those old guys were absolutely right. When we returned, there was no sign of our dolly anywhere. Daniel was angry. I was ecstatic. I never wanted that cursed cart in the first place and felt like this was a blessing in disguise. So, our final trial run was a mixed bag of experiences. The good news...we had a comfortable weekend in our new home away from house, and everything worked. The bad news...the solution to our towing situation was not going to be solved before we left home.

When I married my husband, I told him I'd follow him anywhere, and with no towing solution in sight, it looked like my first destination would be Ohio. And away we went...

Vicariously Yours,
Traci

Our last night in Indianapolis was terrible. With no furniture in our home, we slept in the street. Okay, so we slept in our motorhome, but it *was parked* in the street. The house was almost empty except for the last-minute items that needed to be packed in the bus—somewhere. While Thomas slept on his new sofabed, Daniel and I stayed up loading vitamins, canned goods, milk, soda, clothes, and whatever else we thought we might need. Packing for a year? Not an easy thing to do. How many pairs of socks would I really need? Which CDs should I have packed when there was only room for 20? How could I choose just eight pairs of shoes for an entire year? Should I have bothered bringing jewelry? Would we need winter coats, hats, and gloves? Surely not.

It was June 3 and I was trying to plan what I would wear every day for the next year, what music I would listen to, and whether or not I would be cold in a place I hadn't yet decided to visit. Even for a person with strong organizational and planning skills, this was quite the stretch. The pots, pans, dishes, and silverware were tucked away in the kitchen storage. The golf clubs, roller blades, pool toys, and baseball gloves were stored in the "sporting goods" section. Our Christmas ornaments were boxed and ready for use when we landed in Florida in six months. Even our luggage was stowed for a possible trip to Hawaii in the spring.

We left home on the morning of June 3 for our year-long adventure around the country and I have to admit something: I was exhausted and not quite sure this whole "living in a motorhome with my husband and child" thing was going to work for me. Not that anything bad had happened yet, but I can assure you that nothing good had happened, either.

For the next 12 months, I would be living outside of my comfort zone and it wouldn't matter what shoes I wore, what music I heard, or what food I ate because nothing would feel like home to me. Or would it? I didn't know what to expect other than a lot of the unknown. As I followed Daniel to our first destination, I couldn't even begin to imagine what this year would bring. I did know without a doubt that I was in the right place...even if I was scared, incredibly tired, and already just a little lost.

We began the trip by dropping our new home off at the dealership for some service work. We'd just go to the local amusement park and hang out for the day while we waited on the bus. What we failed to consider was the distance between the dealership, the amusement park, and our campground. Oh, and the fact that we had only slept for a few hours the night before. We walked around Kings Island like zombies, temporarily perking up after a quick ride on a roller coaster and a chocolate sundae with sprinkles. Several hours later, we checked into our first campground...our first home away from home. We could barely keep our eyes open as we plugged cords in and hooked hoses up. We were in Lebanon, Ohio, not far from home, and yet, it felt like a different world.

Two days passed and I already needed a post office. I checked the internet and was no closer to finding one, so I asked a pleasant man at the local ice cream parlor. "Yeah, it's just four blocks up the street," he said. Thomas and I canvassed a 16-block area for two hours and never did find the post office. I hoped this wasn't a sign of things to come, but figured it probably was.

The week was hot—each day more than 90 degrees—and we learned that cooling a motorhome is complicated. The campground charged a nominal fee of $2.00 per night for guests to run air conditioners, which we happily paid. We would have paid much, much more. Thomas and Daniel don't do well in extreme heat, especially with only one computer and a nine-year-old boy who couldn't understand why dad's work-related activities trumped his computer games between 9:00 a.m. and 5:00 p.m. I needed to find something for my boy and me to do. Should I have whipped out the school books already? I opted against it. No need to begin that battle until later in the summer.

"Let's go swimming," I said. Thomas moaned but gave in when I reminded him through gritted teeth how much fun we would have.

Four days into the year-long journey and I was already thinking about taking the car back to Indianapolis for a little break. My friends said I could stay with them if I needed some alone time; however, I'm sure they meant after being gone for several months, not four days. So, I stopped being a wimp, slathered on the sunscreen, and headed to the pool to hang out with other campground folks.

There was a grandfather there with his two grandkids and they could not have been friendlier. While Thomas splashed around with the boy and girl, I talked with Joe, a nice elderly man from Alabama who was missing one arm. When we returned to the bus and my husband asked me what I did that afternoon, I told him I sat and chatted with "One-armed Joe." I don't know that he would have minded the nickname; he had nicknames for everyone in his family, including the two kids playing with my son. The boy was called "'Bama" because he was born in Alabama but lived in Georgia, while the girl was called "Peach" because, yes, she was born in Georgia but currently lived with her family in Florida. Joe also told me about a granddaughter living in Atlanta whose nickname was "Poo." He didn't tell me where she was born, but with the pattern of how these nicknames were given, I silently guessed at what she was born *in*.

I spent the afternoon learning about Joe's family and they invited us to a campfire that evening. Even though it was totally out of character for me, I accepted the invitation and headed back to the bus to tell Daniel. He laughed at me...not because he didn't want to go, but because the previous night when he had accepted an invitation by a different family to roast marshmallows, I had let him know how uncomfortable I was and that I had no desire to spend my evenings wearing bug spray, eating blackened jet-puffed sugar, and talking to strangers in the dark. You do remember me saying that all of this was outside of my comfort zone, right?

So why did I accept One-armed Joe's invite? Because I realized that this trip wasn't about living inside of a zone that kept me from growing and stretching. I was going to have to push myself to become the person I knew I could be, and roasting marshmallows with strangers just seemed like a good first step. And it was. We had a wonderful evening with Joe and his family—learning about them and hearing their stories of travel around this country of ours. We also learned some pointers on how to "full-time" in our motorhome and Joe convinced Daniel that we needed to tow the car "four wheels down." I wanted to kiss that one-armed man!

So what else did we do in Lebanon, Ohio, besides become acquainted with campground etiquette? Well, we grocery shopped and I learned yet one more lesson about my new life: my favorite food outlet doesn't operate outside of Indiana. This was almost tragic. Where would we find our familiar products? I thought every grocery store carried Dannon Coffee-Flavored Yogurt, Aunt Millie's bread, and Olivio margarine. It was only Ohio and already we had to find alternative foods. What would it be like in Wyoming? Or California? And, would I really need to shop at Wal-Mart?

Daniel told me that shopping at Wal-Mart was part of the RV lifestyle. I had no idea that the ubiquitous discount retailer not only catered to RV'ers but welcomed overnight parking—something called "boon-docking." Although I already missed my SuperTarget with its Starbucks, well-designed layout, and plentiful cashiers, I was willing to learn how to shop at America's favorite place to save money. It would take some getting used to; the aisles were narrower and I was forced to navigate like a NASCAR driver to avoid getting "into a wall." The check-out lines were notably longer, which not only allowed extra time for me to catch up on the latest gossip in *People,* but also the most recent alien abductions and human oddities in those *other* publications. It wasn't as difficult as I thought it would be. And, I did like and appreciate the warm welcome by a blue-vested man as I walked in the door. Yes, I could get used to that.

During our first week on the road, we visited Kings Island several times because it was comfortable, almost like home. On our last night in town, we chose to do something different and took in a show called the "School of Rock." It was cheesy, but then I didn't expect Broadway. I thought some of the performers could have been on *American Idol*: William Hung was on *American Idol*, so that wouldn't necessarily be a compliment. The show did include a full range of performers including a band, which was very good, and a few scantily clad female back-up singers who danced more provocatively than I expected at a family amusement park. I thought their "act" was more befitting a Vegas production—somewhere off, off, off the strip. Where was Spongebob Squarepants when I needed him?

No, it wasn't a glamorous start to a year of adventure, but it was *only* the beginning. And, each night of that first week, we slept with smiles on our faces and few cares in our minds. We had said we would leave everything behind *and we did it*. How many people do that—do what they say, I mean? Yes, in this little town in Ohio, not more than 150 miles from home, we started our low-stress, laid-back life. So far, so good.

Vicariously yours,
Traci

Our new campground near Columbus was nice. Not that we had much experience in rating places like this, but when compared to the other five we had visited over the past few months, this one scored very well. One amenity in particular excited me: a 24-hour laundry room with new machines. Of all the things I could have missed about home, my washer and dryer were the two that pained me the most. I didn't miss people yet. I didn't miss my dog yet. I didn't miss my gym, my church, or my house. But, my bright white and graphite Kenmore high efficiency washer and dryer duo (minus the coin slot attachment)— well, those two I longed for already. Doing laundry became a chore that I didn't like, but at least here, I could not like it 24 hours a day.

Thomas was depressed that the campground didn't have cable and was short on "satellite friendly" campsites. What that meant for him was that other than sightseeing and sleeping, he would be bored to death for the next four days. What that meant for me was that I was going to have to entertain my son or, at the very least, listen to the whining. I took him out of the bus for an afternoon excursion into the great unknown. Guess what we found? A Wal-Mart. It was time to test my new shopping ability again. With time to kill and a child to entertain, I parked the car and entered Mr. Walton's discount store.

As much as I loved the grinning greeters, I had to wonder why this store was so disorganized. I wasn't even looking for anything in particular and I couldn't find it. I started longing for my SuperTarget again where I could meander—Starbucks coffee in hand—through wide aisles, but all I could find was this neighborhood Wal-Mart where someone had spilled coffee on the floor. Thomas and I walked around for a while trying to find something to buy, but the check-out lines were so long that I decided to leave empty-handed. There was a theater down the road so we caught a movie while Daniel feverishly worked back at the bus. We searched the listings at the theater for something kid-friendly and Thomas chose *Shark Boy and Lava Girl in 3D*.

Thomas loved the movie and chattered on the way out that he couldn't wait for the sequel. I mentioned to him the possibility that the first movie might not bring in enough money to support the making of a second, to which I got "the look" and a snappy comment about my not understanding the broad appeal of the characters Shark Boy and Lava Girl. I was convinced we should have stayed at Wal-Mart where we could have watched "Only-talks-in-expletives boy" and "Hair-defies-gravity girl" making googly eyes at each other over the spinning wieners at the snack bar—in 3D.

The weekend began with a trip to COSI, the incredible science museum in Columbus. Instead of paying an entrance fee, we purchased a membership package that included both admission into *this* science museum as well as many others around the country and Canada. Five hours later, our family had seen every exhibit at least once with extra time spent in our favorites. Thomas loved the unicycle suspended on a cable hung high above the entrance so much that he rode it several times. Daniel discovered another adult who loved playing with fire and making things go "BOOM" during the "How Fireworks Work" show. I was fascinated by the Life Exhibit, or more specifically, the part showing the effects of preservatives in food over time. The display included several items, but it was the Twinkie that caught my eye. I like Twinkies. I always have. I grew up near a Hostess Bakery where my dad bought them right off the line. As I studied the display, I noticed that the Twinkie, which had been exposed to the elements for some time, still looked good. Heck, I'd eat it. But not the homemade brownie. No, it looked like something I'd avoid stepping in, if I saw it first.

I read the signs on the exhibit one by one, thinking about how preservatives maintain a "like new" appearance in foods, and a question came to mind. If we ate preservative-full food over an extended period of time, say 60 years or more, would we inherit that same "like new" quality? Now, I'm no scientist, nutritionist, or doctor, but by stuffing ourselves full of preservatives, wouldn't we by default be self-preservationists? No mortician needed. After much reflection and thought, it occurred to me that the effect of preservatives in Twinkies was very much like those of Botox and cosmetic surgery. Think Pierce Brosnan versus Michael Jackson, or Lauren Bacall versus Joan Rivers—and I think we all know who the Twinkies are.

On Sunday, we visited a local church near the campground (one chosen on the internet for its "get lost in the crowd" size), and enjoyed the service very much; however, I kept thinking how mortified my grandmother would have been had she been there. Sure, the music was loud with its drums, guitars, and amps working overtime, but that wouldn't have bothered Grandma. People were dancing and clapping in their rows; Grandma would have smiled. Had she spied the male member of the worship team leading the service while wearing a tank top which clearly revealed his hairy, and without a doubt sweaty and stinky, armpits— well, I think Grandma would have dropped to her knees and prayed that God would bless that man with sleeves before his next leadership opportunity.

A trend of contemporary, coffee-shop church services had swept through the nation, which enabled many who felt uncomfortable with formal worship to find a place "just like home." Unfortunately, with casual church came casual dress and a somewhat slippery slope where modesty and respect got pushed aside in favor of increasing tolerance and acceptance. "Come as you are" church shouldn't mean that you dress as you would for the state fair or annual family canoe trip. Church was still church, whether it took place in a grand building with stained glass windows or a rented space in a strip mall next to the bagel shop. In a society where many schools were mandating dress codes for our students in order to boost self-esteem, discipline, and test scores, we witnessed an adult worship leader wearing a tank top, cut-off shorts, and flip-flops, acting as our intercessor with God. Yes, I realize that He knows what we all look like without garments and adornment, but shouldn't we shine ourselves up a little bit before entering God's house? At the very least, shouldn't we cover our armpits?

As soon as the service concluded, the three of us made a beeline for the parking lot in hopes of avoiding any amount of incidental fellowship, something I'd never be able to do in my home church without severe social repercussions. Besides, we had a ship to see.

The city of Columbus, Ohio, was named for the famous explorer, Christopher Columbus, the man who discovered North America and in the process earned himself a national holiday, though not a day off of school as my son reminds me each October. Anchored in the Scioto River in the heart of Battelle Riverfront Park is an authentic replica of Columbus' flagship, the *Santa Maria*. People of Columbus call it authentic; experts disagree. One minor discrepancy was the exact length of the *Santa Maria* (no one really knows) and so, from Portugal to Texas you could find exact replicas ranging anywhere from 66 feet to 98 feet. In terms of replicating the size of a historical ship, wasn't "giving or taking" 30 feet quite a large discrepancy?

Regardless of this inconsistency, we boarded what the literature claimed to be "the world's most authentic, museum-quality replica." The crew was dressed in period-appropriate attire, I thought, but then my sole reference to historical sailing came from *Pirates of the Caribbean* and *Master and Commander*. I suspected that because it was a Sunday, the adult shipmates were home mowing the lawn or washing the car while the strapping teenage crew tended to the guests on board. Maybe that was why the conversation began with discussions of toilet facilities—a topic of particular interest to me. Not once in *Master and Commander* did Russell Crowe use the toilet and I wanted to know how it might be done if he had. Now maybe the teenage boys were just having fun, but they told us that the crew would step out onto a ledge on the outside of the boat, about six inches in depth and, while holding onto the side, do their toilet business. If any personal cleaning was necessary, the crew member would grab hold of a rope that had a whisk broom attached to the end and when finished with it, toss it back in the ocean where it would glide along, getting rinsed off just in time for the next user. This crude device was called the "bitter end," or so we were told.

With a crew of 40 members, the Santa Maria was lavishly equipped with four of these so-called hygienic wonders of the sea. We were told Captain Columbus never hung his hind end over the side of the ship, but instead had his own personal pot (and probably something a tad more squeezably soft than a bitter end), which had to be emptied by some unlucky cabin boy. Not even for Russell Crowe would I touch or come within sniffing distance of that chamber pot or else the contents of the pot wouldn't be the only thing heaved over the side of the ship.

We continued our tour and listened as the crew told stories of their plight on the sea. The tour ended, yet the crew never once mentioned the fate of the flagship *Santa Maria*, which involved an unfortunate grounding of the ship on Christmas Day, 1492. It was dismantled and used in the building of a fort on modern-day Haiti. Wow, while I supported the concept of reducing, reusing, and recycling, I hoped they didn't repurpose the four bitter ends into something useful for the kitchen.

Our last day in Columbus was uneventful. Daniel, a telecommunications broker, was back to work in the bus selling T-1's, DS-3's, and PRI's—which, to me, sound like robots from a George Lucas film—to his customers back in Indiana. While Daniel burned up his phone and laptop, Thomas and I drove to the Columbus Zoo where we spent the day staring at animals sweating in the 90-degree heat while they stared at us. When we arrived back at the bus after working hours, Daniel was ready to break camp and move on to Cleveland. Evidently, he had some business calls that needed attention in the morning and didn't want to spend that time driving from one city to another. What this meant to me was a long drive in the dark and our first night camping in a Wal-Mart parking lot. I said, "No problem." I figured it would be fun...and *almost* adventurous.

We left Columbus at 9:30 p.m. and began driving north. The drive should have taken just over two hours, but at midnight, we realized that we were hopelessly lost. The directions from a mapping website were straightforward and yet somehow we ended up in a very dark and unknown place. Since the two of us were driving separately, I called Daniel on his cell phone and tried to figure out what to do. We needed a place to turn around, but we were in a forest and stadium-sized parking lots were in short supply. Suddenly, Daniel saw a sign for a Visitors' Center and abruptly turned into a parking lot. When I looked up at the sign, it read, "Happy Days Welcome Center." The irony was too much.

Daniel and I looked once again at the mapping website and decided to head in a different direction, back toward the highway where we sought some help. One truck stop and 45 minutes later (at 2:00 a.m.), I caught sight of a magnificently bright Wal-Mart sign. I could have cried. It was to me at that moment more beautiful than any lighted Christmas display I had ever seen and I hoped it wasn't a "driver fatigue" mirage. We pulled in, parked, and passed out; however, when boondocking, you are never fully able to sleep because other buses and tractor trailers are pulling in, as well. So, our first experience sleeping in a parking lot was littered with the constant sound of diesel engines, truckers opening and closing their rigs, and customers yelling into weather-beaten speakers about needing "fries with that."

Why would we subject ourselves to that kind of night when there were quiet little campgrounds hidden somewhere in the woods? In our limited experience, pulling into a campground after dark wasn't a skill Daniel possessed, and besides, we felt like being a bit daring. It may not be exciting enough to become a series on the Discovery Channel, but RV'ers from around the country travel this way, so why not us?

Just after 10:00 a.m. the next morning, we pulled into our new campground and got set up once again. Daniel went straight to work, which left Thomas and me to explore a new town. We found Kent State University, Blockbuster and a grocery store with 50 kinds of yogurt. There were many things on the schedule for the week, which was fortunate, because we were going to be there for quite a while. The towing situation would be fixed so that when we left this KOA, I would be in the motorhome with my family instead of trailing behind in the car.

I wasn't sure where we were, but it was somewhere between Akron and Cleveland. The camp store had a sign advertising the events for the weekend: a chainsaw artist, balloon animal specialist, pancake breakfast, and marshmallow roast. Ah, yes, more opportunities to stretch my limits and hang out with strangers. Though the scenery hadn't changed much in the past week, I can assure you that I had. Why, just a few days ago I ridiculed Wal-Mart and last night I happily called it home.

Vicariously yours,
Traci

Have you ever driven for an hour just to eat at a specific McDonald's? I hope not, but I must confess that my week in Streetsboro began in just that way. At some point in my planning for this trip, I picked up a book called *Kids Love Ohio*, filled with an incredible wealth of kid-tested and mother-approved Buckeye activities. On Wednesday when Daniel's workday was completed, we began looking for something to do and, as I thumbed through the book, I came upon an entry for "The Most Magnificent McDonald's," featuring a grand piano, elevator and atrium. I can't explain why we opted to go. McDonald's had never been a destination back home except when Thomas was very small and the Happy Meal toys were those Inspector Gadget body parts—a genius marketing move because in order for a child to have the anatomically complete action figure, parents had to visit the burger joint on at least a half-dozen occasions. Although my husband was fine with Thomas having a "special needs" action figure, I insisted that we spend the next several weeks stopping at 10 McDonald's drive-thru windows in search of a missing arm and leg.

In Ohio, we were in search of Ronald's fast food finery when we discovered that once again we were lost—now a common occurrence for us—and in an area of Cleveland that reminded me to lock my door. Daniel stopped at another McDonald's to ask the whereabouts of its fancy-schmancy likeness and the counter person looked at him like he had just ordered a snickelfritz sandwich with cheese or, at the very least, a Big Mac plain. "This…this *is* McDonald's," he said as he motioned to the surrounding cash registers, fellow employees, and waiting food. Daniel tried to explain exactly *which* McDonald's he was looking for. "You know, the nice one—with the piano and elevator." "Yeah, that's not this one," quipped the fry guy. No kidding. Even Ray Charles would have known that. Finally, after several minutes and a short interview with each available employee, Daniel received enough information to set us on our way uptown to a neighborhood where the "golden arches" were accented by a substantial fountain, meandering walk, and two-story glass entry.

Once inside, Thomas made a beeline for the children's game center where there were Nintendo systems set up and ready to play. Though the menu and food were the same as any other McDonald's, it was nice to take the elevator up to the second floor atrium and munch our French fries while listening to the music of the grand piano. So it wasn't a "Cheeseburger in Paradise," but it was a far cry from zipping through the drive-thru in Fishers, Indiana, looking for a go-go gadget limb...with fries and a Coke.

When planning our trip through Ohio, I was very excited to visit Cleveland. I love Drew Carey and figured that if he thought Cleveland rocked, well, then I would, too. Located on the south shore of Lake Erie and a mere 60 miles from Western Pennsylvania, Cleveland was named for General Moses Cleaveland, a surveyor who in 1796 stepped onto the banks of that Great Lake and, upon taking in the incredible view of a pristine forest and nearby river teeming with life and vitality, uttered the words, "This is a perfect spot for a city—rip out all of those trees," or something to that effect. And so began the planning and dividing of the land into parcels and lots, which grew into the Village of Cleaveland, a settlement of about 150 inhabitants by 1820. Within the next decade, the Village of Cleaveland had grown enough to warrant the establishment of a local newspaper, the *Cleveland Advertiser*. Hopefully, you noticed that the spelling was changed by one letter, an "a" that was arbitrarily dropped when the editor of the paper realized his nameplate was only so big and, I suspect, thought no one would notice anyway. In time, the city became a manufacturing mecca due in large part to its proximity to ample waterways and railroads. By 1920, it was the fifth largest city in the nation and home to Standard Oil's John D. Rockefeller, or at least much of his fortune.

The home of the Indians and Browns became known as the "mistake by the lake" when it defaulted on its loans in 1978, the first major city to accomplish this since the Great Depression. Not exactly something you want to put on a license plate. Fortunately, much has been done to revitalize the image of Cleveland, including the additions of the Rock and Roll Hall of Fame, Great Lakes Science Center, Jacobs Field, and Cleveland Browns Stadium. In fact, the once disparaged town has now become the "Comeback City."

Sitting on the shore of Lake Erie, the downtown area offers a beautiful view across the water and for us, a show of sorts complete with two hot-dog jet skiers who took turns submarining their rides and nearly drowning in the process. We also found a great skate park where about 20 kids basked in the afternoon glow of the metal grinding rails and smooth, fast concrete. I stood watching these boys of all ages doing things on wheels that I could never begin to do if Tony Hawk himself coached me, and as many of them hit the concrete time and time again, I silently thanked God that Thomas limited his kick flips and ollies to video games.

Next to the Rock and Roll Hall of Fame sits the Great Lakes Science Center, a must-do for families and yes, our COSI membership paid off, with free admission. The Cleveland Zoo, located just outside of downtown and known to have the largest collection of primates in North America, was also a wonderful place to spend an afternoon. All in all, we spent three days wandering through the attractions, up and down the streets of downtown Cleveland, trying to gain an understanding of what "Clevelanders" love so much about their city. What's not to love? Doesn't everyone appreciate a good story where against all odds and media scrutiny, someone battles back from despair, humiliation, and near destruction to find themselves stronger for having done so and prouder still of what has been accomplished in spite of it all? Don't we all cheer for the person who overcomes the most difficult of circumstances?

Those who worked to revitalize and renew can now be proud of this place that welcomes visitors with beautifully designed streets, walkways, green spaces, and buildings. Museums, theaters and sports arenas offer a myriad of things to do, but it's the people of the city that make you feel right at home. So, was Drew Carey right? Does Cleveland rock? I would have to say that it does.

When not wandering the streets of Cleveland, searching for fast food, or relaxing at the campground, we were charmed by a little town just a few miles from Streetsboro called Hudson. If you have seen any movie where the neighborhoods are full of pristine, white two-story homes with black shutters, winding driveways, lush lawns, and manicured landscapes next door to red brick two-story homes with black shutters, winding driveways, lush lawns, and manicured landscapes, then you have seen Hudson, Ohio, too. Without exaggeration, this town could very well be the movie set for any number of films. I kept expecting to see Steve Martin stepping from the front door of any number of houses, briefcase in hand, hopping into his suave Saab or Volvo, but not before giving a gratuitous wave to the neighbors out watering their heirloom roses in matching Burberry garden hats and gloves. Affluence oozed from the power lines and sidewalk cracks in this picturesque hamlet complete with a central square that Rockwell himself would have found worthy of painting. On Friday night, there was an ice cream social and art fair in the square, as well as a men's chorus performance under the gazebo. If a little town called "Perfect" ever existed, this was it.

It was Father's Day weekend, our first holiday away from home, and I treated Daniel to a massage at a local spa. So, on Saturday morning, Thomas and I checked him in for 60 minutes of deep tissue kneading. With nothing to do for at least an hour, Thomas and I ambled over to the local coffee shop for a shot of caffeine and perhaps some conversation with strangers. We checked out the art fair and various shops on the square before spying a bench to sit where we could finish our drinks and people watch. It hadn't been more than a few minutes before a woman walked past us, tripped on the sidewalk, and hit the concrete. Because her hands were full, she neglected to break her fall, leaving her face to take the full force of the accident. She cursed and got up, but her face was covered in blood. Thomas, always the Scout, jumped to help gather her belongings while I tried to sit her down on the bench.

In between expletives, she apologized for being so stupid, insisting that she was fine; she had no idea how badly she was bleeding. Universal precautions aside, I tried to stop the flow with a tissue, but it was just too much, so I sent Thomas into the local restaurant for a supply of napkins and ice. Her forehead began to swell with a knot the size of a golf ball and she kept trying to pinch her nose, convinced that she just had a simple nose bleed. I pried her hands away from her face and forced her to look into my eyes as I told her that she had scraped quite a bit of skin from her forehead, nose and chin and no amount of pinching would help. Thomas returned as several passersby stopped to see about the commotion, offering assistance in the way of a 911 call, to which my red-faced friend yelled, "No!" I think she was embarrassed enough without adding to it with flashing red lights, attention-getting sirens, and a team of medics.

With the bleeding stopped and ice on her forehead, I held her motion-less while she introduced herself. She mentioned that she had been shopping with a friend who should be coming along any moment, when suddenly the friend appeared and, shaking her head said, "Now what did you do?" Surely things like this don't happen to her often, do they? Her friend took over the first aid and both ladies thanked us for the help. As we walked away, Thomas grabbed my hand and said, "Now that was something you don't see every day," and I thought to myself how odd it was that in this picture-perfect little town something so messy could happen right in front of us. Then it occurred to me that we were there to help and comfort her precisely when she needed someone. In a town that was perfect, our timing was, too.

Our second week on the road was spent at a KOA in Streetsboro, Ohio, home of the nastiest water in the Midwest. That wouldn't make a good license plate, either. The water was so bad that after a week of shower-ing and washing our clothes in it, we smelled like thru-hikers on the Appalachian Trail instead of faux-campers in a luxurious motorhome. On the upside, we no longer had leakage problems with our hose con-nections because the water rusted all of the fittings.

While here, we did touristy things in Cleveland, Hudson, and Cuyahoga National Park as well as everyday activities like grocery shopping, laundry, and fighting over the remote. It was a week of continuing to learn how to live together in a space smaller than our old family room. A handful of times during the week, we gathered around the fire pit to watch the flames dance in the night breeze…listening to the chirp of the crickets and to each other for a change.

Sitting around the campfire telling stories was an activity we all enjoyed and yet never did back home. I imagined that each destination would bring new experiences, good and bad, that could add to the breadth of tales to tell our friends and family. For example, when

Daniel and I began the process of tearing down camp and getting ready to leave, we discovered that the sewage system at our campsite was full. No wonder our site smelled like a latrine all week. The staff told us not to dump our tanks at our own site, so we had to move over to the dump station to take care of the nasty necessities. Good thing Daniel noticed the problem before he attempted to empty our tanks—imagine how messy that would have been.

After leaving the campground, we parked and slept near Akron, Ohio, in anticipation of getting the tow bar for the bus. When we left, the three of us were traveling together for the first time in our home on wheels and, as Daniel watched his car follow in tandem, I realized that it only took a month after the loss of the dolly, some advice from a one-armed man, and a few thousand dollars to make it happen. Don't you just love when things come together?

Vicariously yours,
Traci

Subject: A Smokin' Amusement Park

The drive to Sandusky was easy and I must admit that riding with Daniel and Thomas in the bus rather than following behind in the car was a pleasure. We found our campground, unhooked the car and set up camp in what must have been record time because the local mosquito population had evidently been waiting on us for their evening feast. It had been a long day and the sleep we had been running on was wholly inadequate, so after a quick dinner inside the bus, we fell into our beds and rested for the next day at Sandusky's famous amusement park, Cedar Point.

Daniel had been talking about Cedar Point for years. He couldn't wait to take Thomas there and show him the big thrill rides—Cedar Point isn't called the "Roller Coaster Capital of the World" for nothing. Finally, the day arrived when Daniel could introduce our 9-year-old to the baddest, fastest, highest collection of coasters in the country. I, too, liked thrill rides, but no amount of motion sickness medicine could have prepared me for that park.

First, it was a blistering day and, regardless of how we tried to cool off with tall, icy drinks, large ice cream cones, or soaking water rides, the heat made us miserable. Not only was it sweltering, but Cedar Point's smoking policy allowed the habit throughout most of the park and the addicted were taking full advantage. As a former smoker, I understood the necessity to take a few drags here and there to medicate the craving, but Thomas was intolerant of the toxic intrusion on his good health. So here we were at Cedar Point and it was hot and smoky. While Daniel was having the time of his life, Thomas and I were dodging cancer causing clouds and ultraviolet rays. Oh, we enjoyed a few rides, but for the most part, Cedar Point was a day for Daniel. Though Thomas was tall enough for most of the coasters, he was only nine and not quite brave enough to tackle the rides that made grown men scream. While Daniel rode everything built to cause involuntary bladder movements, we spent our time on the train, Ferris wheel, and bumper cars. That was okay with me because at 9 years old, you don't have to tame all the steel monsters in the "Roller Coaster Capital of the World."

There were things in Sandusky other than Cedar Point, but we didn't see them. Ironically, as Daniel and I were sitting down on Friday, June 24, planning our next stopping place, we realized that we were suddenly very behind schedule. Yes, I know, there was no schedule; however, we had made reservations in Niagara Falls, Ontario for June 30 and we were not going to have time to stay in Sandusky through the 26, stop in Dearborn, Michigan to see the Henry Ford thing, and do anything in Toronto. Time was too short for all of these stops, so we chose to leave Sandusky early, skip Michigan altogether and head straight to Canada.

The afternoon we pulled out of Sandusky was another 90—degree day. It was also the first time we operated the towing system without professional supervision (or even a curious old-timer) to help us if we messed up. Sweat dripped down our faces as we crouched over the car parked on the hot asphalt, trying to remember what those guys had told us at Summit Trailer. We were missing one crucial step and couldn't figure it out. Then Daniel remembered the video he had taken and we dashed back into the air conditioned bus to watch and learn. Success! Within five minutes, we were on our way to Port Huron, Michigan where we parked near the Canadian border at the Port Huron Wal-Mart.

After choosing our spot for the night, we disconnected the car, and headed off to eat and catch a movie. Luckily, the mall across the street had a theater showing *Herbie Fully Loaded*, a hit with Thomas and a two hour break from the intense heat for us. The next morning we woke up expecting to brush our teeth and wash our faces, or at the very least, use the restroom; however, there was a problem in the fresh water tank. Nearly every drop of water we had stored before leaving Sandusky was now soaking into Wal-Mart's asphalt, leaving us with the inability to take care of any personal hygiene. We threw on some clothes and headed out to a local restaurant for breakfast where we used their water to clean up—much to the chagrin of the other patrons.

The last thing we did before heading into Canada was call our family and friends to let them know we would be "unplugged" for a few days. Daniel and I had traveled to other countries, but the drive into Canada marked for us the true beginning of our year of adventure. It was the unknown, if only because of the currency exchange and their insistence on using the metric system. With smiles on our faces and excitement in our hearts, we drove across the border to meet our Northern neighbors.

Vicariously Yours,
Traci

The trip into Canada was easy. We expected a long wait at the border, but it took a short 10 minutes to answer a few questions about firearms and firewood before we were on our way. We found the campground on the north side of Toronto and couldn't believe how fabulous the facilities were. Everything looked brand new. On Monday, it was my job to exchange currency, buy postal supplies, and find a grocery store. For some reason, I was freaked out about doing daily chores in Canada. Yes, I realized that it wasn't an exotic foreign country—everyone did speak English, although with a funny accent—but I was intimidated nonetheless. In my desperation, I made Thomas go with me to run errands. I thought I'd be braver with him by my side. Not that at his age, he was a tower of strength, but having him with me did prevent my wimpy tendencies to run back to the bus and have my husband help me.

We waited in a long line at the post office and bank before making our way to the small grocery store in town. Things had gone well so far. The locals were helpful and kind and didn't laugh in my face when I asked for repeated explanations about the exchange rate and descriptions of currency. Foreign money confused me. It always had…but then I sweated through economics and math classes in high school and college. I was the girl who loved music and English. It would require more information than the people of that small Ontario town could give for me to understand Canadian currency. I gave up and decided to forget cash and utilize credit. Plastic I understood in any environment.

The market in town was an ancient IGA where we discovered that time had stopped and possibly reversed. The store was smaller than many convenience stores I had been in and the selection of products was shocking. There were two kinds of soda, one kind of bread, a few miscellaneous snack items, and a refrigerated section that rivaled the one in our motorhome. Obviously, no one in the area really shopped there, right? I had interacted with many people at the bank and post office and they all appeared to be of average weight—not starving—so I assumed they got their sustenance from somewhere else. I picked up a loaf of bread and a snack for Thomas and made my way to the checkout where I noticed a "cash only" sign. Curse my mathematically challenged brain. I asked the cashier if she would help me by taking whatever funds she needed from my stack of alien money. She obliged. I couldn't be certain, but I think she tipped herself. Oh well, it was my fault for being an inexperienced American traveler.

Another currency mishap occurred in the laundry room. I was just getting used to the idea of doing my laundry outside of my home and learning the etiquette of public laundromats when I was thrown a curveball at the Toronto KOA. I had my dirty clothes in the washing machines already dripping with soap when I discovered that the machines at this particular campground (costing $1.50/load) required one Canadian dollar coin plus two quarters. I didn't even know there was a Canadian dollar coin. My experience with coin-operated laundry machines, though somewhat limited, led me to believe that quarters were all that was necessary to wash and dry. I stood there in the laundry room, staring at two washing machines full of dirty clothes and liquid detergent, unable to figure out what to do while Thomas was tugging at me to hurry up. He had a new-found friend waiting at the pool. I didn't have the right coins. I don't know why, but I almost cried. I realize it was just laundry, but I had tried so hard to figure everything out that day, preparing for the necessities of daily life in this new place, and I blew it by two stupid coins. The obvious thing to do was drag myself into the office and exchange my Canadian quarters for two Canadian dollars, which I eventually did, but the feeling of being unprepared caused me to pause and question whether I was capable of making it on this trip. Note to self: stockpile some dollar coins. Although Americans treat them as collectibles, Canadians wash their clothes with them.

While there were many fun and interesting things to do in and around Toronto, my husband and son wanted to visit an amusement park called Canada's Wonderland. With my experience at Cedar Point, I wasn't psyched about going, but agreed if only to get hold of a big pretzel to eat. The park had a familiar feel to Kings Island which made sense because Paramount owned both properties and, though the rides were thrilling, many of them were duplicates of attractions in Cincinnati. After a couple of rides, I was done; however, Thomas and Daniel wanted more G-forces to test their stomachs' ability to keep breakfast down.

As I sat outside the entrances to various rides, I noticed that the dress policy in Canada's Wonderland was more liberal than in the Ohio park. I admit it was insanely hot, but never had I seen girls in bikinis walking around an amusement park outside of a pool area. I began thinking about these bikini-clad girls boarding the various metal and plastic rides that had to have been hotter than an active cook top and I wondered if any had suffered burns in discreet places. And then I thought about how sweaty people get in 92-degree heat, where the only thing protecting thrill riders from sitting in someone else's perspiration was fabric and I wondered if the minimally clothed ladies had considered this. My last thought about the bikini-clad girls was this...why was it that I didn't know anyone with high enough self esteem to walk around an amusement park in a bikini? I would almost be willing to pay you $100 to do it. Of course, that would be Canadian currency.

On a trip into Toronto, we came across the Ontario Science Center and checked to see if our COSI Membership was valid there. It was. Opened in 1969, it was the first of the interactive science centers in North America. The Exploratorium in San Francisco was modeled after Ontario's layout. With the addition of touch displays, it was a popular destination for tourists and locals in the 1970s; however, over time, the public began to lose interest in the old exhibits and by the '80s, many had fallen into disrepair. It wasn't until the 1990's that funding was made available for a massive rejuvenation, a project that continues to this day. In fact, 45 million dollars was raised in order to transform at least 30 percent of the public spaces inside and out.

Thomas loved the museum, especially the "Science of Roller Coasters" display, where guests had the opportunity to test their ability to fight motion sickness. One of the more extreme parts featured a ride where visitors could strap themselves onto a bicycle and, pedaling forward and backward as hard as possible, build enough momentum to complete a full-circle revolution. Thomas was too small and Daniel and I were too dazed from the other dizzying parts of the presentation. We did watch a few young men gather enough speed to make themselves go upside down several times. I had to look away. I was reeling from the tunnel with spinning walls. After three hours, many more exhibits and a quick bite to eat at the Valley Market Place, we made our way back to the car and began our drive to the next destination for the day, the CN Tower.

The CN Tower, designated by the American Society of Civil Engineers as one of the modern "Seven Wonders of the World," was built in 1976 by Canadian National and, at just over 1,815 feet, stands as the tallest building in the world. It serves as both tourist attraction and, more importantly, telecommunications hub with sky-high receptors and antenna allowing for crystal-clear communication in Toronto. The area surrounding the structure was a pleasure to stroll through with many shops, restaurants, and parks, but it was the tower that commanded attention from tourists and locals alike. We went as close to the top as we could, visiting Sky Pod, the world's highest public observation deck, at 1,465 feet in the air. Another observation area with a glass floor was located at just under 1,300 feet and this was where you could find crazy people stomping and jumping on the glass as they looked down onto the street below. Daniel wanted Thomas to lay down on the glass for a picture—something my son had no interest in doing—but he did it anyway despite his fears. Of course, Daniel practically threw himself on the floor for his own picture…thrill seeker that he is.

On our way back down the elevator to the main floors, the attendant asked us to guess the thickness of the glass panels that we had just walked, stomped, and lay on. We were shocked to learn it was a mere two and a half inches thick. Two and a half inches—and people were jumping up and down like they had just won the lottery. I think it is best they tell people that bit of trivia on the way down, don't you think? We stopped on the main floor to watch the film, *To the Top: the Movie* and play a simulated LEGO Racer game with Thomas. It was dinnertime and we were in need of a place to eat. We checked with two different staff members at the Tower and they both recommended the same place—it had to be good. And it was. Richtree's Market was a wonderful surprise of great food, selection, price, and atmosphere. The day had been long, but well worth the effort and energy to spend it tooling around such a unique city.

We left Toronto and drove to Niagara Falls, Ontario, an attraction making a list of its own: "The Seven Forgotten Natural Wonders of the World." Who could ever forget such a watery beast? We set up camp and headed out for our "discovery" drive, something we did each time we arrived at a new location in order to find the life necessities of grocery stores, Wal-Marts, banks, and post offices. We made one wrong turn and ended up driving right to the Niagara River and had to stop. I had no idea that you could drive, park and walk right up to edge of the falls. I had expected an entrance gate with an exorbitant fee or, at the very least, barricades blocking the view. I was wrong. Peering over the waist-high stone wall, I gazed at the three different water features that make up Niagara Falls and couldn't believe my good fortune. It was spectacular. We closed our eyes and let the mist fall on our faces for several minutes before remembering that we had other errands to run.

On the way back to the car, we heard many people talking about a celebration with fireworks on Canada Day, but we didn't know much more than that. We needed information. I approached a couple of strapping young "Mounties" and asked my naïve American tourist questions. The young uniformed men were gracious, filling us in on local news and trivia. Did you know that a 65-year-old man walks across a high wire between two very tall hotels by the falls twice daily? Before we left the Niagara Park that day, we looked up in the air and saw him. I was going to like this place! We had many more days at Niagara, full of much sightseeing and fun. The next day was Canada Day and when in Canada we would act as the Canadians do...but first we needed to learn exactly what it is that Canadians do.

Vicariously yours,
Traci

Have you ever had a day that was just special? One when you woke in the morning and spent each hour doing such incredible things that you knew that that day would be one of the most memorable in your life? Have you had that kind of day? You might be thinking about your wedding day or the day your children were born, but for us, it was something different. We had been on this trip for a month and we weren't yet having fun. It had been harder to adjust to this transient lifestyle than we expected. We all have had good days and bad, but for the most part, Thomas was miserable. I didn't blame him...I wasn't sure how I felt just yet about this way of living. Daniel worked a lot and we were doing far less sightseeing than I wanted. Our time in Canada had been good with the exception of experiencing limited cellular coverage, a challenge for my husband, and his telecommunications business. In spite of that, we had one of those special days—the kind that become a memory that you look forward to talking about again and again—that bring to mind nothing but pure joy.

July 1 was Canada Day, a holiday I knew nothing about and had never thought to celebrate since I am not Canadian and had no idea when the celebratory day of the country's dominion took place. We chose to make a full day of super-touristy activities, so we booked a tour on a double-decker bus and headed out of the campground at 9:30 a.m., a feat for us. Since leaving home, we had been waking closer to 10:00 a.m. every day. We were certain that the loss of sleep would be worth it.

The tour began with a drive through the Niagara Falls Park with stops at many destinations along the way, including the Floral Clock, Butterfly Conservatory, and the Botanical Gardens. Each of these stops served to verify that Canadians love their horticulture! When the Niagara Parks Commission was established in 1885, it was charged with creating a public park adjacent to the Canadian Horseshoe Falls. The need for added land maintenance and beautification required more expertise, which led to the development of an educational program and the founding of the Niagara Falls School of Horticulture. This school offered a three-year program and allowed students the incredible experience of maintaining the grounds of Niagara Park. The Botanical Gardens, located on Niagara Parkway, boasted thousands of plant and floral specimens, as well as a world famous rose garden with over 2000 prickly beauties. Not to be outdone, the Floral Clock, built in 1950, was a behemoth of an attraction at 40 feet wide and comprised somewhere between 15,000 and 20,000 plants. With the thousands upon thousands of living things needing watering, pruning, and weeding, it was a wonder the students at the School of Horticulture had time to eat and sleep.

Sure, the flowers were pretty and the butterflies were nice, but what we really wanted to see was the falls—up close and personal. The highlight for me was the *Journey Behind the Falls* tour, an expedition that began hundreds of years ago with brave souls climbing down steep embankments and over large boulders, and evolved into high-speed elevators, concrete tunnels, and biodegradable ponchos. Our tour began with an elevator trip 150 feet down through solid rock, followed by a long walk through winding tunnels ending at various observation decks. As we made our way through the tunnels, the sound of the falls became almost deafening. We reached the opening just feet away from the location where the Niagara River plummets 13 stories and realized that staying dry was not an option. We stood in awe of the power resonating from the water and couldn't imagine what it must feel like to be even closer. We were about to find out.

Our next stop was the Maid of the Mist, a tour named for the large diesel engine boats that take passengers within spitting distance of the American Falls, Bridal Veil Falls, and Horseshoe Falls, and guaranteed a thorough soaking of those brave enough to stand on the open deck. The first Maid of the Mist (*Maid of the Mist I*) launched in 1846 and was the beginning of what some claim as the longest-running tourist attraction in North America. We boarded our boat along with 597 of our closest acquaintances and, after donning our bright blue ponchos, began the slow trek toward the first of the three waterfalls that make up Niagara. American Falls was completely within the boundaries of the state of New York and was the second largest (or smallest, depending on whether you are a "half-full" or "half-empty" kind of person) water feature in the park. Because Daniel, Thomas and I chose to stand right by the rail at the bow of the boat, we got our first shower after arriving there. Next stop: Bridal Veil, the smallest of the three and the closest to the Canadian Horseshoe Falls, with only Goat Island separating the two. Goat Island was a small, uninhabited land mass that earned its name from a herd of goats kept there long ago by a pioneer named John Stedman. Although the goats were killed by a ferocious storm in 1780, the name stuck and the area now served as a prime viewing location of the natural wonder from the American side. We never made it to Goat Island, or the American side of the falls, but were told that there were many trails and observation decks available—for a prime American fee.

As we approached the Canadian Horseshoe Falls, the sheer force of the water reminded us that this was indeed the "big daddy" of Niagara's threesome. Ninety percent of the water from the river flowed over Horseshoe, leaving just 10 percent to pass over American and Bridal Veil. Throughout the first two stops at the base of the smaller falls, it was easy to stand at the rail and do our best *Titanic* imitation, but as the *Maid of the Mist V* edged ever-closer to the base of the BIG waterfall, we struggled to hold our positions. The sound was louder than any rock concert I had attended and I had to cover my ears, but it was the thick drenching mist that sent Thomas and me running for cover. Our ponchos were worthless against the effects of that much water plunging hundreds of feet in front of us, but Daniel stood his ground and took fabulous photographs in the midst of the mist. As I cowered behind the throng of fellow wet onlookers, I realized just how much this experience would forever be etched in my mind. I felt so small and insignificant in the shadow of that colossal waterfall—it was humbling and yet comforting to know that the same power that created these thunderous falls works in my life daily.

After the tour ended, we dried off at the bus, changed clothes, and drove back down toward the river for the Canada Day celebrations. There were thousands of people lining both sides of the Niagara Parkway as well as seated in the large lawn areas in anticipation of the evening festivities. Each night throughout the year at 9:00 p.m., the parks service illuminates the falls with colored lights, but this was no ordinary day. It was Canada Day—and additional merrymaking was in order.

There had been musical entertainment throughout the afternoon and evening performing on a stage in the park, but as the sun retired for the day, a large orchestra took to the platform and began playing wonderfully harmonic pieces. At precisely 10:00 p.m., fireworks began exploding over Niagara Falls to the rhythm of the symphony. The three of us shared a small piece of curb, just across the street from Horseshoe Falls, and as the show gathered momentum, goose bumps formed on my arms. The combined sounds of the roaring waterfalls, booming fireworks, and energetic orchestra created such a moving atmosphere that Daniel and I couldn't help but feel honored and blessed to share in the event. The wonder we felt as we sat there with the people gathered was something I've only experienced a few times in my life. Within seconds, all of the difficulty that we had faced getting to this destination faded away and we remembered why we left home in the first place.

Up to this point in the trip, nothing truly special had happened and we were beginning to wonder when the good stuff would come. When would we experience the joy of being free...the joy of RV'ing? Sitting side by side on the curb of the Niagara Parkway was all we needed to be convinced that this was the beginning of an incredible adventure. I realized that it was just music, fireworks, and splashing water—things that we had seen and heard before—but we had been planning this trip for so long, talking about what it might feel like to be in a place like this, and now...now we were there. Yes, as we went to bed that night, we knew that this day was one of those days...the kind that stays with you forever and ever.

We explored the town of Niagara Falls for the next few days, checking out shopping areas, tourist attractions, and local haunts, but on July 4, we drove to Niagara on the Lake, a historical town located where the Niagara River and Lake Ontario meet. The town was settled after the American Revolution by loyalists to Britain and was virtually erased during the War of 1812 when the Americans set it on fire. The drive from Niagara Falls was striking, littered with charming houses, prosperous wineries, and breathtaking water views. We saw many cars pulled off the side of the road, with people picnicking along the river, as well as cyclists and pedestrians exercising on a waterfront trail. After finding a place to park, we explored the area near the marina to see what we could find. In the distance, we saw an old fort and knew we had to tour it.

Jumping back in the car, we drove to Fort George and discovered a wonderful way to spend an afternoon in this small town. As we wandered through the fort, we learned that it was built by the British when the 1783 Treaty of Paris gave ownership of Fort Niagara, in New York, to the Americans. The stronghold housed British soldiers along with their families and was the site of many skirmishes during the War of 1812 until it was overtaken by the Americans during the Battle of Fort George in May, 1813. The tour was fascinating and the interpreters were generous with their time and knowledge; however, the musket demonstration impressed us the most. Peter, our mock British/Canadian soldier and guide during the demonstration, was gifted in both trivia and wit. For example, he said that British soldiers never retreated, they simply "advanced to the rear." Good show. We had no idea. He shared interesting and comical tidbits about a British soldier's life and told us the history of the particular musket he was about to shoot, including the beloved nickname of it...the Big Brown Bess. Instantly, Daniel and I looked at each other and knew this was the name we should give our home on wheels. You see, when we left home, many friends asked us if we had named our motorhome—similar to naming a boat—and, although we wanted to, nothing meaningful had come to mind...until now.

From that point forward, our big brown bus would be called Bessie. As Peter continued to display the proper technique for adding black powder and round shot to his weapon, he mentioned that muskets were inconsistent, meaning that they did not fire in a reliable or predictable fashion. Case in point: it took Peter four times to get his gun to fire. It was both hysterical and a little frightening. Could you imagine being a soldier of that era with advancing troops nearing your position and your weapon won't fire? That would be slightly more than frustrating, don't you think? I might even advance to the rear. The rest of his show was informative and funny and as he wrapped up, he nodded to Daniel and said, "Would you like to come to all of my demonstrations?" Daniel had laughed and slapped his knee after every joke. Evidently, our thespian appreciated the responsiveness.

We stayed until Fort George closed and headed into town to grab a quick bite to eat at a place called the Stagecoach Family Restaurant, where we enjoyed egg sandwiches served with Canadian bacon—or ham, as it's called there. As we drove back to the bus, we talked about what a phenomenal experience the day had been and we laughed again at the antics of our British soldier, Peter. Our time there was over and all that was left to do was laundry, grocery shopping, and cleaning. But first, I needed to see a particular waterfall one more time.

The border crossing back into the U.S. was uneventful; since we left our drugs, firearms, and pet moose at the campground, there wasn't much room for concern. One of the first pieces of business we needed to attend to in New York was replacing my cell phone, which Daniel lost during the Canada Day fireworks. With that in mind, and a 12-hour drive ahead of us from Buffalo, New York to Bar Harbor, Maine, we decided to overnight at the Batavia Wal-Mart. Soon after parking, we re-discovered the leak in our fresh water holding tank. After several trips to discount and home improvement stores, Daniel plugged the hole in the outlet pipe and arranged to refill our water tank at the Home Depot Garden Center. The next day, I got a new phone and we began our trip east.

I won't bore you with the details of the long drive, with the exception of a few things. We spent the next two nights at Camp Wal-Mart in Albany, New York and Waterville, Maine and learned that when the blinds were closed, a good night's sleep could be had in the middle of a parking lot. Secondly, internet mapping sites did not know where Wal-Mart was and should not be consulted ever again. Thirdly, the front bumper of the bus had nothing behind it. How do I know this? Good question. Let me set the stage for you. It was a dark and stormy night—well, it was dark, anyway. We stopped in Lowell, Massachusetts, where Daniel checked email and worked a few hours. After dinner, he felt like driving as far as Bangor, Maine, where we would camp a short hour away from our weekend destination of Bar Harbor. We got Thomas settled with his travel entertainment and set off down I-95. All was going well. We had been in four states that day— New York, Massachusetts, New Hampshire, and Maine. It was about 10:30 p.m. when Daniel and I began getting tired and eager to reach our home for the night.

There standing in the middle lane of a long, dark highway was a doe, a deer—a female deer. We looked at each other and knew we were going to hit her. Just the night before, Daniel had been reading an article in *Men's Health* about what to do when confronted by a deer in the middle of the road, and we laughed about the author's recommendations. In an instant, the suggested actions came flooding back to Daniel which provided some comfort. He slammed on the brakes, but when driving a 28,000-pound bus at approximately 62 mph while towing a dinghy (or automobile) weighing in at 4,300 pounds and trying to stop within a distance of no more than 10 feet—do you have the answer to this story problem? No, he couldn't stop in time and no, Bambi's mom didn't make it.

We were in the middle of a dark Maine highway with no cars around us and carnage on the front of the bus. I sent Daniel to investigate. Oh come on, you didn't think I would go, did you? He found no sign of the animal. She must have been thrown completely off of the road upon impact. We lost the passenger side headlight, though, and now had a rather large gaping hole in the front bumper. Wow, fiberglass shatters spectacularly when hit at a high rate of speed with a deer butt.

With only one headlight pointing five feet in front of the bumper, we pulled our wounded bus into the first Wal-Mart lot we could find and fell into bed. The next morning we continued on our way to Bar Harbor and made camp at the head of Mt. Desert Island at the KOA. Bar Harbor was stunning. The weather was not cooperative though, and we would have to leave the island before we wanted to because of meetings with RV service and insurance people. Unfortunately, the new front bumper would take a month to arrive which meant we were somewhat stuck in the New England area. I could think of worse places to be stranded for a month. We would spend the next few weeks eating clam chowder, lobster, blueberries, and whatever else happened to be a local specialty. We might also be looking for retail outlets stocking elasticized pants, too. We were in luck though—I heard L.L. Bean pants are generously sized.

Vicariously yours,
Traci

When we pulled into the Bar Harbor KOA and began to set up camp, the first thing we noticed was the size and number of local island mosquitoes. Apparently, the chickadee was getting some competition from the blood-suckers for the title of state bird. After being nearly eaten alive, we walked through a few campsites to find the beach. It didn't take long to realize that this beach was unlike any other we had ever visited: it was rocky instead of sandy. The only beach Thomas had ever seen was in San Diego a couple of years ago and this was nothing like it. It was a chilly 67 degrees, but he wanted to play in the water, if only to look for tiny sea creatures living in the rock pools. As we jumped from rock to rock, something happened that reaffirmed why we were on this trip. Thomas said, "Dad, how about you show me the finer points of skipping a rock." Daniel spent the next 20 or 30 minutes showing him, no detail being rushed. I don't know who was more excited the first time Thomas successfully skipped a stone more than twice on the water's surface. We cheered like he had scored the Superbowl's winning touchdown. Leisurely father/son moments didn't happen at home—not with three business phones ringing and email messages demanding attention. The rain began to fall and we headed back to our campsite, but those few precious minutes as Thomas learned to skip a rock on an Atlantic Ocean rocky beach were more than worth the 12-hour drive from Buffalo—and the gaping hole in our bumper.

On a drive from our campground to Wal-Mart, we passed a sign on the road that said something about a lumberjack show. We were intrigued, so we pulled over to check it out. Each night at 7:00 p.m., rain or shine, the town of Trenton, Maine, hosted The Great Maine Lumberjack Show. We found our entertainment for the evening. When we arrived just before showtime, a large crowd had already gathered in the exposed metal bleachers despite the rain. At precisely 7:00 p.m., our host for the show—who wore a red and black flannel shirt, jeans, work boots, and a ponytail—entered the stage area and yelled, "Yo Ho!" He cupped his hand behind his ear and listened as if someone was supposed to answer him. Again, he said, "Yo Ho!" This must have meant something to a few people in the audience, because a meager "Yo Ho" answered his call. After another try of getting the entire audience to say "Yo Ho," our host explained that this was the official lumberjack greeting, which would explain why we had never uttered it: we weren't lumberjacks. Further greetings were extended and then the lumberjacks and lumberjill were introduced, followed by the rules of the games. There were two teams competing that evening with three members on each, and the events included cross-cut sawing, ax throwing, log rolling, underhand chopping, speed climbing, and power sawing. Thomas was practically vibrating in his seat. Each of the events was incredible to watch and the skill of the lumberjacks and lumberjill amazed us. When we left home in June, I had no idea we would ever have the opportunity to sit among the woods of Maine and watch expert wood cutters chop, saw, and roll their way to victories in a sort of "Olympics of the Forest." Thomas got to work with one of the lumberjacks using a cross-cut saw. Not only did we see a great show full of physical prowess, regional history, and comedic bits, but we also had the chance to take home a great souvenir—a bundle of firewood chopped by a real lumberjack.

Since the weather was uncooperative near Bar Harbor, we had to wait until the following week to participate in the "must do" event in the area: a whale watch tour. We left Bangor on Friday afternoon to take an evening tour on the *Friendship V*, a large catamaran that held 200 people and traveled at a good clip. We left the harbor at 5:00 p.m. and instantly understood why they recommend bringing warm clothes. It got mighty chilly and I was relieved that we had extra jackets with us. Captain Larry sped along the route while Sasha, the naturalist on board, narrated historical facts and informative tidbits.

We stopped near an island and saw harbor porpoises, puffins, and seals. Thomas realized that viewing these animals in their natural habitat was infinitely better than any zoo exhibit he had ever seen and he was impressed. We ventured out further into the ocean and were told to watch carefully for spouts of water that would indicate whale breaths. Sasha said she would use a "clock" system for spotting the animals and then Captain Larry would drive the boat toward the sighting so we could get a closer look. As we all stood at the rail trying to see a gush of water somewhere, anywhere—Sasha yelled that there was one at 1:00. Which side of the boat was 1:00? We headed in that direction, but then remembered that Captain Larry drove toward the spot, thereby changing the clock. Within minutes Sasha called out, "Whale at 11:00." We shuffled over to the other side of the boat. I was confused. If the captain turned the boat each time nature girl called out a number, wouldn't 11:00 become 12:00? Sasha blurted, "3:00 Captain Larry!" I was getting seasick from the waves and the racing back and forth from one side of the clock to the other. Planting myself at 10:30, I waited patiently for my mammoth mammal to blow its greeting, and when I saw it, I told no one. That humpback was mine.

Another sighting was announced and then Sasha excitedly uttered something about a "terminal dive." Was that a bad thing? No, but it did mean that the star of this show was diving and wouldn't reappear for another 7-9 minutes. Within that time, the super swimmer could travel anywhere and the likelihood of seeing that one again was slim to none. Whale spotting was tedious and required too much patience—like fishing.

The hours of studying the surface of the ocean coupled with the seasickness made me hungry, so I went inside to get a snack. When I sat down, there was a woman at the next table with her head down. I thought she was asleep. To my surprise, she opened her eyes and lifted a barf bag to her mouth and heaved. Over and over again, she vomited at the table next to me in the galley. I kept thinking, wouldn't she rather do that in private? Her actions didn't bother me. I had lots of bulimic friends in college that had me hold their hair while they threw up. What repulsed me was that she was sitting in the eating area continually throwing up into an overused baggie and acting like it was nothing. I decided I didn't need a snack. It was time to leave the good ship *Friendship* and head back to my campground where people threw up in the privacy of their own coaches.

We spent several days in Bangor, the third largest city in Maine, and came to know the city well. There weren't many local attractions with the exception of a small downtown area where the Maine Discovery

Museum was located. Thomas was still young enough to appreciate a good children's museum or even a mediocre one. He would admit that he is hard to impress—he has visited the Indianapolis Children's Museum countless times—but he was willing to try to have fun. Within 30 minutes, he was bored. We left and spent a few minutes walking in the downtown area, but soon realized that to stay occupied we were going to have to leave town.

I had read something in a travel book about Old Town, Maine, a small hamlet best known for its manufacturing of canoes and kayaks, and an event called Canoe Hullabaloo. I had no idea what a "hullabaloo" was, but figured that with a name like *that*, it had to be more fun than sitting at The Pumpkin Patch in Bangor. We found the cute town and the location of all the excitement with ease. The festival celebrated the cultural heritage of the community—also known as Canoe City—by featuring the famous boats as both artwork and sports equipment. When we arrived, a crowd had gathered, which indicated to us that we needed to join them to see what was going on. It didn't take long to find out. We saw two men carrying a canoe, running down the sidewalk, climbing down the riverbank, and paddling away followed by another team and another team—all moving at an amazing pace. The crowd began to disband when someone yelled that another team was coming and we turned to see a man and woman—resembling couch potatoes instead of athletes—walking with their boat, ambling down the riverbank, and slowly paddling down the river. And that was it. The people walked away and the three of us were left standing there trying to figure out what had just happened and what all of the "hullabaloo" was.

I convinced Daniel and Thomas to let me walk around and check out the arts and crafts, but with the intense heat of the summer, even I was ready to leave within a few minutes. As we drove through another tiny community several miles away from Old Town, we almost collided with a couple of guys running down the road with their canoe. We stopped and watched them dart down the riverbank and paddle away. We waited a few minutes just in case the other teams were close behind. When no one appeared, we continued on to Bangor. I wouldn't say that we had wasted our time in Canoe City, but I would admit that choosing an activity just because the name sounds fun probably won't happen again. Although, I did hear something about a Blueberry Wing Ding sometime in August....

Spending several days in the same place got boring, but it allowed us the opportunity to live a "normal" life for a week, anyway. While in Bangor, we found a church to visit, Calvary Chapel, and were blown away by the pastor there. He was a passionate preacher and first-class singer/musician. The congregation was young and made us feel comfortable. They were, however, 100 percent Caucasian. The preacher acknowledged it one Sunday and we laughed because we had just talked about how "white" the state of Maine was. As I mentioned before, we had been living sort of a normal life in Bangor, meaning that we went to the grocery store, post office, bank, gas station, and restaurants where local residents visited and we never saw a single minority person—ever.

Why were there so many Caucasians in Maine? Heck, even the deer were white-tailed. Not that all of the white people bothered me—I am white people—but I have spent my entire life around minorities and it struck me as odd that there weren't many non-whites in the entire state. I didn't even see a black bear. What I did see, though, was a multitude of perfect landscapes just waiting to be photographed. Prolific wildlife, lush evergreen woods, charming lighthouses, and ocean views were all there waiting to share their majesty with us. And although the people of Maine may not be of color, they were colorful, offering a glimpse into a lifestyle that centered on the great outdoors instead of a cubicle or corner office. When you come to Maine, leave your dry-clean-only clothes and fancy car at home—no one has use for them here. Want to pass as a local? First, relax and then dress yourself in L.L. Bean and rent a Subaru. And while you're at it, strap an Old Town canoe to the top—I hear another hullabaloo is just around the corner.

Vicariously yours,
Traci

Our eight-night stay in Bangor was painful only because it became too familiar to us. Daniel and I discovered that as soon as we figured out the streets and locations of the bank, grocery store and post office, it was time to go. When we pulled up stakes and drove to Old Orchard Beach anticipation was high. We didn't know what we would see and do in this new place. All we cared about was that it was somewhere we hadn't been yet.

When we told the caretaker at The Pumpkin Patch (our semi-permanent home in Bangor) that we were headed for Old Orchard Beach, he looked at his wife and made a face—the scrunched up kind made after eating something far too sour. We couldn't understand why he would have such negative feelings for his sister city to the south. It was located in his home state and enticed thousands of tourists each year. I had to know what the issue was. He told us that Old Orchard was for "young people" and families. Weren't we a young family? It sounded perfect.

The drive was easy with the exception of finding our campground. It wasn't that we got lost, but Daniel couldn't remember where we were staying and there were at least a dozen RV parks within a few miles of each other. We wanted to stay in town for five days, but no property had more than two consecutive nights available and the best we could do was split our time between two different places.. Our first home was called Wild Acres. It was true to its name. The slips and roads were teeming with swimsuit-clad people speaking French. It almost felt like a different country, especially when compared to Bangor or Bar Harbor, and I began to wonder if the cute old man at The Pumpkin Patch had been right in trying to dissuade us from going there.

Thomas was thrilled and couldn't wait to play in the sand. The sun was beginning to go down, but we agreed to walk to the beach and let him at least see it before going to bed. As we turned a corner near the shore, we witnessed an unbelievable sight…the full moon coming up over the water. It was so bright that it lit up the boardwalk and buildings for miles. Daniel and Thomas took their shoes off and were wading in the water when a big wave rolled in and, before they could turn and run, they were soaked. I laughed until my stomach ached. I hoped it wouldn't be the last time on this trip that the ocean took my boys by surprise.

Hundreds of residents from Quebec escape to southern Maine each summer. As I lay on my towel, it was difficult to believe I was anywhere other than France because no one was speaking English. As I mindlessly watched my fellow sun-worshippers, I was reminded of a book, *French Women Don't Get Fat*, and wondered if the same applied to French Canadians. I hypothesized that it did because the number of svelte "le français" speaking women was entirely unfair. I also guessed that where beautiful swimsuit ladies congregated so did hairy-back men in Speedos. I've never seen a study on this, but I believe that few American men—outside of the Iron Man competition or the Olympics—would dare to wear briefs at the beach. Why was it that European men had such high self-esteem? I wouldn't encourage someone to be emotionally distressed, but sometimes a healthy dose of self-consciousness would prevent the general beach-going public from seeing things best left concealed. For example, as Daniel and Thomas dug holes in the sand and splashed in the ocean, I spied a gentleman wearing a bikini brief who looked to be performing a stress test on his swimsuit material. The only saving grace for my eyes was the oversized fanny pack covering what the fabric didn't. It was obscene.

I also saw a guy who was performing gymnastics and was thankful he wore a more modest swimsuit. He did several back hand springs, layouts, flips, and flops which were impressive. As talented as he was, he may also have been a little crazy. He performed for several groups, but as the spectators tried to walk away, he blocked their escape by doing another flip. At one point, a beefy guy looked like he was going to pummel him if he didn't leave him and his girlfriend alone. Maybe he was trying to work for tips—like a street performer—but he had nowhere to stash money. If only he had been friends with fanny pack guy.

Old Orchard Beach consisted of a seven-mile stretch of sandy oceanfront as well as a central pedestrian area based around The Pier, a boardwalk that extended into the Atlantic Ocean several hundred feet. The Pier had been in existence since 1898, but was rebuilt several times after being destroyed by natural disasters. The current structure was completed in 1980 and housed wonderful restaurants, shops, and attractions. Since Daniel and I love seafood and could eat it every day, we walked to the boardwalk to check out the evening entertainment and dining options. With a carnival atmosphere, the pedestrian area in Old Orchard offered many family-friendly activities and taste-bud-tempting edibles. I was looking for lobster, but a shack advertising fried dough caught my eye. Although I didn't eat any, I appreciated the fact that they didn't try to fancy up this diet-sabotaging snack item by calling it an elephant ear, funnel cake, or doughnut. It was just called fried dough. People were so honest in Maine. We walked along the street and found a stand with a giant fiberglass lobster on top. The long line told me one of two things: the food was excellent or this was the only place to get lobster on The Pier. Either way, I jumped in line and ordered a lobster roll (a hotdog bun stuffed with lobster meat) while Daniel chose a haddock sandwich. We inhaled our dinners. It was that good. Thomas didn't care much for the fair food, but he wanted another chance to play in the sand. He met a mother and her five-year-old son digging what looked like a lap pool and Thomas jumped in to help with the excavation. As the tide filled the hole, both boys plunged in and sank into their own beachfront hot tub.

Old Orchard Beach was quirky. Tourists didn't wear sunscreen and walked around sporting the kind of crispy red skin that won first prize in a human lobster contest. Mosquitoes were undeterred by repellant, leaving each of us with groupings of bites rivaling the largest constellations. The town also had no Coca-Cola products. This was the most tragic oddity of all. I was dumbfounded. I couldn't have a Diet Coke for 5 days and I really needed one. I would rather have third-degree burns and 1,000 mosquito bites than another 5 days without a Diet Coke. Au revoir, Old Orchard Beach.

Vicariously Yours,
Traci

We left Maine on Saturday morning and drove south to New Hampshire. Daniel and I both forgot that we didn't have campground reservations for Saturday night, so thank you, Camp Wal-Mart in Portsmouth. On the way there we passed Kittery, Maine, where there was outlet shopping along with good food and a big, shady parking lot where Daniel and Thomas could access both the internet and Direct TV. After some speed-shopping and a lobster roll, we were on our way again to Portsmouth. I don't know if Daniel and I were just getting experienced or if our intentional ignoring of internet mapping sites in favor of real paper maps was the reason, but we hadn't gotten lost in quite some time. We rolled into Wal-Mart, dropped the jacks, opened the slides, unhooked the car and went out to dinner—all in about 15 minutes.

It amazed me how peaceful a parking lot could be. Well, that was until they started the cleaning process. Did you know that Wal-Mart cleans their parking lots at about 1:00 a.m.? And, they do a thorough job. I wasn't sure how close they got to our vehicle, but it sounded like they were scrubbing asphalt just inches from our heads. It became soothing after a while—kind of like train horns and Harley Davidsons.

We skipped worship on Sunday because the only church we found in the area offered Indonesian services. Besides, we had gone the week before, so it wasn't like we were going heathen or anything. We couldn't go to our campground yet because check-in was 2:00 p.m. What did we do when we had four hours to burn? We headed to the Visitors' Center in Portsmouth where Daniel picked up piles of information along with questionable directions. This would be interesting.

We toured a Portuguese fishing boat, a tall ship called the *Gazela*. The boat was fine, but there was no tour per se, only a self-guided one which left us struggling to educate each other about the vessel. There were actual crew members there you could talk to, although none of them appeared to like people. When compared to the replica of the *Santa*

Maria in Columbus, Ohio, this ship was luxurious. There was a flush toilet with bath tissue...no bitter end in sight. That was an improvement anyone could appreciate.

Exhausting the nooks, crannies, and restroom facilities, we disembarked the sailing ship and drove through downtown Portsmouth in search of Fort Constitution. Do you remember reading about Fort George in Canada and how awesome it was? Well, keeping that in mind, Fort Constitution was nothing like that. I knew there were many forts in the United States and federal funding was lacking for preservation efforts, but come on—the only way we knew we were in the right place was because of a small sign affixed to a utility pole. That and the distressed, crumbling walls that looked old enough to be a fine blue cheese.

After finding a piece of grass to park on, we made our way over to a lovely, albeit rocky, spot on the beach where we sat and watched Thomas and two other boys skip rocks and look for crabs. It was heaven. The waves lapped near our feet, the smell of salt water was in the air, a flock of gulls chased fishing boats across the gulf of Maine....

On Monday, Daniel and I went for a brief walk where we climbed hills near our Barrington, New Hampshire campground. In the shade of the mature trees, we could tell it was going to be a sweltering day. Daniel was going to work in the bus for a few hours while I took Thomas on a paddle boat ride. I had rented the boat for an hour and was convinced this activity would be thrilling. The lake was huge and there were big rocks just under the surface that we had to avoid. There were several motor boats out that day, which only made it more difficult to propel through the choppy water. Add to this the fact that Thomas was too short for the pedals, leaving me to do the majority of the work and you can understand why I only lasted 35 minutes, can't you?

After lunch and a rest, Daniel suggested canoeing. Again we hit the lake with vigor—an hour of tranquility in our private watercraft with just the three of us; what could be better? Ten minutes into our excursion and my back was aching. I had no recollection from my last outing (in college) that paddling was hard work. We bottomed out on a large boulder in the water and I started to panic. A million childhood memories of getting overturned in a boat and being nibbled by fish came flooding back. Maybe I'm not the outdoorsy type, after all.

On Tuesday, Thomas and I took the car into Portsmouth and toured a submarine called the *U.S.S. Albacore* and visited the Seacoast Science Museum. Thomas claimed he could never live on a submarine so small...while I claimed I could never live on one that wasn't yellow. The gentleman at the ticket office had served on the vessel for some time and was a wealth of information and trivia. Finishing at the sub, we drove to the waterfront science museum. With our experiences at the large museums in Ohio and Canada, we were somewhat under-whelmed with the one in Portsmouth, with the exception of an exhibit featuring a blue lobster. Now *that* was something. Did you know that a blue lobster is extremely rare—like one in five million? This partic-ular lobster was found by a fisherman and donated to the Seacoast. My question is this: what color is it after you cook it?

Thomas and I headed outside to sit on the rocks by the ocean and this was where the day became perfect for me. My son doesn't like to sit still for more than a 30-minute cartoon unless he has a portable game system in his hand—and you know what? We sat on the rocks for 45 minutes and watched the tide come in—the water held his attention for that long. He said, "Mom, this is way better than any video game." I melted. I was happy to sit there with him and watch the water splash the rocks, make tide pools, and chase the gulls off of their perches—until I had to go to the bathroom. I held it for as long as I could, not wanting to ruin the moment, and when we left he made me promise that we would come back later to see where the water was...and we did.

A few quick observations about New Hampshire: their license plate says, "Live Free or Die." Wow, we had corn stalks on our Hoosier plates. I think our state slogan should be "Live, Eat and Die." We do have the twelfth highest number of restaurants per capita, and we are one of the fattest states in the country. Also, New Hampshire had wacky names of establishments. For example, a beauty salon called "Convertible Hair"—which brought to mind a hairstyle that wouldn't move in a strong wind—and a restaurant named "Fat Belly's." I elected to forego a visit to the salon, but we did visit Fat Belly's, where we ate burgers and bought t-shirts. There were signs along the roads that said, "Drive Courteously, It's the New Hampshire Way", and I have to say that it was absolutely true. People drove the speed limit, let other cars get in front of them, and stopped for pedestrians crossing the street. Fascinating! Sure, people in New Hampshire protect their right to carry guns, but when it came to driving, courtesy ruled.

Vicariously Yours,
Traci

Leaving New Hampshire on Wednesday afternoon, it was 90 brutal degrees hot—and although most folks have experienced these temperatures, I didn't expect it in the Northeast. It never occurred to me that it could be this hot in New Hampshire or Maine and I hoped that in Vermont, the weather would be milder. As we drove north, I could feel the temperature dropping. We stopped just inside the state line at the Visitors' Center so Daniel could check email while I ran inside to grab some brochures. When I opened the door to leave the bus, I was startled to feel the chill in the air; it couldn't have been more than 65 degrees outside. I was so excited for the crisp temperature that I grabbed a cup of fresh hot Vermont coffee inside the building.

It was raining as we pulled into the entrance of the Apple Island Resort, our home for the next few days. Daniel headed in to register while Thomas and I hung out in the bus avoiding the downpour. He popped back in the bus with a big toothy grin, which in my experience means either something very good is about to happen or just the opposite. Daniel announced that we would need to double back in order to get to our campsite because it was outside of the campground. What at first seemed like a bad thing turned into one of the loveliest experiences yet on this trip because our slip (though only containing a spigot and outlet), had a perfect view of Lake Champlain. We pulled in and set up camp just as the rain stopped and, after opening the blinds, we saw the sun breaking through the clouds, along with a beautiful rainbow. *Welcome to Vermont*, I thought. We slept with the windows open so we could hear the boats bobbing up and down at the marina—it was a very, very good sleep.

On Thursday, Thomas and I visited the Vermont Teddy Bear Factory, a company started by a father and son in their garage in 1980. They now have two factories in Vermont that ship "Bear Grams" all over the world. Thomas and I were both a little old to get excited about fuzzy-wuzzy plush toys, but it was fun to see how they were made and hear the history of the company. After watching the bears get stuffed, we stopped at the Shelburne Museum which was similar to Conner Prairie, a living history museum in Indiana, but much bigger. We toured a steam-powered ferry that was built in 1906 and used for 42 years on Lake Champlain. It was immaculate! Thomas was unimpressed though and we headed back to get Daniel so we could do the really fun thing of the day: tour Ben & Jerry's Ice Cream Factory.

Daniel and I have eaten Ben & Jerry's for 13 years, so we were thrilled about seeing the stuff made *and* getting samples. The factory was in a town called Waterbury, Vermont, and was exactly what you would expect it to be with cows greeting you at the entrance. Even the trash cans and benches had been given the Holstein treatment and were painted with the familiar black and white pattern. The tour itself was shorter than I would've liked—only 30 minutes—but the short video of the history, view into the manufacturing room, and free samples along with bits of trivia, were well worth the drive. In the sample room, they had the "skinniest" mirror I have ever seen. It must have taken off 20 pounds, which was why I wanted to buy it. No luck with that, though.

After we purchased a souvenir (New York Super Fudge Chunk for me, Triple Caramel Crunch for Daniel, and a chocolate shake for Thomas), we walked out to the "Flavor Graveyard" where they listed all of the discontinued flavors since the company began. My very favorite flavor was out there—Bovinity Divinity—and it was both sad and funny to read about its demise. Other flavors seemed destined for the graveyard: Honey Apple Raisin Chocolate Cookie for example, or Lemon Peppermint Carob Chip. I wouldn't even accept a free sample of those. When we finished our ice cream, Thomas played on the giant swing set while Daniel and I sat in Adirondack chairs and watched the sun set over the Green Mountains. After stuffing our bellies with Ben & Jerry's, we had a light dinner at a campfire, complete with roasted turkey dogs and vegetables from the farmer's market in New Hampshire. As we watched the fire burn in the granite fire ring, the moon shone on the water in Lake Champlain and we had to wonder what on Earth would ever make us want to go back home. At only two months into our 12-month adventure, it was hard to imagine.

Friday, our last day in Vermont, we drove to the harbor at Burlington where we took the ferry to Port Kent, New York. This was an experience like none other in my life—my first ride on a ferry. We maneuvered the car onto the boat and got out so we could stand by the rail for the hour-long trip across Lake Champlain. Daniel and I enjoyed the wind blowing in our hair and the slight smell of fish rising from the lake. As gulls squawked from a nearby perch, we talked about how much we loved the trip and wanted it to last forever.

After we docked in New York, we left for Lake Placid. We had been told that this was a must-see so we drove through curvy, narrow backroads to find the place where the Olympic athletes train. We bought our tickets and took the van up to the 1/2 mile start of the 1932 Olympic Bob-Run—where we rode in a wheeled sleigh, reached speeds of 70 mph and hit 4 Gs (that would be four times the force of gravity against your body, for those who don't ride coasters). We did have to sign a waiver and have a medic precisely fit helmets on our heads, but other than that it wasn't scary. Okay, it was terrifying and we couldn't believe how fast we were going and how hard our sled hit those curves. I have a new respect for the athletes who bobsled, luge, and skeleton. I thought it wasn't much of a sport—I mean come on, other than the guy who has to run and push, don't the other people just ride? Not so. There is much more to maneuvering down this hill than meets the eye. I don't know what it is that makes a great bobsledder, but surely a strong neck is one requirement. I did it once and needed a chiropractor. So much for this Olympic hopeful; maybe I'll try a summer sport.

As we traveled through several states, it amazed me the different kinds of signs we saw along the road. We had all seen the "deer crossing" signs in Indiana, but had never seen these before—*Lobster Crossing* (Maine), *Moose Crossing* (Maine and New Hampshire), *Dairy Cow Crossing* (Vermont), *Tractor Crossing* (Vermont), and believe it or not, *Athletes Training* (Lake Placid). With regard to the sign in Lake Placid, was it really a hazard? Did athletes run with such reckless abandon that cars needed to beware of their sudden presence?

In Vermont, fetching views were around every corner and curve. Everywhere we looked, there were lush green mountains surrounded by

idyllic farms with bright red barns, white houses with big front porches, and cows or sheep in the pasture. I couldn't understand why so few
people lived there. I could only guess that it was the long, harsh win-
ters. Thomas said that people didn't live there because there was nothing to do. As we drove by a cemetery on our way out of town, Daniel
noted the hundreds of crumbling grave markers and how disproportion-
ate it appeared for such a small town. Thomas quipped, "I know what
killed all of those people…boredom." I suppose he had appreciated
enough trees for a while. So, we were off to Lake George, New York,
where they had many amusements just for him and maybe some historical stuff for Daniel and some inspiring scenery for me.

Vicariously Yours,
Traci

We stopped at the Hubbardton Battlefield on the way to New York. Why, you ask? Good question. Daniel had (in two months) developed an affinity for American history—specifically Revolutionary War history—so he wanted to visit as many significant places as possible while we were "in the neighborhood." The way to the battlefield was anything but easy. We had to drive Bessie, the bus, with the car in tow up a 6-mile road called Monument Hill. Considering how difficult the drive was, we expected to be "wowed" by the noteworthy site. Hmmm...not so much.

We arrived in Rutland in the early afternoon, but discovered that Camp Wal-Mart was full. The town was having a "Sidewalk and Ethnicity Fair" and the parking lot was packed with cars, food stands, and hundreds of people. As we joined the festivities, I was baffled at the name of the event. Vermont was colorful; its people weren't. The only ethnicity was the food: tacos, gyros, Polish sausage. They did have some funky music playing and a group of people line dancing in the street and it was possible that their clothes were made in China or Turkey or Pakistan, so *technically* the fair was full of ethnicity. We left Vermont in favor of New York, a state that not only celebrates multiculturalism, it carries a torch for it.

The campground in Lake George was the largest we had stayed at and by far the nicest. There were several swimming pools, tennis courts, bocce ball courts, and bike trails, as well as theaters where they showed family movies each night and had special talent a few times a week. Thomas was swimming and heard an advertisement for the hypnosis show later that Sunday evening, and he wanted to go. I had never been to a hypnosis presentation. I thought it was a bunch of hooey, but we went. We watched a 90-minute show where a professional hypnotist led a group of about 20 people (volunteers from the audience) to act like complete goofballs—hollering like Tarzan, forgetting their first name, losing their bellybutton, dancing, crying, screaming—it was the funniest thing I had ever seen. I could not imagine being one of those people

and having 100 strangers see me act like that. There were moms dancing Britney Spears-style in front of their kids while old men thought
they were in labor and teenage spies needed to find and answer the
shoe phone in the audience. After it was all over, a kid who had been
on stage came down and sat with his mom and brother. When asked by
his mom, "So, how was it?" he answered, "I don't know, it didn't seem
to work." Really? I thought he was one of the kookiest acting people
up there. Then again, maybe he wasn't entranced—maybe it was just
adolescence.

Daniel and I celebrated our 12th anniversary on August 1 with a family bike ride down to Lake George. The bike trails in that area were fabulous and followed historical routes, with plenty of signage so you
could read about what happened along the way. It was about six miles
from our campground to the beach so we stopped to get a drink, go to
the bathroom, and play a round of mini-golf before heading back. We
didn't have our locks with us, but the bike rack was right in front of the
golf place and we thought as long as we kept watch, everything would
be fine. My bike got stolen. Daniel was beyond mad and I felt pretty
crummy myself because I loved my Marin *and* I wasn't quite sure how
I would get back to the campground. Daniel offered to ride ahead and
get the car, but I insisted walking the six miles—I figured God was trying to tell me something, like I needed to be less concerned with material possessions...or maybe I should be more concerned with them so
other people can't steal them. Either way, it was not a nice thing to
have happen on any day let alone our anniversary—but it did make
choosing a gift for me easy for Daniel.

We visited a restaurant called "The Log Jam" for our celebratory meal.
We knew there would be great food, but we had no idea there would be
entertainment, too. There was an elderly lady who stumbled to the
bathroom and berated the bartender for refusing to serve her additional
drinks. There was also a couple at the table next to us who might have
been grandfather and granddaughter, but I don't think so. I've never
seen a granddaughter wearing that kind of dress (with a visible thong)
and platform lucite shoes.

And then there was Fort William Henry where you could learn about the attack on the British/Colonials by the French/Indians, a massacre that Thomas had no interest in whatsoever, and who was I to blame him? I love history, but I have a hard time letting him watch violent cartoons, let alone see graphic depictions (although historically accurate, I'm sure) of killings and scalpings. Thomas and I kept moving throughout the fort while Daniel took his time. Not to be un-American, but Fort George in Niagara Falls, Canada was much more fun and child-friendly.

I don't know about you, but I love to watch Food Network—especially Rachel Ray, who hosts a shows called *$40 a Day*. She hails from near Lake George and did an episode where she visited a few local attractions, promoting the food. Well, I had to visit at least one of her recommendations, The Painted Pony, the country's oldest weekly rodeo. I had no idea that upstate New York was so country—and I do mean *country*: cowboy hats and boots, twangy stories put to music, and stores bursting with all things Western. We thought it would be great to experience this unique New York cowboy spirit and take in the Texas-style barbecue for dinner and then stay for the rodeo competition. On her show, Rachel just raved about the food and I was anxious to taste it.

The crowd at the barbecue was huge and the food smells were mouth-watering so we were eager to "git" some of that grub. The food was not fabulous; it was just okay. But, there was still the rodeo, right? Thomas loves cows, and part of the competition involved roping calves. This did not go over well with my son. As Thomas watched the first rider rope his calf, throw it to the ground and tie it up, his mouth dropped and his eyes welled. I felt terrible. It might as well have been a puppy out there, because he did not like the cowboys treating the calves that way. At intermission there was a children's activity called "The Boot and Shoe Race" where young ones removed their left shoe and threw it into a pile at one end of the ring. When the announcer said "Go" the kids sprinted to the mountain of footwear, found their shoe, and ran back to the starting line. I watched in amazement as one excited girl ran through a fresh cow pie and slipped that dirty sock into her shoe. Thomas didn't win the race. He didn't care. All he wanted to do

was go back to the bus and wash the rodeo dust off of his feet. I agreed.
It was time to go.

Vicariously Yours,
Traci

We made our way back to Maine in preparation for getting the front of the bus fixed and the remnants of our clash with our deer friend erased from all but our memories. The drive to Bangor was about 400 miles, so we split the trip into smaller segments, allowing Daniel to get some work done during the day. We tried the Rutland Wal-Mart again, but the parking lot was still full so we pushed on to somewhere in New Hampshire. The next morning when we woke up, I had no idea where we were. There were people milling around the bus and talking very loudly. We left the windows open because it was too costly to run the air conditioning and probably against some town ordinance, anyway. Daniel had to work a few hours before we pulled out again, which meant that Thomas and I needed to find something to do either inside the bus or within the parking lot—unhooking the car for a "look-see" around town sounded like too much work in the heat. Our choices were limited to reading, playing a game, or starting schoolwork, none of which sounded fun because the bus felt like an oven.

Looking outside, we checked for any local attractions within walking distance and a grocery store was the only real option, so we threw on some almost-clean clothes and went loitering. We didn't need anything at the store. We just didn't have anywhere else to go, and the air conditioning felt sensational. Thomas and I studied all of the fruits, vegetables, and bakery items before perusing the freezer section to get some intensive relief from the heat. We snacked on food samples and walked the aisles one by one for as long as we could before getting bored or freezer burned.

Forty-five minutes later, we were on our way to a familiar spot: the Portsmouth Wal-Mart. We had stayed there before and slept extremely well with the exception of the pre-dawn arrival of the asphalt scrubber whose job it was to not only vacuum the parking lot, but also buff it to a glassy shine. He spent 90 minutes driving his roaring machine back and forth, making certain that he didn't miss an inch of blacktop. Regardless of that minor inconvenience, we parked, unhooked the car and sped away to our favorite spot on the rocky beach where we sat for two hours watching the tide. While we climbed the rocks and chased the gulls, Daniel caught sight of a young bride and groom a short distance from us. It was such a beautiful scene—they each had their shoes off and were wading out into the shallow surf where they climbed a big rock and, against the early evening sky, had a wedding photograph taken. The bride's dress blew in the ocean breeze as her groom helped her climb down from the rocky perch and soon the couple was joined by the wedding party. It was a Friday and as I watched them smile and pose, the thought occurred to me that this was quite the way to start the perfect weekend. While Thomas skipped rocks on the beach, Daniel and I watched the happy couple, even sneaking our own photographs from time to time. We didn't know them, but the location of their wedding told much about what kind of people they were. There was no fancy church nearby and no exclusive restaurant to host the event. What we saw was a young couple dressed in simple attire standing barefoot on a rocky shore in Portsmouth, New Hampshire, with nothing more than a large reception tent full of tables, chairs, and well-wishers. It wasn't exactly a chapel in Vegas, but it was a far cry from traditional and, I thought, a promising way to begin a new life together.

The weekend was spent preparing the bus for its much-needed trip to the body shop where the front façade would be replaced along with a headlight. We were to drop our home off on Monday morning and then drive the car to Bar Harbor where we would stay at a hotel for a couple of days before picking the bus up and heading south. We had made reservations in Massachusetts and New Jersey; however, when we called the repair shop on Monday morning to confirm the appointment, we were told that our parts had not come in and it would be another week. Excuse me while I scream! At the risk of offending the good people of Bangor, Maine, the last thing I wanted was to spend another week in a town we had already done—quite thoroughly, in fact. Besides, we had reservations at a hotel in Bar Harbor and campgrounds in two different states. My flexibility and patience with the RV service industry was being tested. After stomping around the Pumpkin Patch campground for a while, I realized that the only thing left to do was cancel our previous reservations and find somewhere else in Maine to spend the week. We had been north in Maine and south in Maine, which left somewhere in the middle for us to explore.

We spent three days in Rockport and I have to say that if we had never been to the mid-coast of Maine, we would have missed what I consider the very best of what the state had to offer. As you drive south on Highway 1, quaint towns roll by at a dizzying rate—Bucksport, Lincolnville, Belfast, Camden, Rockport, Rockland, Thomaston.... These towns represented Maine so well that I felt like Bar Harbor was the Gatlinburg or Branson of this beautiful state, just tourist traps with about as much authenticity as a platinum blonde with dark brown eyebrows. Also, there were the most ideal and accessible lighthouses that we had seen.

The first one we visited was called Breakwater Lighthouse and sat at the end of a rocky wall built in the late 1800s in the shape of a trapezoid, 170 feet wide at the base and 45 feet wide at the surface. It was made out of huge pieces of granite, a material that was as plentiful in Maine as L.L. Bean clothing and Subarus, and used just as often. The pathway was over a mile long and challenging to walk across, especially at high tide when the water was just inches beneath the top of it. We had a blast sitting on the huge rocks watching the boats come in, smelling the salty sea air, and listening to the hungry birds squawk as they attacked helpless crabs. After an hour or so at Breakwater, we trekked out to Owl's Head, a peninsula with a stunning lighthouse and fabulous rocky beach, which was another thing discovered on this trip. I learned from Thomas that there are many things to do on these pebbly shores (skipping stones, hunting creatures, watching water) *and* you don't get sand in your shorts.

We ventured onto a larger peninsula that had the Atlantic Ocean on one side and a scenic river on the other. Our destination was a distant lighthouse that we had been told about, so off we went, traveling from the middle of nowhere to the remotest parts of anywhere. Along the small roads were houses that dotted the area and I wondered what these people do with their time, especially in the winter when the roads are impassable. We finally found the lighthouse and had a challenging time climbing the rocks down to the water where we stood within inches of the ocean.

On the way back, we passed a place called Tenants Harbor, a real working harbor with fishermen pulling in their catches, and a restaurant we had heard about called Cod End. There was nothing fancy about it—just a dock with a small building that had a counter and a blackboard menu of local favorites, along with picnic tables for dining al fresco—but the food we ate there was divine. While in Maine, I had eaten lots of lobster and lobster rolls, but after eating at Cod End, I swore off my crustacean friends because nothing could be as good. The return drive to the campground was long and by the time we got back, there was a message from the RV dealership. The part was in and they were ready to work on the bus. Our plans to spend the weekend at the Blueberry Wing Ding would have to wait. We rolled out of the campground in Rockport Thursday evening and sped back to Bangor where we spent the night at Camp Wal-Mart preparing for yet another scheduled appointment with the service guys.

After dropping the bus off at the shop, we drove the car to Bar Harbor where we rented a hotel room for the weekend. The only room available was in an annex building with a restaurant on the main level and a few rooms on the second floor. Our "hotel" room was disgusting—sub-standard electrical outlets, a grungy bathroom, and the strong stench of grease wafting up from the restaurant...I couldn't believe we were paying $120.00/day to stay there. I had to go to the store and buy cleaning supplies and air freshener just to get through the night. The location of the hotel was great though, only a 10-minute walk to the harbor, which we took full advantage of many times.

After checking the tide schedule, we hoofed it down to the marina to try something a little more adventurous—climbing the rocks surrounding the shore of Bar Harbor—something we discovered was great fun for all of us and good exercise. Three hours later, we had tired out and gone as far as we could along the shore. We returned later at high tide so we could see how far the water had risen and unbelievably, most of the rocks we had climbed on were completely submerged in the ocean. We also found a couple of girls (about 14 years old) in bikinis laying on a rock letting the waves crash over them, and Thomas insisted that we station ourselves where we could watch them. Daniel and I tried to get him to sit in another area, but he would not budge. He sat there for at least 20 minutes watching them. I wasn't sure if he was enjoying hearing them scream as the frigid water rushed over them or if he was hoping their swimsuits would come undone. Either way, I was astonished. He would be ten on Monday and his interest in squealing girls has already started. Yikes!

Daniel and I got up early on Sunday to watch the sun rise—which happened at 5:38 a.m. We drove up to the summit of Cadillac Mountain and found a group of no fewer than 50 people waiting for the same thing. There was an Asian couple taking pictures of each other taking pictures. There was also a family that brought their toddler who insisted on throwing rocks over the side of the mountain and screamed horrifically when told to stop. That killed the serenity for me. There were cameras on tripods and king-size zoom lenses just waiting for the big moment and I started thinking, how do you know when to leave? Do you wait until the sun has fully climbed into the sky or is it okay to leave when either boredom has set in or your behind starts hurting from the rocks you've been sitting on? It should have been romantic and awe-inspiring, but watching the sunrise surrounded by 50 strangers was weird. Unfortunately, the morning we chose to roll out of bed before dawn was overcast leaving us to ooh and aah over not so much a sunrise but a few glowing clouds. Did you know that the summit of Cadillac Mountain is the first place the sun shines in the United States between October 7 and March 6? We had hoped to catch the sunset, too, but it rained. There would be other sunsets, like Key West at Christmas. I suppose planning ahead does have its benefits, but only if you're willing to accept that sometimes the best plans are written in pencil.

Vicariously Yours,
Traci

We shouldn't have been surprised by the increased traffic congestion in Massachusetts. Maine was less populated, with the possible exception of white-tailed deer and, without opposable thumbs, they don't drive. In Bangor, someone shared a gross generalization with us that people in Massachusetts were rude. I disagreed. We found the people to be gracious despite three recent Superbowl wins.

We stayed at a campground a short 15 minutes from Plymouth, Massachusetts. Our first attraction, the *Mayflower II*—an exact replica of the Pilgrim's ship—had been given to America from the British after World War II. It was luxurious in comparison to the *Santa Maria* that we toured in Columbus, Ohio. During its voyage from England to Massachusetts, there were just over 100 passengers on board along with 30 savory crew members. The current "crew" of the ship was knowledgeable and spent a lot of time answering our questions like, "Where did they go to the bathroom?" I just needed to know things like that.

We learned they used ceramic pots which were dumped into bigger pots and, when full were pulled up from the "hold" to the deck by the crew and disposed of. No wonder the crew was savory. Could you imagine being in cramped quarters with 100 other men, women, and children and squatting over a flower pot to "go"? I just don't think I could do it. There's a saying, "The pioneers get the arrows and the settlers get the land." I now understood that the pilgrims got little more than a pot to pee in.

After the Mayflower, we walked down to Plymouth Rock. Thomas asked what the landmark was and I explained the significance, but he wasn't convinced. "So it's just a big rock?" and I said, "Yes." Wow, and to think the state of Indiana considers me qualified to homeschool my son. Upon closer inspection, the boulder was smaller than I expected and had large cracks. Was the stepping stone of our young country falling apart? I had to know, so we located a salaried mineral expert, or ranger, and asked. She had extensive information on the rock and told us that the cracks occurred when it was moved and subsequently dropped. Boy, that must have been a big "Whoops!" She also told us that once a month, during the full moon, the tide submerged the stone.

With great luck, the day we arrived in Plymouth there would be a full moon. We went back to watch the tide come in and yes, we saw Plymouth Rock slowly succumb to the ocean. It was a memorable thing to see. However, as the tide came in, so did the litter and soon the historical monument was surrounded by Styrofoam cups, cotton swabs, and used prophylactics. Shouldn't someone take care of that irreverence? At the very least, shouldn't there be a net or something next to the rock so visitors can fish out the junk—maybe take home a unique souvenir? Maybe not.

We jumped aboard a trolley to get a tour of the city and hear more trivia about the people, buildings, and monuments. Within a few minutes, we suspected our tour guide might suffer from a disorder. He couldn't finish a complete thought or sentence. Daniel and I guessed at the cause—perhaps ADHD (Attention Deficit Hyperactivity Disorder) because he not only forgot to finish his sentences, but was distracted by anything shiny. He also answered his cell phone several times during our tour which really annoyed me. It's bad enough when someone answers their phone in a restaurant or elevator, but when your guide does it during a tour that you paid a considerable amount of money for.... I'd only been in town for 24 hours and I could have been a more efficient tour operator.

Of course, it wasn't just the mentally defective narrator who made us crazy during the trolley ride. The driver was unaware that faster wasn't better when showing people around your city. While circling a particular monument, Daniel yelled, "Can you please stop so I can get a still shot?" The driver slammed on the breaks, dramatically sighed, and watched the dashboard clock while my husband and several other shutterbugs captured the moment. With Daniel still out of his seat, Speed Racer hit the accelerator and we were off again to see something else zoom past us in historic Plymouth.

I've had longer, more enlightening tours in some closets. The one positive thing that came out of the worst tour on Earth was a visit (although a quick one) past a beautiful monument. We loved it so much that we went back on our own, taking the long way around, and photographs from every angle.

Forefather's Monument, the largest solid granite monument in the world, was stunning. It was a significant tribute to the ideals of the Pilgrims: faith, law, liberty, morality, education. The statue was meant to be a twin sister of Lady Liberty; however, funding was difficult and Faith, the figure's name, was built at 1/3 the original specifications. Had it not been for thousands of individual donors, the memorial would probably still be unfinished.

On one side of the granite was an engraved manifest of all who sailed on the *Mayflower* and a statement by Governor William Bradford, who led the settlement for 33 years, that gave me chills. It said, "Thus out of small beginnings greater things have been produced by His hand that made all things of nothing and gives being to all things that are; and as one small candle may light a thousand, so the light here kindled hath shone unto many, yea in some sort to our whole nation; let the glorious name of Jehovah have all the praise." Those words were immortalized in stone for the purpose of inspiring generations of visitors and yet, few guests in Plymouth know where to find them.

What bothered me most about Forefather's Monument was its location on a hill far off the beaten path and the apparent disregard for the surrounding landscape. The ground was ugly with knee-high weeds and thinning grass. Why wasn't this landmark cared for and fussed over by a team of historical enthusiasts? Millions of dollars were invested in a living history museum called Plimoth Plantation—which showcases every bowl, spoon, and pot used by the Pilgrims—but a 50-year-old granite tribute to the very heart of the fathers and mothers of our nation, "gets no respect," as Rodney Dangerfield would say. Daniel and I sat beneath the gaze of Faith and wondered how we could fix the situation. We wish we knew.

The next day, we took the train to Boston for more excitement and history. Again, we did the trolley tour because Thomas loved riding them and it prevented too much whining over excessive walking. We ate breakfast at Fanueil Hall/Quincy Market because Rachel Ray suggested it in one of her books. Fanueil Hall was the place where Sam Adams (yes, the beer guy) stood and voiced the need to revolt against the British—big and brave words. I'm sure the beer came long after that speech, or maybe right after it. The food was incredible. It was so good that Daniel and I didn't stop eating until our plates were clean. If I had a higher metabolism, I would have sprinted back for seconds and thirds.

After breakfast, we took a harbor cruise to the *U.S.S. Constitution*, or *Old Ironsides*, the oldest commissioned warship still afloat in the world. If you saw *Master and Commander*, the swift enemy ship that confounded many seamen was fashioned after this old beauty. The producers of the film took pictures and measurements to get the ship just right. Owned and operated by the U.S. Navy, the 50-man crew took it out into the harbor while we were there to set five of the sails. After more than 200 years, the ship was in perfect condition, maintaining 15 percent of its original wood and most of the original copper produced by Paul Revere.

We walked the Freedom Trail to Bunker Hill where Thomas convinced us to climb the 294 stairs, or 22 stories, to see the top of the tower. Warning signs were posted in several places letting you know how many steps there were in the monument but I didn't grasp the feat that we were about to undertake—I mean, how hard could it be? It wasn't so much the steps that got me, but the lack of fresh air. I have claustrophobia and I had to do a lot of praying after step 100 to get myself to the top without having a conniption. To my dismay, when I got there, fresh air was non-existent. There were no open windows. I wanted to shout, "Are you kidding me?" I tried to smile through my panic, but Daniel knew I was in trouble. He took three quick pictures and lunged with me for the stairs and our only way out.

Again, I prayed the whole way down because I was close to losing control of my civility. Each time someone passed me, crowding me in the confined stairwell, I struggled to maintain my composure. By the time I reached the bottom and walked into the open air, I was shaking so much that I hit the ground. The things we do for our children, right?

Although my legs felt like noodles, I needed fresh air, so instead of jumping on the trolley, we walked the Freedom Trail. We visited the Old North Church and discovered that the scene in *National Treasure* that took place at the church could not happen in Boston because the roads were too narrow for film crews. Also, the gal working at the church said that the movie was filled with misinformation regarding historical facts. Don't film producers have the money to work on details like that? If not, I'd be happy to volunteer my services...for a fee, of course.

After leaving the Old North Church, we continued our walk along the footpath to Paul Revere's Mall (no, there's no shopping) where there was a fantastic statue of him on his horse. It was amazing to learn how important this man was in the Revolution and why he was chosen as a courier for the Sons of Liberty. The King of England had enacted the "Quartering Act", which meant colonists had to house and feed the British soldiers. Paul Revere had 16 children so no soldiers could live with him, giving him the freedom to come and go as needed. His house still stands in Boston as the oldest in the city. Hard to believe since Paul had so many children living there. They must have been very well behaved or all very handy at home repair.

We walked further on the Freedom Trail and then jumped back on the trolley to see the rest of the city. That trolley driver was a fabulous guide. He didn't stop talking the entire time we were on board and he drove as slowly as he wanted, stopping when necessary to show us something important. We loved that! He sounded like Gilbert Gottfried, though, which was unnerving. I couldn't imagine trusting the annoying comedian to drive me anywhere other than crazy. Daniel could not stop laughing as the screeching driver yelled at other motorists, calling them bums and telling them to go work for the Yankees. It was an experience unlike the one in Plymouth—that was for sure.

My calves woke me up the next morning—a reminder of the 294 steps I climbed at Bunker Hill. "Let's take a drive and do something easy," I said to Daniel. He agreed, so our last day in Massachusetts was spent driving to Cape Cod—specifically Provincetown—to see where the Pilgrims first landed. In looking at the map, Cape Cod is shaped like an arm making a muscle with a fist at the end and we needed to drive all the way to the tip of the fist to find Provincetown. We read about another Pilgrims' monument and hoped to avoid any stair climbing, but drill sergeant Thomas refused to listen to our excuses. As we entered the Visitors' Center, I was relieved to see open windows in the tower and followed my boy up to the top. With the clear sky, the view was stunning with beaches, boats, lighthouses and the distant Boston skyline.

We left the monument in hopes of walking to the lighthouses, but quickly discovered as we made our way through town that this was not a good place for Thomas to be. Why? Well, the atmosphere in P-town that Friday afternoon was reminiscent of Mardi Gras, but slightly twisted. The first character we saw was a gentleman wearing a tall turquoise feathered head-piece paired with a matching bikini top and bottom along with "break your neck" platform heels. Thomas asked me what it was and I vaguely remember saying, "A very big hat." Daniel told him it was Big Bird. There were many more costumed characters walking the streets and, as much as we wanted to see the lighthouses, we felt like we had to get Thomas out of there. We just weren't ready for those conversations yet. I had been told that Provincetown was different. *That* may have been the understatement of the year.

Leaving Massachusetts was difficult because we liked it so much, but we knew we would be back. We enjoyed experiencing firsthand our country's history and foundational beliefs there. The Pilgrims traveled here long ago in search of religious freedom and, although they sacrificed much, ultimately found it. The Sons of Liberty sought independence from a distant monarch who wanted to quash their spirit. Whether walking the Freedom Trail or gazing on Founder's Monument, it was impossible for us to spend time in Massachusetts and not contemplate the importance of our "inalienable rights." We were so moved that we forgave the residents of this New England state for their insistence on cheering the local NFL team. Freedom should be extended even to Patriots fans.

Vicariously yours,
Traci

Sent: Sunday, August 28, 2005
Subject: One Week in My Life

Daniel's best friend from his youth lived in Hamden, Connecticut with his family, so we spent the weekend with them. We rolled into town and found the closest Wal-Mart to Mike's house and made camp. After a quick reunion in the parking lot, we went out for a tour of the town including part of Yale University. Daniel's friend is a faculty member at Yale in cancer research, toxicology and lots of other stuff that I really didn't understand. He is a brilliant scientist and doctor and I am so thankful that there are people like him in this world. As we toured his lab, he explained what this was and what that was and after several minutes, I was thinking about dinner, shopping, and ibuprofen. Daniel must have been wearing the same confounded look because the good doctor stopped his monologue and said, "Well, it doesn't really matter."

New Jersey was our next destination because Daniel wanted to ride some roller coasters and Six Flags had a location in Jackson. Trying to be a good, supportive wife, I found the closest campground in the area and made reservations. To be blunt, the campground stunk and we regretted paying in advance for three nights. The roads and campsites were the consistency of kitty litter, which was impossible to keep outside of the bus. The bugs were so numerous and persistent that each time we opened the door, a cloud of them swarmed the opening and invaded our space. Even the laundry room was sub-standard. There were no doors on two of the four machines, rendering them inoperable, and the others were rusted and covered in an inch-thick layer of soap residue. The lesson we learned: when in doubt, choose a KOA campground. They are consistently clean and well-kept.

The attractions at Six Flags were fun, but we were miffed by the number of people who considered line-jumping acceptable. While waiting on one ride in particular, a dozen guests cut in front of us. Not that Daniel or I would ever say anything; confrontation is not something we enjoy. Besides, it was too hot to spark an altercation. The agony and frustration, though, was worth the family picture we got from the Superman roller coaster. There's just something special about capturing moments when your faces are contorted from fright, wind, and G-forces.

Exhausting what little there was to do in Jackson, New Jersey, we were thrilled to learn Philadelphia was a short 60-minute drive from our campground. We couldn't resist. I can't emphasize enough to you how much fun we were having discovering the history of our young nation. Philly was fabulous! We spent the day touring the city, taking in as many sights as possible—or as much as Thomas's short legs could manage. The Liberty Bell has some serious security around it. Guests have to go through a checkpoint similar to one at an airport and there are several guards throughout, watching your every move. The building surrounding the famous landmark was designed by Kevin Bacon's father, Edmund, who also restored much of Society Hill, the area in town where several members of the Continental Congress once lived, including James Madison and his lively wife, Dolly. As we toured downtown, our guide told us that William Penn planned the city for the illiterate people who lived there. The streets running one direction were numbered second, third, fourth, and the perpendicular streets were named after the trees that were planted there. Why did William Penn do that? It was easier for non-readers to give and take directions if they were looking for a home at 4th and Elm. All they had to do was walk to the fourth street and look for the elm trees. Because there were no addresses, each home on a street painted its shutters a different color. Directions to your friend's house might sound something like this: "Go to the sixth street, turn left at Walnut and look for the purple shutters." I would have been lost. I don't know the difference between a walnut and a beechnut. And what happened when the leaves fell off in autumn? Thank goodness I can read.

There were many "wow" moments for me in Philadelphia and touring Independence Hall was one of them. It was amazing to stand in the same room that George Washington, Ben Franklin, Thomas Jefferson, James Madison, and so many other brave men stood, the room where they debated what our country believed in, and where they signed the two most important documents of our nation's history. Washington's chair still sits in the exact place it was when he used it. The highlight of the day was the "Lights of Liberty" tour. It began late in the evening, after the sun had gone down, and involved a multi-media dramatization of events beginning with the First Continental Congress and ending with the reading of the Declaration of Independence. It was a walking tour of the historic buildings, enhanced with video and sound. Everyone wore a headset and was ushered through the streets of Philly by illuminated guides. We stood outside Ben Franklin's court and heard a dramatization of the uproar over the Stamp Tax imposed by the British. On the soundtrack, a mob of people were arguing and calling for Franklin's home to be burned while we watched hand-painted images depicting the story, projected on the tall buildings surrounding us. The combination of the soundtrack and video created a drama so palpable that I wanted to run to Deborah Franklin's side and protect her from the angry protestors. There were five of these scenes on the tour.

After being led through a maze of buildings, we came out into an open space and heard a group of young Continental soldiers shouting to their comrades that they were being engaged by the enemy. Smoke from the explosions made it difficult for them to see and the sound of bombardments was deafening. We were watching pictures of these men and listening to their terror and bewilderment when someone shouted, "They're behind you! Turn around. They're behind you!" We were instructed to turn around and there facing us was a line of British soldiers, guns at the ready, and then…they fired. I realized it was just a video production, but I could have sworn I felt the blast through my body. Tears streamed down my face as I thought about how frightened those young men must have been. War was an ugly business.

Thomas had his own headset and his audio was not the same as ours. The tour included a children's version, so Thomas did not experience the level of emotion we did. I was not interested in terrorizing my son for the sake of a history lesson. I asked him after the tour ended what he heard when the soldiers got shot and he said that someone told him to duck. Thank goodness.

The last scene of the tour took place behind Independence Hall. Projected on the back of the building were images of the townspeople and the members of the Continental Congress—on the headsets, we heard the debate over the desire for liberation. At last, a Congressional representative walked out of the hall and read, for the people, the Declaration of Independence. The townspeople and representatives cheered. The tour ended with our group standing behind Independence Hall watching the members of the Continental Congress (George Washington, Ben Franklin, Thomas Jefferson, and James Madison) as well as the people of Philadelphia cheer and celebrate the separation from Britain. It was an incredibly moving experience—not just for me, but for all of those adults standing around me. This group of strangers wearing headsets began to sing along with the people on the screen and as we mouthed the words "God bless America, our home sweet home," I looked at those to my left and right and noticed I wasn't the only one crying. It was an experience I will forever treasure in a city that touched my heart.

There isn't a day that goes by that I don't learn something. I learned that when asked a "who did it" history question, nine times out of ten the answer is Ben Franklin. He was a brilliant and hard-working man. As one guide told us, "It's amazing what a man can do when he doesn't watch television." You got that right. I learned that to be a member of George Washington's private guard, a man had to be a Virginian land owner who was no taller than 6'4"—our first president wanted to be around those he could trust and intimidate. We visited Gettysburg and there I learned more. We were told that Robert E. Lee did not believe in secession—meaning that he did not believe the South should leave the union. I was stupefied. How could a man fight for four years, sacrificing thousands of lives, and not believe in the cause of the conflict? For Lee, it was more important that he answer the call of his beloved state of Virginia than hold fast to his own beliefs.

The battlefield at Gettysburg was 25 square miles and yet, the highest number of casualties in the entire war happened within a small, one-mile area in only 50 minutes. We purchased a CD to listen to in the car as we took the self-guided auto tour. The audio was not only informational, but dramatic. The sounds of war were savage and terrible. Listening to the dramatization as we drove from skirmish point to skirmish point, I could only imagine what it was like on that field. I was reminded of how grateful I am to those who fought for this country and those who continue to do so.

We finished our tour of the Northeast with Washington, D.C., a city that is the culmination of the historical places we have been. After spending time in Boston and standing in the very spot where the first shot of the Revolutionary War was fired, and visiting Philadelphia where George Washington, Thomas Jefferson, and Ben Franklin argued the language of our nation's founding documents, it only made sense to come to the capital. Thomas will have a more meaningful encounter with the monuments and memorials here because he knows these men. He has been to the planning rooms, battlefields and encampments. Washington, Lincoln, and Jefferson are real to him, not just pictures in a book or characters in a story. I only hope that as he gets older, he will remember this trip and the significance of the places and people. For the time being, we took him to an amusement park to help him remember that he was only ten years old and school was out for the weekend.

Vicariously Yours,
Traci

The campground in College Park, Maryland, was almost as well appointed as the one in Lake George, New York, with a pool, laundromat, dog park, wireless internet, cable television, and fire pits. It was nicer than our first home. I was amazed that the campground even existed, considering the large amount of acreage it required and its prime location. We were a short 40 minutes from downtown Baltimore, 30 minutes by train from Washington, D.C., and 60 minutes from Richmond, Virginia—a perfect location to spend 10 days.

With much ground to cover and an unusually long list of things to do, a plan seemed like the first order of business. The National Mall, Smithsonian, National Archives, Arlington Cemetery, and Capitol Building were must-see attractions for us, but where should we begin? Having just spent several days immersed in history, Thomas begged for a day of roller coasters, cotton candy, and mindless fun before submitting to the marathon tourism week looming in front of him. Within a short distance from Washington, D.C., were two amusement parks— Six Flags and Kings Dominion—and we treated Thomas to both. With school in session, the parks were deserted and we were able to ride roller coasters to our heart's content, or until our stomachs gave way. There was plenty of time for history later in the week.

Monday began Daniel's workweek and, because his sales numbers were looking good, the three of us were able to hop the train in the afternoon to D.C. We went without much of a plan because we wanted to get the "lay of the land" on foot in order to see whether we could walk everywhere we wanted to go or if we needed to buy trolley tickets. Boston and Philadelphia had been so easy to walk around that we naively assumed D.C. would be, too. We did realize that our nation's capitol was bigger than the previous cities, but what we didn't know was just how resilient Thomas would be with the increased amount of walking here. He wasn't. He didn't like walking mile after mile in 98-degree heat over blistering concrete while looking at government buildings and historical landmarks. Who knew?

It was sweltering everywhere we had been since leaving Indianapolis. From Ohio to Toronto and Bar Harbor, Maine, we could not escape the dog days of summer. Maybe there *was* something to this global warming thing. Despite the temperature and Thomas's lethargy, I had already decided before we got to the National Mall that we would walk from the Capitol to the Lincoln Monument and then on to the White House. I don't know officially how far that was, but it felt like 20 miles. The three of us were sweating like turkeys the day before Thanksgiving. I felt like my feet had melted into my shoes. Although I had used deodorant in the morning, no product could be expected to perform under those conditions. It was in this reeking state that we shuffled into ESPN Zone for dinner. The hostess winced for a moment but seated us anyway, although far away from other customers. We made sure to leave our server a big tip.

On day two in our nation's capital, we went back into town, but instead of aimlessly walking in the cruel heat, we toured the air-conditioned Smithsonian. I had a somewhat shadowy memory of being there as a child, but no real recollection of what it was like. First of all, I didn't remember that the Smithsonian was a collection of more than a dozen different museums and buildings. How I forgot that, I will never quite understand, but then when last I visited Washington, Jimmy Carter was president. When I informed Thomas that we'd be visiting the Smithsonian that particular day, he pictured one large building where he would follow us around for a few hours, nod his head as if he were listening, and say things like, "Yeah, that's really neat," and "When are we leaving?"

Imagine his surprise when he realized that the Smithsonian included many buildings filled with displays of old things. I thought for sure he would love the Air and Space Museum—and he did—for about 45 minutes. At that point, even Daniel was getting a little overwhelmed with aeronautical terms and space exploration explanations. Realizing that this was an incredible educational opportunity for Thomas and remembering that I was responsible for his 5th grade curriculum, I tried my best to entice his interest in the various exhibits, being certain to read all of the plaques, note cards, and signs. I must admit, I had never taken the time for any of that before and after a short while, even I was losing my desire to be there. A change of scenery and subject matter was just the thing we needed.

We walked across the mall to the American History Museum and were taken in by all of the incredible stuff (a highly technical term for all things on display) there. The first thing we saw was the American flag that had hung from the side of the Pentagon after 9/11. I found it much more awe inspiring than the Wright Flyer. Not that what the Wright brothers accomplished was unimportant or unworthy of a place of honor in history, I just didn't care. Maybe it was because I wasn't alive when it happened. The flag, however, pulled me in and reminded me of that moment in time when the attacks on our soil began and I felt an emotional connection to it. It was surreal to be standing in front of it after seeing it on television. I thought about Orville and Wilbur's plane while I stood there and wondered if I would have been more awestruck if I had seen the famous flight replayed while Tom Brokaw discussed the likelihood of it ever happening again. Probably not.

The exhibits at the American History Museum were phenomenal, but one in particular took my breath away and it wasn't the Hope Diamond. Instead, it was a large exhibit focused solely on the military history of our country, a display that caused emotional reactions from many an onlooker that day. As you would expect, there were pictures, uniforms, and equipment from the various wars, but there was something else. For the later conflicts, there were stories recorded by the soldiers who had been there. It was difficult to listen and watch these heroes relive the events that brought them both great honor and agony. Their voices trembled and faces contorted as each recalled painful memories. Some of the men cried while others looked as if they had simply run out of tears. As visitors to the museum listened through headsets to these stories, watching the storytellers, some of them cried, too.

The list of things to do was long—presidential monuments, war memorials, historical buildings, national museums, and regional landmarks—and all offered unique experiences in our nation's capital. We saw the Declaration of Independence and Constitution, the documents written by our founding fathers as they defined America. We stood in the shadows of men of greatness at the presidential monuments and read powerful words each had spoken or written...words that changed our small, developing republic. We visited men and women of valor at the war memorials in hopes of somehow honoring the lives sacrificed for our freedom. Silently, we walked through Arlington Cemetery, noting the sea of white grave markers spread out in every direction, each representing someone's son or daughter, husband or wife, father or mother. As the ceremony of the Changing of the Guard occurred at the Tomb of the Unknown Soldier, Thomas raised his hand in salute while we stood reverently behind him.

Walking through the streets of Washington, D.C. was like stepping into an American history book still being written. The past was available for us to peek at under glass or read on a plaque, and yet the future continued to unfold within the walls of the White House, legislative buildings, and Supreme Court. Our National Mall reads like a "Where's Where" with the Capitol Building at one end and the Lincoln Memorial at the other with the Washington Monument in between. There are so many monuments and memorials in the city that little, if any, open space remains to honor any others. I noticed that the only place with room to grow was Arlington Cemetery and I doubt anyone is lobbying to get in there.

Have you ever watched a movie or television show where Washington, D.C. was the backdrop and some character, needing time to think, found solitude sitting on the steps of the Lincoln Memorial or on a bench in front of Jefferson or Washington? After spending a few days surrounded by these men of greatness forever immortalized in granite, sandstone, and marble, it now made sense to me that someone looking for inspiration or courage or peace might seek it in the shadows of these former leaders—these men of character, intelligence, and determination—and find it.

On one of our trips aboard local transportation in D.C., I saw a poster that made me think, "Only in Washington." The picture was a group of people, all wearing milk mustaches, trying to get into a bathroom and the caption said, "Got Lactose Intolerance? 75 percent of people are lactose intolerant, especially those of color. If you are lactose intolerant, you may have grounds for a lawsuit." Have we come to this in

America? In recent years, we learned that coffee served in the drive-thru window is extremely hot, fast food eaten in excess can cause obesity, and claiming you found a finger in your meal only works if you didn't put it there. I spent a few minutes on their website and read that this concerned group believes people who are allergic to dairy are coerced by the "Got Milk?" advertisements. What do these people think—that the average American cannot ignore a marketing campaign? We do it with politicians all the time.

We took Thomas to something called "Medieval Times" for a post-birthday celebration since we didn't do anything fun for his special day other than drive from Bangor, Maine to Portsmouth, New Hampshire. Thomas loves all things related to this time period, especially swords, fighting, and jousting, so this place was everything he could have hoped for, with the exception of donning some armor and sparring with them. The "castle" was at the mall near Baltimore and, upon entering; we were greeted by "serfs" in full costume and led to an area where guests were photographed with the King and Princess. After perusing the castle and its many gift shops complete with faux and genuine fighting equipment, royal polyester apparel, and all manner of regal knick-knacks, we were summoned to watch the "knighting" of a select few. Thomas was enthralled the entire time and stood as close to the happenings as he could. After the ceremony, we were called into the dining area by groups depending on the color of our crown. Yes, we all wore paper crowns, which was why I forbid Daniel to purchase the souvenir photo. He looked like the fry cook who had just clocked out from his shift at Burger King...an unflattering picture for sure.

Our "wench" greeted us and explained how the dinner would be served without silverware. However, the well-dressed couple next to me needed further explanation. As I motioned with my hands, I said, "Well, your left hand is your fork and your right hand is your spoon." Daniel, Thomas, and I did just fine eating with our hands, but then we have been living in a bus for three months. We didn't even sit at a table.

The show began, and what a spectacle it was. The men who acted as the knights made me think two things: the band wasn't working out and money was tight, or playing Dungeons & Dragons as a pre-teen made them wish they had been born in an earlier time period. They took their roles seriously and gave the crowd a night of impressive horsemanship and heavy weapons battling. The founding company of Medieval Times began in Spain in 1973 and expanded to our continent with a premier location in Kissimmee, Florida—a smart choice. Since the success of the central Florida location, the company opened other castles in California, Toronto, South Carolina, Texas, Illinois, and New York and has entertained over 35 million guests. That's a lot of mouths to feed—no wonder they skip the silverware in favor of the original five-finger method.

Daniel called Indiana Senator Richard Lugar's office to arrange a tour of the Capitol building which was to take place on Friday at 9:45 a.m. We arrived right on time and were quickly sent on our way with our guide. Our host had just graduated from Indiana University and had been working in Lugar's office for all of five days when given the task of leading us through the Senate buildings and Capitol. Wow! We got the new guy...we felt important.

He was a history major in college, which meant he knew four years' worth of information about the makings of our great country; however, five days into his internship was too little time to learn about the buildings he was guiding us through. He got us lost twice and stopped by security once, which wasn't bad for his first tour. The highlight for Thomas was riding the "Capitol Choo-choo," a small train inside the underbelly of the Senate buildings that transported people between those buildings and the Capitol. Daniel and I thought this was a total waste of taxpayer money, estimating that the walk couldn't take more than eight or ten minutes. Apparently, the Senators and staffers need the train to shave off precious time, ultimately getting them where they need to be in less than five minutes. Quick, someone call Brian Williams: I think we've been fleeced!

The National Statuary Hall Collection has an assembly of 100 statues donated by the 50 states, honoring two notable persons in each state's history. For example, Virginia was represented by Robert E. Lee and George Washington. Texas had Stephen Austin and Sam Houston. These names I knew. The two statues from my home state of Indiana meant absolutely nothing to me. I had to look them up on the internet to figure out who they were. Imagine my surprise when I discovered that Lewis Wallace had not only served in the Civil War, but had also written the best-selling novel, *Ben-Hur: A Tale of the Christ.* Wow, where have I been? The Hoosier state's other statue was Oliver Hazard Perry Morton, who I found out was the governor during the Civil War and a strong supporter of the Union.

After doing a bit more research, I learned that the statuary collection became law in 1864, shortly before the end of the Civil War, and our statues were donated in 1900 and 1910. No wonder two Civil-War-era leaders were chosen to be honored in bronze. Kansas removed one of their statues and replaced it with a new one in 2003. I guess Governor George W. Glick had been voted off the pedestal because after 89 years, Dwight D. Eisenhower took his place. Politics: even in death, it never ends.

There are many more stories about each of the monuments and memorials, museums and cemeteries that we visited, but the most important story is really your own. What will it be like the first time you visit the capital? Watching the Changing of the Guard at Arlington Cemetery, reading the names, seeing the faces, and counting the stars on the war memorials, studying Thomas Jefferson's words on the Declaration of Independence and Constitution—these are things that you must do in your lifetime because they will give you a sense of belief in your country that sometimes wanes when you watch the news and hear what bad things have been said and see what bad people have done. Why visit Washington, D.C.? Because all that is good and bad is remembered here and yet it is all charming in its own way for it is the story of the making and re-making of our nation...and isn't it only right that you should somehow participate in that?

Vicariously Yours,
Traci

Sent: Monday, September 19, 2005
Subject: Back Home Again in Indiana

It was a long and difficult drive from Washington, D.C. to Indianapolis for Daniel. The slow upward climbs on the mountains were offset by the screaming quickness of the downward grades, and by the time we got to Columbus, Ohio, he was exhausted. It was nice to wake up in an almost familiar area the next day and we celebrated by taking the car to Graeter's Ice Cream shop to watch our favorite sweet treat being made. We stocked up on several half gallons of Black Raspberry Chip to share with friends and family. We didn't spend much time tooling around Columbus. There were still three hours of driving ahead of us before hitting the KOA in Indianapolis. It would be bizarre to return to our hometown and not be able to stay in our house, but it had been sold.

The closer we got to Indiana, the more we noticed the boring, uninteresting landscape. Interstate 70, a marvel of modern highway with its numerous smooth and straight lanes, made our temporary return to Indy faster, but it wasn't scenic. As Daniel and I drove into town we talked about how the billboards accented the many fields along the interstate and how distracting lush groves of trees would be—I mean, who would want to look at nature instead of an ad for Crazy Ron's Gas & Grub? I am proud of where I come from and boast about the wonderful things in our state—the Colts, Children's Museum, Indy 500, zoo, and great shopping—but I have never thought that the landscape of Indiana stood above the rest of the country. In truth, I've always thought it was just a little plain. A trip to New England didn't help change my mind. I have seen the Green Mountains in Vermont, Acadia State Park in Maine, and countless picturesque places along the coast and, I must admit, I wish the Hoosier state had that scenery, too.

I spoke with a man in the laundry room at Cherry Hill Campground just outside of Washington, D.C. who asked where I was from. When I told him, he got a big grin on his face and said, "I love Indiana. It is so beautiful." I looked at him in amazement and asked him what part he had seen. We talked for several minutes about the Hoosier State and I must admit that I don't see my home through the eyes of a tourist. I have lived here too long to notice the things that make Indiana special and different. Over the next several days, I intended to look at those familiar surroundings—the ones I have passed thousands of times and stopped noticing—and try to see it all for the first time...to see the beauty that my Maryland friend did.

Why did we come home after three months? Thomas missed his friends, Daniel's customers missed him, and I missed, hmmm, surely there was something. Truthfully, I wasn't ready to come home. I was emotionally prepared to not see my family and friends for at least 12 months, so when this visit home became a reality, I felt like the child who'd gone off to college amidst a flurry of fanfare and well wishes only to return home within a week to do laundry. This trip was my opportunity to change and grow and in three months' time; the only thing that had grown was my behind from eating too much lobster, ice cream, and blueberry pie. It wasn't that I didn't want to see my friends, but I felt like I didn't have anything new to say. No profound wisdom had entered my brain yet in the first months of the trip, and I hated to admit it.

Daniel spent the week meeting with customers and vendors while Thomas stayed with a friend as much as possible, leaving me alone in the bus or tooling around the city. We had spent so much time together over the past few months that I felt entirely disconnected and lost without them. Leaving town the second time meant that we would be alone again, just the three of us. I also longed for the most unexpected gift of the trip so far: anonymity. It allowed me to walk out my door and not care who saw me wearing the same thing I had worn for the past two days. Yes, anonymity was good.

Before we could hit the road again, many details had to be attended to, including errands and appointments for Thomas and me. One necessity was a trip to the dentist for both of us. I had scheduled our appointments while in Washington, D.C., and the day Thomas and I jumped in my car to see the good doctor, something surprising happened. I got lost. I have lived in Indianapolis for 35 years and have been seeing the same dentist since 2002. I can't even explain what happened as I was driving, but all of a sudden I found myself sitting at a stoplight on the north side without a clue as to where I was going. I asked, "Thomas, where are we going?" He raised an eyebrow and answered slowly, not sure if it was a trick question. I turned the car around and made my way to the appointment, but arrived an hour early. My watch was set for a different time zone. This long-term traveling thing was harder than it seemed. I was learning American history and geography, but sacrificing key information. Let's hope I retain enough to make it home next June.

They say that absence makes the heart grow fonder and this might very well be true because when I took Thomas to have his teeth cleaned on Wednesday, the dentist and hygienist came out to hug me in the lobby of the office. I never got that treatment before and I only see them every six months. What gives? Was it because I had been so far away? Or had they never hugged a real campground person before? Either way, I appreciated the enthusiasm for our temporary return. Just imagine how they'd react after we'd been gone for nine more months and had been as far as California. I was hoping for a free family cleaning.

I admit, it was nice to be missed and it was good to catch up with people before heading off again. Did I miss my friends and family in Indiana? The simple answer was yes, but no amount of longing for their companionship would make me want to stay and forfeit the rest of this opportunity for adventure. It was time to go again and when we left, we wouldn't be back for a long while. This trip had already changed us and I expected that over the next several months, we would change even more. Life was different on the road, a far cry from being at home, and although we may not have known what day it was, what time it was, or where we were at any given moment, we did know that we were exactly where we wanted to be at exactly the right time. Home for us now was wherever the bus happened to be parked.

As for the beauty of Indiana that my friend spoke of, I saw it, and guess what? It wasn't in the landscape, architecture, or development. No, the beauty of Indiana could be seen in the people who live there—good, honest people who care enough to say hello and ask how you're doing today. No mountain, forest, or ocean view could compete with that.

Vicariously Yours,
Traci

Sent: Saturday, September, 24, 2005
Subject: Bourbon, Beer, and a President

After spending a week in Indianapolis, we pointed the bus toward Frankfort, Kentucky and sprinted. The return to our solitary, anonymous lifestyle was well worth the two nights spent at a campground more suited to mobile homes than recreational vehicles. It surprised me to see so many permanent residents sharing living space and lifestyle amenities with transients. The site resembled a trailer park more than a campground. I liked it. My life had changed in four months' time: I used to be a suburban housewife living in a "starter castle" and now...I slept in a trailer park. My parents would be so proud.

The Jim Beam Distillery was across the street from our Kentucky home. It was within walking distance and a tour was tempting, but I couldn't figure out how to include it in Thomas's curriculum. Would it fall under science, social studies, or home economics? After much thought, we spent our school time on board-of-education–approved subjects, English and math, instead of learning how to make liquor. I figured Thomas would have plenty of time in college to study that supplemental training.

We left Kentucky at the stroke of 1:00 p.m. on Tuesday, traveling through splendid horse country. The hills rolled along as we passed expansive green pastures with well-tended white fences; magnificent galloping thoroughbreds tossed their manes in the wind. This was the Kentucky I wanted to see. Thomas and I had never ridden a horse. If only there had been time to stop and spend precious minutes with these glorious animals. I promised Thomas that before returning to Indiana next summer, we would ride horses together. I hoped I could keep my promise.

We drove three hours to Charleston, West Virginia, where we stayed at Camp Wal-Mart. I did my homework this time and found a 24-hour store where parking wouldn't be an issue. When we arrived, though, there was a sign in the corner of the stadium-sized lot prohibiting overnight parking. I turned on the computer and began searching the internet for alternative accommodations, but Daniel chose to stay and see what happened. I was not comfortable with this arrangement. Having one incident involving a late-night knock on the door by a sheriff was enough for me. Daniel felt like taking a risk.

I didn't sleep much that night. I kept thinking someone was going to make us leave. Also, there was a group of twenty-somethings sitting in the beds of their pick-up trucks until 2:00 a.m., not more than 30 feet from our bus, debating the finer points of crushing beer cans and spitting long-distance loogies. As riveting as the conversation was, I couldn't imagine that there wasn't a better, more interesting place to spend an evening. At the very least, they could have parked in the opposite corner of the empty mile-wide lot. Where was a pop-up thundershower when I needed one?

After a sleepless night, we drove to Charlottesville, Virginia, home to Thomas Jefferson's beloved Monticello and the University of Virginia. Charlottesville, named after the wife of England's King George III, was deemed the best place to live in America according to the book released in 2004 by Bert Sperling and Peter Sander, *Cities Ranked and Rated*. The authors used 10 categories to determine which cities in our country were the most livable, but admitted that three things—cost of living, climate, and quality of life—most influence our daily lives. Rounding out the top five favorites were Santa Fe, San Luis Obispo, Santa Barbara, and Honolulu...not a bad list of vacation destinations, let alone places of residence.

Thomas Jefferson would be proud of his hometown, but then, he had much to do with what has made Charlottesville an outstanding community. It was his idea and spirit that drove the creation of the University of Virginia, a testament to his passion for higher learning. When the first classes met on campus in March 1825, students were given a unique opportunity to specialize in studies different from the doctrine of the day. While pupils at other institutions were restricted to medicine, law, and religion, those at Jefferson's school were free to choose from architecture, astronomy, botany, philosophy, and political science.

His pride in the college was so great that this man of eloquent words and great intellect, this man held in high regard by kings and queens, who earned a myriad of accomplishments desired only three things be remembered about him on his tombstone: "Here was buried Thomas Jefferson, author of the Declaration of Independence, of the Virginia Statute for Religious Freedom and father of the University of Virginia." If only he had had a giant, blue and orange foam finger to stand high atop his grave marker, ensuring that all who visited knew he, the third President of our nation, was the Cavaliers' number one fan.

Before visiting historic Monticello, we settled in at the Misty Mountain Campground, chosen by Thomas because of its likeness to a place in *The Hobbit*. Knowing very little about Charlottesville, we listened to the stories of our next door neighbors when they dropped by our evening campfire. They told us that quite a few celebrities lived in the area including Dave Matthews, who just last weekend had a concert at his home across the street from Misty Mountain. And to think we were just hours away when it happened. We also learned that Sissy Spacek, Jaclyn Smith, Neil Diamond, John Grisham, and my personal favorite, Howie Long, lived right outside of Charlottesville. Who knew that Virginia was home to more than aging and dead politicians? I shouldn't have been surprised that celebrities called this place home. It *was* ranked as the best place to live in America.

Though our original intent of having a peaceful campfire had already been altered by talkative and friendly neighbors, I was flabbergasted when another camper, out for an evening stroll with his pooch, stopped to join the conversation. It wasn't that I disliked those people; I just wanted them to go away. I tried to become more comfortable making small talk with strangers, but my success was minimal. In my experience, when strangers stopped to chat with us, they would ask a question or two about our trip and then disregard our answers as they began talking about themselves. That wasn't a bad thing. It just didn't feel like real conversation to me. With its one-sided nature, it more closely resembled therapy. Forty-five minutes later, our three chatty friends had run out of things to say and bade us goodnight. I should have charged them for my listening ear or at least taken notes so I could relay the fascinating details of their childhoods to you. Next time....

No trip to Charlottesville would be complete without a visit to Monticello, Thomas Jefferson's home. Featured on the back of the nickel, the grand mansion was designed by Jefferson when he was 26 years old. The grounds of the original estate consisted of thousands of acres including two mountains; however, after his death, most of his holdings had to be sold to pay off debt. Though our former president lived well beyond his means, those who admired and respected him bought his land and belongings and returned them to the Thomas Jefferson Foundation.

He lived in the house with his wife, Martha Wayles Skelton, and their children until Martha died in 1782. Only two daughters—Martha Washington Jefferson and Mary Jefferson—lived past the age of three. Thomas Jefferson never remarried and when given the opportunity to move to France to serve his country after his wife's death, he accepted. When he returned to Charlottesville, he redesigned his home, inspired by what he had seen and learned in Europe. The remodel of the home began in 1796 and was completed in 1809; however, he was constantly thinking of ways to improve either the house or the grounds.

Walking through the door of Thomas Jefferson's home left me speech-less. Having visited Mount Vernon, the home of George Washington, I was amazed at the extravagant style of Monticello. Both buildings were large and situated on thousands of acres; however, that was where the similarities ended. George Washington's home was simplicity at its finest, while Jefferson's was detailed and fussy. Though many of the materials used in the construction process of Monticello—including the bricks and nails—came from the surrounding land, it was obvious that no expense had been spared. No wonder he had financial difficulties.

While admiring the beauty of his home and gardens, I was shocked to hear the tour guides talking about the controversial subject of Jefferson's alleged affair with one of his slaves. One staff person specif-ically said, "DNA evidence does confirm Jefferson's fathering of a child by Sally Hemmings." What? I knew I missed something while perusing the collection of books in the library. What began in 1802 as a personal political attack on Thomas Jefferson's character turned into a provocative story, causing over 200 years of debate and study. I read much about the account while in Charlottesville and I still didn't see the big deal. Why had so many people devoted time, money, and effort to prove the parentage of the Hemmings children? Standing in front of an exhibit at the Monticello Visitors' Center, I looked at pictures of many people ranging in hue from vanilla to chocolate brown, all claiming to be a descendant of the great Thomas Jefferson. Assuming it was all true, what did it get you? At the risk of offending you, would it really matter if your great-great-great-great-great-great-great-great-grandfather might be Thomas Jefferson?

Even though Jefferson died in 1826, Sally in 1835, and the two remaining children as late as 1877, a book regarding the controversy was recently published stoking the fires of the tale yet one more time. The author questioned Jefferson's ability to father a child due to a particular dysfunction he might have suffered. Whether the former president fathered his slaves' children shouldn't matter. As an adopted girl with no knowledge of my own father, I have to say that life goes on just fine with or without a definitive answer. However, since my biological father hasn't come forward to claim me, I would be happy to assume that I, too, am somehow a descendant of Thomas Jefferson. Now, what do I get?

One afternoon, we drove into Charlottesville to see the "historic downtown district" publicized on the highway. Our experience from other towns led us to the Visitors' Center where abundant information could be gathered. We were greeted by a kind lady about 70 years old and I asked her for suggestions of things to do and see in her town. I should have known we were in trouble when she smiled and paused for several minutes. Trying to help her gather a few thoughts, I mentioned the Civil War Trail and asked if we should start there. "Well," she said, "It isn't that the trail isn't important. It's just that they have made it out to be more than it is." Really? She went on to say that the trail was nothing more than a bunch of plaques noting every statue, skirmish, and landmark in the area. She explained that a historical marker had even been posted on the local Burger King.

With our limited time, we asked about other local attractions. She continued to think, drumming her fingers on the desk and gazing up as if the information would fall from the ceiling. Several times she started to say something but stopped. We could almost see the wheels turning in her mind and it didn't look promising. I wondered if she was new to her position. Heck, maybe she was new to Charlottesville. I found a map, noticed a boardwalk, and asked "Ms. Knows Very Little" if we should meander over that way. A light bulb flickered above her head. With great enthusiasm she pointed at us and said, "Yes, that's a pedestrian walk. It runs through town and there are some shops and restaurants that you might like." She shot out of her chair as she remembered something else. "Oh! There's an old building down the road with a Civil War guy and, I think, a few cannons. You might like to see that." She fell back into her chair, exhausted from the mental exertion and released an audible sigh.

Before we made it out the door, she asked us where we were from and, after hearing our answer, fumbled through several stacks and file cabinets before handing us a couple of brochures regarding the Civil War. As I looked them over, I wondered what information we would have received if we had been from the South. Were our pamphlets written in Yankee? As much as I would have loved to stay and chat with her, there was an old building, a Civil War guy, and some cannons to see.

We discovered that the old building was the original courthouse where Thomas Jefferson, James Madison, and James Monroe practiced law together, a significant place to be sure. The Civil War guy was Thomas "Stonewall" Jackson and the cannons were…cannons. Visitors' Centers had served us well until now. In historical Charlottesville, we learned a new lesson: sitting behind an information desk didn't make you helpful any more than sitting in a garage made you a car.

Vicariously Yours,
Traci

Sent: Thursday, September 29, 2005
Subject: Very Virginia

Within the Williamsburg area, there were fascinating attractions to see, including the Yorktown Battlefield where a pivotal victory occurred in the Revolutionary War. There is the Jamestown Settlement—the first permanent English community—and the mammoth 18th century living history museum, Colonial Williamsburg. Our time at the Williamsburg KOA coincided with the last week of the month which, for anyone in sales, spells trouble if the numbers aren't in yet. Daniel worked much more than usual, which allowed less time for sightseeing. "More time for school," I told Thomas. He wasn't excited.

We did get to the Jamestown Settlement on Sunday before the work-week began and were intrigued to learn that the pilgrims were not the first settlers in the New World. The people in Plymouth, Massachusetts claimed that the first permanent settlement was in their hometown. Now that we were in Virginia, we were told that a group of colonists arrived in Jamestown 13 years before the pilgrims. Funny, no one in Plymouth mentioned anything about Jamestown. Not only did we learn that Jamestown was indeed the first permanent settlement in the New World, but also that Pocahontas was 10 years old when she had her fling with Captain John Smith.

When did history become so confusing? And, why didn't Disney portray Pocahontas as a young girl instead of a blossoming woman? To think that I watched the animated movie and felt warm and fuzzy inside as the happy couple started falling in love. Gross. What I didn't understand was why Pocahontas' father, Chief Powatan, chose not to scalp Captain Creepy for wooing his pre-pubescent daughter? I surmised that the young girl's interest in John Smith was related to her father's inability to show love and affection—meaning that she was seeking a father figure. Or at least, that's what I believed Dr. Phil would say.

Thomas liked talking to the knowledgeable guides at the Jamestown Settlement, but felt that costumed characters working in living history museums on occasion took themselves too seriously. Interpreters sometimes refused to step out of their roles to answer questions posed by guests if the information fell outside of what their character would know. The charade would be complete if it weren't for all of the ringing cell phones and two-way radios.

Did you know that the Virginia community was responsible for the first planting of Spanish tobacco? We were told by our guide that the only reason slave labor was brought to the New World was to work the fields of tobacco because it was too strenuous and time consuming for the English. Weenies. Also, had it not been for the tobacco crop, the company in England that funded the voyage and settlement would have left Jamestown due to the danger involving the Native Americans and lack of profit there. Our guide encouraged us to consider what might have been different in our country's history—no tobacco, no slaves, no Civil War, no 600,000 deaths.

I thought about her hypothesis for a day or two after leaving and couldn't help wondering if Abraham Lincoln would have been the president he was if there had been no Civil War…had he not been so challenged by the idea of secession and emancipation. It was something to think about, huh?

One day, while Daniel was working, Thomas and I sat at a picnic table to have school. When a fellow camper walked by with a miniature dachshund, my boy threw aside his pencil and raced toward the animal. He loves dogs! This was a defining moment for me in the Williamsburg KOA because this woman was also a mom of a ten-year-old boy who happened to be on a year-long RV trip with her family. She introduced herself and invited us to a campfire later in order to get to know one another and possibly coordinate our calendars so we could get together along the way.

We went that evening to meet and greet and roast marshmallows over a roaring fire. The family was from Albany, New York, and had been on the road since July. Our stories were somewhat alike as we discussed why we had made the decision to leave our homes, but that was where the similarities ended. The plan for their trip was contained on a spreadsheet, complete with reservations and activities booked months in advance. We had a loose plan—a limited vision of where we would be next week, let alone two or ten months from now. They planned their trip for five years; we flew through the process in less than twelve months. The longer we talked to this family, the more I understood why our friends and family thought we had lost our minds when we left town.

With all of the Revolutionary War reading Daniel had been doing, it was never a choice of whether or not we would visit the battlefield at Yorktown. Daniel was still interested in anything related to the making of our nation and with these landmark visits came opportunities for Thomas to learn firsthand history lessons. Mixing homeschooling with sightseeing was a beautiful thing.

Yorktown was a pivotal battle in the Revolutionary War only because it was the most decisive victory for the Continental Army and served to break the confidence of the English. It was here that the French Navy fought the redcoats and forced the ships carrying supplies and reinforcements to turn back, leaving General Cornwallis alone and outnumbered—giving the Americans and their allies the opportunity they needed. There wasn't much of a battle because once the Americans and French had trenches dug and artillery in place, a sort of colonial "shock and awe" took care of much of the British troops.

Fighting occurred in only a couple of places where the British had dug in and built earthen barriers surrounded by long pointy sticks called "fraises" and prickly bushes, or bramble. The French stormed one of these "redoubts" and the Americans, led by Alexander Hamilton, stormed the other. It lasted 15 or 20 minutes and casualties were minimal. Daniel loved this particular campaign because it was the first and sole opportunity for Alexander Hamilton to lead a military operation. Hamilton had wanted to fight for some time, but Washington wouldn't let him. He valued Alexander's attributes and didn't want anything to happen to him. If only George had been around to protect him from Aaron Burr some 30 years later.

Because there wasn't much of a confrontation at Yorktown—compared to say, Gettysburg—the museums must have had a difficult time filling their exhibits with stuff. The federally owned National Park Visitors' Center had a table used by Cornwallis, but then, so did the state-operated Victory Center. I assumed the leader of the Brits could have used two tables for planning his imminent surrender, but then why would you take two tables into battle? General Cornwallis didn't resign to Washington, because he was ill. I might call in sick, too, if I had to give my sword to the leader of "rabble in arms." On the surrender field, Washington chose not to accept the enemy's sword himself, but sent his second in command while he watched from a distance. Not to criticize Washington, but that decision seemed childish to me, like "Well, if he isn't coming then I'm not going either, so there." Daniel thought it made perfect sense, but then he has the same opinion of George Washington that I hold of Dr. Phil...he's always right.

We chose to leave Williamsburg in favor of Virginia Beach, a decision that took all of two seconds to make. See how easy these things are when you haven't planned too far ahead? Daniel's month had ended and work would be less stressful for the first half of October. I was hopeful that our sightseeing would pick up again. If they didn't, I might have to resort to making an activity spreadsheet and trust me, no one wanted that.

Vicariously Yours,
Traci

"Virginia is for Lovers." At first glance, the phrase would seem aimed primarily at honeymooners or couples but that was not the intent. When the slogan was first pitched by an advertising agency in 1969, it was to read, "Virginia is for _____ Lovers", allowing the tourism board to fill in the blank with whatever activity they chose. Some brilliant mind streamlined the motto and it has stood the test of time for more than 30 years.

In our weeks spent there, we discovered the truth in the expression. Lovers of all things—rich history, accessible culture, diverse landscapes, and hospitable people—could find what they were looking for in Virginia. As the gateway to the South, it bridged the fast-paced world of industry and development with tranquil, welcoming charm. Sound too good to be true? I thought so, too, but I couldn't have been more wrong.

Arriving in Virginia Beach was exciting for several reasons: a new month, a unique festival, balmy weather, and the sandy beach. Our site at the campground was paved and featured a concrete patio and fire pit. Up until this point in my life, I hadn't given much thought to my preferences involving asphalt versus gravel, but now I knew: asphalt ruled. Besides, it made vacuuming almost unnecessary.

Our first night at the campground was sleepless. The next-door campers had ventured out and had fun at some local pubs, and we paid dearly for it during the wee hours of the morning. They came back loud and proud of their drunkenness and shared 60 minutes of frivolity with us through our open windows. They planted themselves on their patio, four feet from our bedroom, and called every single family member and friend in their speed dial. The conversations were incoherent but booming, and could be heard even after closing our windows and turning on the air conditioner. With no one left to call, the happy campers brought out Fido and incited a sing-along with man's best friend. I couldn't quite name that tune, but then it had been awhile since I heard intoxicated people sing with their dog.

Daniel wanted to go out and confront them, but I didn't think that was a good idea. Not to make gross generalizations here, but when was the last time you were able to reason with a drunk person? In my five years of experience at Ball State University, having a serious conversation with someone under the influence of alcohol ended in one of two ways: with tears or vomit, neither of which was fun at 3:30 a.m. Daniel agreed to call the office, leave a message, and try to get some sleep. Here, the management handled disruptive behavior unlike previous places we had stayed—meaning, they did nothing. They encouraged us to deal with the situation ourselves if it happened again. I stood corrected. Maybe in Virginia, it was possible to reason with intoxicated people.

We spent Saturday lounging at the beach. The weather was a mild 78 degrees with clear sunny skies and a light breeze blowing across the Atlantic. Thomas told me before we left the bus that he was not swimming in the ocean, but I made him wear a swimsuit anyway. Lucky for him because he made friends with a few boys and learned to boogie board that afternoon. Daniel and I watched him laughing as he threw himself on the board and rode the waves in. It was the happiest he had been since the beach in Maine and we decided then to keep him on the beach all winter long. The beauty of this trip lay in the opportunity to go where we wanted and do the things we love. We would miss some of the interior portions of the Carolinas, but if Thomas loved the beach, then why not give him three months of nothing but sand, saltwater, and sun?

An annual event with 30 years of history, the "Neptune Festival" celebrated the spirit of the ocean and its importance to the people of Virginia Beach. It also signified the end of the tourist season, something one local told us was the true reason to party. The festivities took place all weekend along the three miles of boardwalk and sand with a surfing contest, beach volleyball tournament, and sand sculpture competition.

The sand sculpture fascinated me and drew the largest crowd of spectators. There were about 15 professional sand artists and 20 amateurs participating. Each contestant, individual or group, worked in an area measuring approximately 10 feet by 10 feet. We stood and watched the masters with their hoses and non-native sand, working to get the correct consistency and hardness, and were amazed at what could be created from this medium. The more elaborate designs began construction on Friday evening to allow enough time to finish before the Saturday afternoon cut-off. The details and varying textures achieved were so crisp and vivid that each sculpture looked as if it could come alive at any moment. Many were based around the character Neptune, however, a few rebellious entrants fashioned something unassociated with the theme, including elephants bathing themselves in a pool, the lost city of Atlantis, the fat Viking lady with braided pigtails singing opera (what's her name?), and the fall of Hades.

After the festival was over, we wondered what happened to the sculptures so we headed back to the beach on Monday night and they were still there. I thought for sure that someone would come along and destroy them—like a child who watches his friend build a tower of blocks only to knock it down two seconds later—but that didn't happen. Sure, some of the details were less visible, but the majority of the art pieces were still there after three days of wind and thousands of onlookers. Could it be that the people of Virginia Beach respected the art so much that not even the local teenage boys would vandalize them? Or did people stay away because the sculpture of King Neptune stood watch over all the others? He did have creepy eyes that followed me everywhere I went.

On Sunday, we drove back to Williamsburg to visit Busch Gardens. We spent our day enjoying all that the theme park had to offer, including screaming thrill rides, laugh-out-loud shows, and all our favorite carnival foods. We did leave early because 6:00 p.m. was the "witching hour"—the time when all of the ghosts and goblins came out in hopes of scaring the guests courageous enough to stay after dark—and Thomas, my dear sweet boy, would still rather watch a dachshund jump through a hoop than a goofy ghoul jump at a giggly girl. Thank goodness!

Thomas thought he would be bored walking through Colonial Williamsburg, but changed his mind after stepping into the Governor's Palace and seeing what was on the walls: they were covered with muskets, bayonets, and swords. The residence served also as the armory. With Thomas's interest in historical weaponry, he hoped I would draw inspiration from this space for his next bedroom design.

We learned that the weapons were kept in the governor's home in case an uprising occurred in the colony, at which point the weapons would be available and ready for use. At least 200 of the muskets were kept loaded at all times. The irony was that when the revolution began and the British leader and his family abandoned their home, Patrick Henry took all of those weapons and distributed them to his men. Smart guy!

After touring the Governor's Palace, we walked through town, stopping to speak with many of the tradesmen. My favorite storekeeper to watch was the cooper, an occupation I had never heard of until we visited the *Mayflower* in Plymouth where I discovered that coopers made barrels. The gentleman at Williamsburg was fascinating to talk to about his craft and even more interesting to watch. We learned that a keg of beer was a different size than a keg of wine and that each "good" had specific and regulated needs. I was astonished that these men could make wooden vessels that were watertight without the use of glue. He said that it took 4 years to learn the proper "fitting" techniques in order to build barrels and kegs. With the ability to package products in plastic, stainless steel, and corrugated cardboard, the need for coopers has all but disappeared. The exception—fine cognac is still stored in barrels made of Limousin oak and sells for nearly $1500.00 per bottle. With a liquid that costly, that had better be one tight-fitting vessel.

Thomas loved the gunsmith the best. A colonial gunsmith required the skills of four different trades—blacksmith, whitesmith, founder, and woodworker—in order to build a gun. Young boys would begin their apprenticeship at the age of 12 in hopes that by the time they turned 21, they would be ready to work on their own. Building rifles was expensive. It was far easier and more cost effective for customers to order an import. With few guns to build, the early American gunsmith often found work repairing other objects. The gunsmith in Williamsburg mentioned that his shop still produced about four muskets per year at a cost of $10,000 each. Yikes! It did take about 400 man-hours to build these complicated weapons, but who could afford to spend that much money on something that would hang on a wall? Although, if you kept it loaded and a rebellion began in your cul-de-sac, you would be ready.

We left Virginia and drove south to Wilmington, North Carolina where it rained for two days. Our first night there, Daniel and I walked to the laundry room after dark when all of a sudden something small jumped in front of me. I thought it was a cricket or grasshopper, but then I saw lots of things jumping in front of me. Afraid to move my feet for fear of stepping on whatever it was, I stood still and studied the gravel road. It was covered in hundreds, if not thousands, of baby toads hopping across the driveway. I hoped no great evil was befalling Wilmington, the constant rain and plague of toads had me worried. Daniel assured me the end of the world was not upon us. Good, I thought. I didn't want to miss out on the rest of the trip. I hadn't been to Key West or San Francisco, Salt Lake City or San Antonio and I really wanted to go.

Vicariously Yours,
Traci

Sent: Monday, October 16, 2005
Subject: Carolina Country

The day we left Wilmington, it was still pouring. The gravel roads and campsites were flooded with a gray soup. In four months, we had never had to break camp in the rain and we were not looking forward to our inaugural experience. But, escaping the profuse precipitation would not be possible during our entire stay, which was too bad. There were countless activities and attractions, but all we saw were the bank, grocery store, and cinema. I had no idea that Wilmington was considered East Hollywood because of the many studios located there. One of my favorite films, *Forrest Gump*, was shot in town. If only the magic of movie-making could have changed the weather long enough to see something interesting.

We made it to Myrtle Beach, South Carolina, a popular destination spot for people looking to bask in the sun and have a good time. Our campsite this week was 20 feet off of the beach and allowed us the privilege to be lulled to sleep by the sound of breaking waves and smell of salty air. Although it did rain some, the weather 90 percent of the time was perfect and we spent hours each day playing in the sand or lounging by the pool. We could have spent our time at miniature golf courses, entertainment venues, and various amusements, but all we wanted to do was relax and enjoy the peace that this week offered. Besides, we had just spent three days in a near flood. It was time to dry out.

If you haven't been to Myrtle Beach, Highway 17 serves as the main road connecting 20 miles of souvenir shops, restaurants, and hotels to the tourists who keep them in business. We helped the local economy by visiting one traveler's hot spot on the strip...Dixie Stampede, Dolly Parton's Civil-War–themed dinner show featuring animals, live music, and country dancing. Our favorite competition was the ostrich race. The birds ran like Olympic sprinters with blindfolds on—lightning fast, but with no idea where they were going. Like Medieval Times in Baltimore, there was impressive horsemanship, dramatic entertainment, and no silverware. I didn't understand why. People had utensils during the Civil War, didn't they? Surely those Southern belles with the frilly dresses and fancy hair didn't eat with their hands. The "Godless North" might have used their hands because they were close to savages, but you can't convince me that those fine aristocratic Southerners didn't eat off of china with the correct fork and knife.

One day at the beach, Daniel was trying to help Thomas with his boogie board, but the surf was different from Virginia and Thomas sank instead of glided on the water. As Daniel tried to coach him, Thomas got frustrated, threw his board at his dad and told him he should try to do it. I watched as my husband was heading out into the surf with Thomas's boogie board in his hands. I had never seen Daniel do this before, so I propped myself up and settled in for a good show. He threw himself on the petite board over and over again, spending more time under the waves than on them. Thomas laughed and yelled, "See, Dad? You can't even do it!" Covered in sand and defeated, Daniel trudged onto the beach, puffed up his chest and proclaimed that the problem was the size of the board, not him. Regardless of whether he succeeded at boogie boarding or not, what struck me was the willingness of Daniel to show our son that attempting something new was fun, even at the ripe old age of 38. My husband was not an impressive surfer, but he excelled at being a father, and for that, I thanked my lucky stars.

Everything wasn't perfect. Even with the beach as our setting for the week, we were still three people living in a space smaller than a college dorm room. Each of us worked hard to compromise our personal desires, making it easier to maintain peace. Daniel and I discovered that we could no longer blame attitudes, language, and behaviors on the kids at school or in the neighborhood. We were our son's only teachers and he watched us 24 hours a day. This became clear when one day Thomas used some of my lines against me. He looked me in the face and said, "Are you trying to make me mad? I don't want to fight with you, so can you please just stop what you're doing?" You could have heard crickets chirping for miles. I stood, mouth agape, not knowing whether to laugh or yell. How could I get angry with him for acting like me?

Some of my quirks were falling away as we continued the journey. My organization compulsion had subsided, since there were fewer items and less space to fuss with. I had exhausted the 16 ways to arrange my four spices. I hoped that living in this oversized closet would bring our family closer, and it had, but I wasn't sure if such limited outside influence might land Thomas on the *Jerry Springer Show* someday. Time would tell.

Homeschooling was proceeding well. We still fought on some school days, but the arguing was less intense and shorter-lived. Since fifth grade was years ago for me, I learned that it's okay to admit to my child that I don't know everything and I discovered the best way to teach Thomas was to learn right along with him. When I removed him from school in fourth grade and informed the principal of our journey, she told me that it would never work. She said that, in her educated opinion, my son would never be able to re-enter school without repeating a grade level. I prayed she was wrong, but felt it was a risk worth taking. Right now, I thought our education plan was working well. And, I had the pleasure of brushing up on my long division.

I read an article in the Charleston paper about a group called the Christian Exodus. They were gathering in South Carolina. They have interesting ideas, similar to those of the original "Republicans," or Jeffersonians, of the Revolutionary War time period. The group leader spoke about the urgency of South Carolina's secession from the Union if the federal government didn't stop imposing "unjust" laws on its people. Stop right there! Haven't we been down this road before? Six hundred thousand deaths and a war that crippled a young nation began with statements like that. Radicalism or not, I loved the South. Beautiful surroundings, wonderful food, nice people, and a sense that you'd better slow down or you'd miss something important along the way...even if it was only a crazy man preaching rebellion.

Vicariously Yours,
Traci

Sent: Friday, October 21, 2005
Subject: Slow Down and Eat

We had been in Charleston, South Carolina; Savannah, Georgia; and Jacksonville, Florida—moving ever southward in preparation of spending the winter far away from freezing temperatures and snow. My expectations for life in the South were true—we were living at an unhurried pace. Though many people thought we were on an extended vacation, life on the road was hectic at times, when trying to squeeze in too much sightseeing with school and work.

We enjoyed the welcoming spirit in the people that seemed inherited, and yet, practiced at the same time, like the performance of a natural-born athlete after years of training. Although hospitality was a natural gift in this part of the country, it was obviously honed by years and years of housing, feeding and entertaining guests of all kinds. Elaborate architecture and historical buildings filled the streets of cities settled long ago by European explorers, picturesque coast lines and luxurious plant life created a stunning setting, and a warm charm welcomed the least of visitors.

Charleston, South Carolina, was the most fetching city I had visited in the past five months. Never in my life had I seen houses like those near the harbor. You could almost hear the rocking chairs and swings calling out from their long, shaded porches, beckoning guests to sit down for a spell and enjoy a tall glass of sweet tea. One in particular, the Edmondston-Alston house, was perhaps the most striking example of antebellum architecture on the High Battery, an elite area of Charleston. It boasted famous guests including General Robert E. Lee, who was in need of a place to stay when his hotel caught fire, and General Beauregard who wanted a front-row seat to watch the Confederate attack on Fort Sumter.

Besides touring grand residences, there is much to do in this historic town including visiting America's first museum. The Charleston Museum, established in 1773, is a valuable resource, if viewing interesting artifacts excites you. One item in the collection that I found fascinating was the very chair that South Carolina delegates sat in when signing their secession papers. Visitors could also learn and visit the exact location of the first shots in the War Between the States, which occurred on January 10, 1861.

Downtown Charleston is a pedestrian's dream with sidewalk shopping, unique eateries, and intriguing sights. We visited the area on three occasions and still walked away feeling that we hadn't seen everything. One fabulous place to spend time was the market square, which housed hundreds of vendors selling their wares including local art and regional specialties. During our travels, we discovered that locals don't always tell the same stories with regard to history. For example, one person told us that the square was the "slave market" where servants used to be sold. Later that afternoon, we were told by the guide on our carriage ride that you wouldn't buy slaves at a slave market any more than you would buy a farmer at a farmers market. "Instead," she said, "slaves sold their goods there. To buy one of *them* you had to go to a different part of town." Well, thank goodness we were only looking for pralines.

As we toured the city, we learned that there are over 180 active church-es in Charleston, a fact that has earned it the nickname of the "holy city." There was only one street in town where you could not see a church in any direction. Ironically, this was once the location of the "red light district." The logic was that if you couldn't see God, then He couldn't see you. I know people who still believe that.

All of the churches were interesting, but two of them in particular had unique stories. One was built in a circular design. The members believed that Satan dwelt in corners so their holy building was built with none. Another was built in such a way that it stuck out into the road. The thought behind this decision was to force the acknowledge-ment of the church's presence on the townspeople by making them go out of their way to avoid colliding with it. I thought it was a good idea. It *did* raise awareness.

Near Charleston, there is a naval museum called Patriot's Point that has a cold-war submarine, World War II aircraft carrier and destroyer, and one of the most decorated Coast Guard Cutters in U.S. history. The destroyer *Laffey*, and sub *Clamagore*, were interesting because each had served in enormous battles, but the aircraft carrier was the hands-down favorite for all three of us. The *USS Yorktown* was old and didn't compare to modern ships; however, we were amazed by the size and facilities onboard. The sign mentioned that the crew would have numbered around 3,000. We had stayed in towns much smaller than that. I kept looking for the Wal-Mart on the various decks. With that many people, surely a discount store was necessary.

I found the kitchen that included a butcher shop, vegetable prep room, and a recipe for 10,000 chocolate chip cookies. I also stumbled upon the dentist's office. I guessed even at sea there was no escaping oral hygiene. While meandering from one room to another, we found the bathrooms and Daniel had to go. Even if he hadn't, I would have encouraged him to use the historical facilities. How many times in your life would you have the opportunity to pee on a World War II aircraft carrier going where thousands had gone before?

While walking in the square one evening, we noticed a Bubba Gump's restaurant. I had never eaten there and, since I loved the movie *Forrest Gump*, I wanted to see what it was like. Daniel and Thomas agreed to try it. I wasn't sure when this particular restaurant opened, but I knew the chain began in 1996 with a location in Monterey, California, and had grown to just under 30 locations in places as diverse as Hong Kong, Denver, Oahu, and Minneapolis. The menu featured abundant shrimp dishes, as well as other Southern favorites like baby back ribs. The best part of the dining experience was playing with the signs on the table that said, "Run, Forrest, Run" or "Stop, Forrest, Stop," depending on whether you needed your server or not. Within just a few seconds of flipping it, someone would stop by our table to see what we needed. The first three or four times, the staff was fast and cheerful. After that, our table was like the boy who cried wolf. We were lucky to get our check.

One mild, starry night, we built a campfire and cooked hot dogs for dinner. Daniel and I had just finished roasting our frankfurters when a large dark animal walked around the back of the bus. Because it was pitch black and I couldn't see what it was, I jumped in my chair and yelled. The animal was quiet but began making its way toward us as we sat near our fire. It looked like a small bear, but, as it came closer, I realized it was a Rottweiler. In our campground experience, aggressive dogs were not allowed on the premises so I assumed the animal was a stray. I was afraid to move. I had seen *Cujo* as a child.

Standing not more than six feet away from my chair, the dog was staring at me...or at my food. He started to approach when I threw my freshly roasted hot dog as far as my arm would allow. In a flash, he darted for the food and Daniel sacrificed his dinner, too, to give us more time to run like scared little girls to the bus. Slamming the door behind us, we told Thomas what had just happened and the three of us peeked outside to see what Cujo's friend was now doing. The dog was walking around our campfire and sniffed the chairs and ground before giving up and leaving. When we were certain he had gone, we went back outside to finish our evening and cautiously roasted a few marshmallows. The next day, we found out that the dog belonged to the owner of the KOA and had broken through his invisible fence. We were told that he was harmless—more teddy bear than terrorist—and he would never hurt anyone. And to think I sacrificed a perfectly cooked turkey dog.

We left Charleston and headed for Savannah, Georgia. We were told by a local in Charleston that we shouldn't expect much from Savannah. I didn't. I was stopping there for one reason: Paula Deen. When watching the Food Network, I learned that my favorite Southern lady owned and operated a restaurant in downtown Savannah and I wanted to go. I consulted the internet and found that in order to get a table, customers should get in line at 3:30 p.m. to put their name on the list. When we walked up to The Lady & Sons, there were already 30 or 40 people in front of us.

Because we had an hour until dinner, we walked around downtown, enjoying the genteel squares and artistic boutiques. At 4:30 p.m., we walked back toward the restaurant and noticed a mob had formed on the sidewalks and street in front of the popular location. The restaurant didn't open for 30 minutes, but the crowd was getting riled. We could almost see the bared teeth of the salivating hungry onlookers as they crowded toward the host with "the list." My mind took me back to the Rottweiler in Charleston and I wondered what would happen if I had a basket of fried chicken to throw. Would some of them run to catch it? At 5:00 p.m., the host elbowed his way into the middle of the street and, with an iron triangle, declared the restaurant open for business. A collective hoorah came from the crowd and they surged toward the door.

Once inside, I was entranced. There were pictures of Paula and her family on the walls and the aroma of butter in the air. Our server had the most pleasant drawl. I could have listened to him read the phone book. The food was good and we all enjoyed our selections. For me, it was much less about the quality of the menu and more about the experience. I had watched Paula on television for some time and there I was sitting in her restaurant in Savannah, Georgia. While Daniel took a picture of his mammoth chicken pot pie, I was struck with the realization that each day on this trip had afforded me the chance to see and do things that others may or may not ever experience. I was humbled and decided that I had better order dessert, just so I could tell you what it was like. It was fabulous!

Vicariously Yours,
Traci

Daniel and I didn't plan on spending most of the winter in Florida, but as the temperature dipped in Indiana, we thought...why not? Why shouldn't we be "snow birds" like so many northern folks who flock to the Sunshine State in hopes of avoiding icy roads, snow shoveling, and arctic temperatures? Committed to remaining in Florida until early January, we would have more than enough time to not only get a great tan, but also explore northern, southern and central parts of our country's fourth most populated state. Did you know that the state song is "Old Folks at Home (Suwannee River) by Stephen C. Foster? Since Florida has more than 50 cities with a median age of 60 years or more, I guess the old folks have found their home, huh? I don't blame them for choosing a fairer climate. I preferred lounging by the pool to shoveling snow, too. Our first few days in Jacksonville involved a lot of soaking in sunshine and enjoying the summerlike weather.

I was in the laundry room talking to a fellow campground mom and she mentioned that she and her family were evacuees from New Orleans. They had been living there for two months. I asked her how they ended up in Jacksonville and she told me that her husband had purchased a used motorhome, against her wishes, just before Hurricane Katrina hit. When they were told to leave their home, they jumped in the RV and drove away without taking many belongings, not considering the hurricane would destroy their home, cars, and possessions. She wished she would have known. Instead, they were left with nothing and had to rely on the generosity of others.

Her husband's company found him a position in Jacksonville, the reason they were at the campground. With limited funds, the family was only able to purchase one vehicle, which her husband used for work. This displaced mother and her teenage son were stranded, 10 hours a day, in an RV park they had come to hate. I could not imagine how difficult it would be to lose your home and all of your belongings, move to a new place where you knew no one except your husband and son, and start a new life in a motorhome. Although our living situations were somewhat similar, what set us apart was that I chose mine. She didn't. As we left the Jacksonville campground and passed their rig, I couldn't help thinking how fortunate we really were. I prayed for that family and for all those who lost so much in New Orleans and Mississippi—and then I checked the weather forecast to see just where Hurricane Wilma was spending her time. It was, after all, still hurricane season.

We drove to St. Augustine, the oldest permanent European settlement in the Continental United States, but we didn't know that at the time we decided to go. All we knew was that our friends owned a vacation home there and would be able to meet us during Fall Break for some fun in the sun with people other than strangers. We couldn't pass up the opportunity. When we arrived on Saturday, our friends had already made themselves at home on the sand, so all we had to do was park our rig and join them.

Our camp site was on the beach, allowing us to open the windows and fill the bus with an ocean breeze and the sound of rolling waves. Blue sky, white sand, and warm water made for a wonderful afternoon splashing in the Atlantic. One of our friends was an "active beachgoer." He liked to do things like play games, swim, and dig for buried treasure. I preferred to focus my activity in the area of lying perfectly still so that the sun browned me evenly. I never intended on entering the surf, but I had no choice. Thomas's raft was well on its way to Cuba and that was a place *not* on our itinerary for this trip.

In the 35 years I lived in Indiana, I never paid much attention to hurricanes. I mean, we've all heard about the horrific damage that Andrew, Hugo, and more recently, Katrina inflicted on the residents of the South, but how many Hoosiers studied every tropical depression and storm that developed in the Gulf? I know I didn't, but then I never looked at a tide schedule before and what an oversight that turned out to be. I lost a car in the ocean, but that was long ago. We started watching the weather while in Jacksonville because Hurricane Wilma was moving toward Florida and we weren't certain when the storm would strike or what the severity would be. The storm stalled over the Yucatan and the people there were taking the brunt of it, delaying landfall in Florida and weakening the impact.   I've always loved the people of the Yucatan, haven't you?

Wilma was due to hit Florida in the wee hours of Monday morning so we left Thomas at our friends' well-grounded house (which by the way was a fabulous vacation home available for rent with 3 bedrooms, 2 bathrooms, in-ground pool, and awesome view) in case the wind and rain were too scary for our young man.   When Daniel called his dad to discuss how to prepare the bus for the imminent storm, he advised us to pull in the slides and hunker down for a rocky night.   Several hours later, we learned that our bus was watertight and heavy enough to with-stand 50 mph winds.   Thank goodness.

There was minimal damage from the storm with the exception of near record low temperatures.   We could live with that.   Our days lounging at the beach were over, but with so much to do, we barely missed it.   We spent our time touring historic St. Augustine and learned once again that history differed depending on who was telling the story.   For exam-ple, some Southerners insisted that the North did not win the Civil War. What?   Who had they been listening to?   Had someone been channel-ing the ghost of John Wilkes Booth?   We learned that the Spanish founded the first permanent colony in North America in 1565?   This was 42 years before the English colonized Jamestown, Virginia, and 55 years before our good friends in black hats and buckle shoes landed on a rock in Plymouth.   I was taught in school that the Pilgrims were the first colonists in our country, but, "No," say the Spanish.   The Englishmen who wrote our schoolbooks forgot to mention the Spaniards and their settlement in Florida.   Instead of eating turkey, mashed potatoes, yams, and pumpkin pie in November, we should be eating tapas, chorizo, paella, and flan in the spring.   I would be willing to honor the English and the Spanish by enthusiastically eating both meals. (Minus the flan.)

The courageous Spanish explorer, Don Juan Ponce de Leon, a man whose name was longer than he was tall, first set eyes on the coast of Florida on Easter, March 27, 1513.   Between 1513 and 1564, the Spanish were unsuccessful in colonizing "La Florida," the Land of Flowers; the French prevailed and established a fort and colony.   King

Phillip II did not like this at all and sent someone more intimidating than 4'11" Ponce de Leon to permanently settle the expanse for Spain and get rid of the French. Enter Don Pedro Menendez de Aviles, an experienced officer in Spain and the newly appointed Governor of Florida.

His first order of business was to name his new community St. Augustine, in remembrance of the day he landed off the coast, the Feast Day of St. Augustine. He then followed his naming ceremony with the expulsion, or massacre, of the French Huguenots. The construction of the Spanish settlement began in earnest, and with it developed a proud history of Spanish culture and architecture. Of course, that came after the British burned the town and the pirates killed nearly all of the settlers.

Flash forward 440 years to modern-day St. Augustine and you'll find a tourist's paradise complete with a wonderful mix of historical and contemporary attractions from the old city gates to Ripley's Believe It or Not Museum. The most prominent landmark in the city is the Castillo de San Marcos, the oldest masonry fort in the country, conceived in 1672 after several wooden structures burned at the hands of the British and, although it took 23 years to complete, the structure proved to be well worth the time and effort. Because the walls were built using "coquina," a locally mined spongey material made of tiny shells and sand, armaments such as cannonballs were simply absorbed into the structure rather than causing damage. Imagine how frustrating that must have been for British naval officers to discover.

The first test for the newly constructed fort came in 1702 when a British governor from newly colonized Charles Town (or Charleston, South Carolina) sailed over to St. Augustine and tried to take the city from the Spanish. After bombarding the stronghold for two months, a Spanish fleet from Cuba trapped the British in the bay, forcing them to burn their boats and walk home to Carolina—not the best day for the aforementioned British governor from Charles Town.

In 1739, the fortress came under siege once again by our British predecessors and, again, the Redcoats were sent packing. The Castillo de San

Marcos was never taken by force and only exchanged ownership through peaceful (if political manipulation can be called peaceful) means. Over the course of the next 200 years, as the Castillo changed hands between the British, Spanish, United States, Confederate States, and United States again, it also changed its name from Castillo de San Marcos to Fort St. Mark back to Castillo de San Marcos to Fort Marion and finally, back to Castillo de San Marcos. As they say, "If walls could talk," I'm sure the stories would be both chilling and riveting.

Two hundred fifty-two years, five flags, and three names later, Castillo de San Marcos was designated a National Monument by President Coolidge and soon after was given over to the care of the National Park Service. Today, millions of visitors walk inside the same walls that protected the residents of St. Augustine for more than 300 years and, as long as they keep their hands off of them, those walls will likely stand for centuries more. You see, though the coquina was impervious to cannonballs, human hands wreak havoc. If only the British had known.

The colonial area of St. Augustine is charming, complete with narrow cobblestone roads, balconied houses, and preservation projects. It was a wonderful place to shuffle along, peeking into the shops, restaurants, and museums. To get a relaxing overview of the layout as well as an interesting narrative, we hopped aboard a trolley and listened to our driver fill our heads with ancient facts, contemporary trivia, and fascinating tales. For example, the oldest street in the country is Charlotte Street. St. Augustine was once a walled city—one of only three in North America including Charleston, South Carolina, and Quebec City, Quebec—and, although the walls have long been gone, the city gates still stand on St. George Street. An unknown Jimmy Buffett started his career in a bar there called Tradewinds before getting fired and leaving town for Key West. With a tour guide and a listening ear, captivating information was just a "ticket to ride" away.

Something else we learned while riding the trolley was that three of the signers of the Declaration of Independence lived in St. Augustine and were under house arrest during the Revolutionary War because Florida remained loyal to the Crown. I was told that the Floridians were in need of protection from Native Americans and the British were happy to oblige, if only to have something to do while most of the real fighting went on up north.

With the end of the war came the beginning of the development boon in Florida, followed by the state's "bread and butter": tourism. Henry Flagler, a partner in Standard Oil with John D. Rockefeller, built a spectacular hotel in hopes of luring wealthy tourists to St. Augustine. Mr. Flagler also owned the railroad that would transport these wealthy travelers. He was an incredible businessman and over the course of several years developed other hotels and businesses in the city, too. His first hotel, the Ponce de Leon, now served as part of Flagler College, a private liberal arts school in the heart of the downtown district.

Because religion played such a large part in the founding of St. Augustine (remember the slaughter of the Protestants by the Spanish), it won't surprise you to learn that the oldest parish in the United States, the Cathedral Basilica, is located in America's oldest city. We took the opportunity to visit the breathtaking church one afternoon. From the 15,000-piece tile floor to the oil paintings and stained glass, the decorative elements were outstanding. There was another church I wanted to see, the First Presbyterian, but we couldn't go in. There was a funeral that day...like that's a good reason to keep out tourists.

I wanted to see *that* church not just because it was well built, but because it was constructed in less than a year's time. In 1891, that was an unbelievable accomplishment. Flagler funded the project and set the deadline because he wanted it completed in time for the one-year anniversary of the deaths of his first wife and daughter. Mary Harkness and Jennie Louise Flagler were buried at the Presbyterian Church and, although Mr. Flagler remarried and moved away from St. Augustine, upon his death in 1913, he returned and was buried next to his family.

The people of the oldest city in the country worked hard to preserve and restore a heritage that began more than 400 years ago. And, it didn't stop with the buildings. As a visitor, we enjoyed listening to the stories and tales told by locals and guides. We heard about spooky, eerie happenings on our evening ghost tour through Old Town and the Castillo and walked through the largest indoor swimming pool-turned-dining room at the Alcazar Hotel (now Lightner Museum). Yes, I would say that Henry Flagler's dream of creating a thriving tourist's destination in little old St. Augustine came true. There may not be a beautiful princess castle, giant singing mice, or anything resembling "a small world," but there was an old masonry fort, the Fountain of Youth, and a town that founded the New World. Maybe you should plan a visit and find out why central Florida isn't the only place to spend your vacation time. If you need a place to stay...my friends have a great rental home.

Vicariously Yours,
Traci

Sent: Wednesday, November 9, 2005
Subject: The Mouse is in the House...and Somewhere Else, Too!

We arrived in Orlando a full month ahead of our original plan. Why? Well, the short answer was because Daniel, Thomas and I love Walt Disney World and couldn't wait any longer to get there. We drove at a breakneck speed to reach our destination. It was still Fall Break in Indiana and we were meeting vacationing friends before they had to go home. The weather had rebounded beautifully from Hurricane Wilma: sunshine, blue sky, and mild temperatures.

Daniel had business to take care of and I had chores to do, like any other day at home, except when we were done, we drove to Downtown Disney. As soon as we crossed onto the property, our faces broke into smiles and each of us let out an energetic "Woohoo!" Our excitement shook the car. There, it was perfectly acceptable to wear a bright pink Tinker Bell shirt, break into song with the Seven Dwarfs, and skip-di-dee-doo-da while listening to Winnie the Pooh music.

I watched *The Mickey Mouse Club* every week when I was a child and dreamed of being a Mouseketeer. I looked into the sky at night for Jiminy Cricket's special star that, when wished upon, would make my dreams come true. When I visited Disney World for the first time with my grandparents, parents, and sister, I marveled at the electric light parade and Cinderella's Castle. I once walked through Epcot with my high school swing choir and sang on a stage there. Daniel and I surprised a five-year-old Thomas with a trip to Disney World at Christmas and watched him jump up and down when he met Buzz Lightyear. Many special memories of the past 35 years involved this place in some way and it was hard for me to walk around any part of it and not feel emotional. Would the magic get old if we stayed for two months? I looked forward to finding out.

On October 29th, we met our friends at Animal Kingdom and had a great day taking in the attractions. For first-time visitors, I always recommended a show called "Tarzan Rocks!" The band and music were awesome and the rollerblading monkeys were incredible, but what I enjoyed most was Tarzan in his loin cloth. I was confused though because while he had bulging muscles, he had no body hair. Wouldn't an ape-man covered with hair make more sense than a sleek and tan body builder? Not that I would rather see a hairy man in little more than a Speedo. No, I appreciated the park's creative license in this instance.

We visited Epcot where the International Food & Wine Festival was going on. Yum! It was the 10th year for the event and drew large crowds of guests interested in sampling the diverse offerings. One thing I loved about the festival was the encouragement it gave Thomas to try new foods. He gave up his usual chicken tenders and tasted Moroccan kebabs, French crème brulee, and Spanish ham.

The international entertainment included a group of three men from Australia who performed a dance commemorating the history of...something. I missed the introduction because when they walked out, Thomas wilted when he saw what they were wearing: loin cloths. Now I liked a good loin cloth, but these guys weren't exactly Tarzan. They were more akin to an Aboriginal John Goodman or Chris Farley. I couldn't blame him for wanting to leave.

Daniel and I surprised Thomas with a Disney cruise to the Bahamas. We arrived at Port Canaveral around 1:30 p.m. on Thursday, November 3, and had no idea what awaited us onboard the *Disney Wonder*. Masters of organization and efficiency, the staff had us checked in and touring the ship within 30 minutes. As we entered the main hall, a cast member asked us our last name and then announced our arrival, which was followed by a thunderous applause by the crew. Talk about a warm welcome. Disney does have a way with details.

The ship was luxurious, but still child-friendly. Lunch was available right away and we walked to Parrot Cay where we had our first experience with a Disney cruise ship buffet. In my former life as a meeting planner, I had seen some artfully arranged and abundant buffets, but none quite like this. The centerpiece on the bread table was a peacock with baguette loaves for the tail plumes. Thomas tried to get me to take one of the baguettes to eat. I told him that I couldn't eat a whole loaf of bread by myself—at least not in broad daylight.

Just before setting sail, the cast member at the Shore Excursion desk told us to take our motion sickness medication soon if we had any issues. We chose not to and lived to regret it later. As we had dinner that night, we struggled through each bite, carefully chewing for several minutes before swallowing. When the ship's photographer came around to take our picture, we smiled through closed lips and hoped his lens would filter our green faces. The next day when we saw the photograph, we snatched it off the rack and threw it away. *No one* needed to see that.

Daniel and I made a deal with Thomas. Since he was ten years old, he could have full run of the ship as long as he ate with us and came home when the kids' club closed. On occasion, we saw him playing basketball and ping pong, but sometimes he strolled around the ship enjoying his independence. The first night, he wanted to go to the premiere of *Chicken Little* at 12:01 a.m. There was no way Daniel and I were getting up to go to a movie at midnight. So, Thomas went by himself. A cast member guided him on his way and made sure he arrived back at the correct cabin by 1:30 a.m.

We crossed into Bahamian water sometime during the night and when we woke and looked out our porthole, we saw pink buildings and sapphire waters. After the boys disembarked to snorkel at Blackbeard's Cay, I headed up to the adults-only pool, "Quiet Cove." I stayed for about an hour before realizing that I felt uncomfortable there. I missed hearing children playing. I also preferred the music that the kids listened to. Give me Hilary Duff or Jesse McCartney over soft jazz any day. I picked up my stuff and found a chair at the Mickey Mouse pool. Ah, the sound of splashing, laughing, and screaming...now *that* was relaxing to me.

I enjoyed my day by myself, but missed my family and looked forward to hearing all about their time with the fish. When they came back, Thomas told me about feeding the manta rays and accidentally stepping on one. He then propped up his toe on the table to show me the trophy wound. Someday, he would tell that story to his friends and search for the scar on his toe as an offer of proof. At the very least, they had a striking picture of the two of them on an exquisite Bahamian beach and an exciting story about an incident with a spiny-backed fish. After dinner we watched the golden sun disappear into the ocean. The sky was aglow with fiery reds, oranges, and yellows, but only for a few minutes and then it was gone. Aboard the *Disney Wonder*, life was good.

Our day at Castaway Cay was brilliant. The island, owned by Disney, is a picturesque Caribbean paradise complete with snorkeling, swimming, boating, parasailing, and eating. We rode a "banana boat" which was a long yellow inflatable contraption that held 12 people and was pulled by a ski boat. It was insane fun. We did learn that salt water stings the eyes. I didn't have goggles, but I was fortunate enough to have a big man seated in front of me and he did a fine job acting as a saltwater body shield.

After the excitement of the boat ride, Daniel and I floated the afternoon away on a couple of rafts in a quiet lagoon while Thomas played on an island "jungle gym." We ate a light meal on the beach and soaked up another hour of sun before it was time to go. We strolled back to the ship, showered, and took naps before dressing for our last dinner and evening at sea. Daniel and I talked about how comfortable our stateroom was. We thought it was quite roomy, but then we *had* been living in a bus for several months.

The live show the last night of our cruise was called *Disney Dreams* and it reminded me why we were spending eight weeks in Orlando, Florida, immersed in a world of make-believe and imagination. Where else besides Disney could a person surround himself with all that is good and lovely? Watching fireworks at night ends the day perfectly; watching Tinker Bell fly in the Magic Kingdom makes us smile; listening to Jiminy Cricket sing "When you wish upon a star..." makes anything seem possible. If you could choose to live in a place where magic happened every day, wouldn't you?

Vicariously Yours,
Traci

This year marked the 50th anniversary of California's Disneyland and every sister park around the world was celebrating, too. I didn't understand why the people in Paris, Hong Kong, Tokyo and Orlando would spend a year commemorating a park that wasn't their own. Wouldn't that be comparable to me observing my birthday anytime someone named Traci, Tracy, Tracie, or Tracey happened to do so? Along with corporate-wide celebrations, Disney offered festivals aplenty. The Festival of the Masters at Downtown Disney was littered with EZ-up tents filled with artistic wares for as far as the eye could see. Musicians played in front of the House of Blues and the Virgin music store, adding a cool vibe to the shopping experience.

I stopped at a woodworker's tent and bought a special gift before wandering over to check out the student art, sidewalk chalk, and Lego creations. I was blown away by the talent in this small area of the country. I loved the chalk art and stood for several minutes watching each piece in the process of being created. The artists sat in heaps of multi-colored chalk dust and I thought the situation would make an award-winning Tide commercial.

Daniel flew to Indianapolis on Tuesday morning for a sales meeting, leaving Thomas and me to fend for ourselves for a few days. I was nervous that Thomas would get bored. Dad was considered the "fun" parent. We were able to get all of our school stuff done early in the days and have plenty of time to visit the parks in the afternoon and evening. We had special "mother/son" time at Epcot on Tuesday and the Magic Kingdom on Wednesday. When I spoke with Daniel, he said that it was cold and snowy in Indianapolis and I almost hated to tell him that we spent the afternoon playing at the pool and bike riding in 80-degree weather. Thomas taught me how to shoot my laser gun on the Buzz Lightyear ride and I scored higher than I ever had. If only I had joined the military after college.

I have talked about the magic of Disney and this week I encountered someone who embodied it. We were leaving Epcot on Sunday when we jumped on a bus back to Fort Wilderness and met a man by the name of Roger, our driver. I knew he was unique when he tried to make Daniel ride on the roof because of his sweatshirt. Evidently, he wasn't an Indianapolis Colts fan. Though he relented and let us onboard, he incited 50 passengers to boo us. Then Roger stood up and announced to the crowd that, although he was a Tampa Bay Buccaneer fan, our team did have the best coach in the NFL. We had found something to agree on. With a wink and a smile, he settled into his seat and pulled away from the loading area.

While riding back to the resort, Roger told us a short history of Walt Disney World and the surrounding property along with interesting and little-known facts. He stopped to show us some of the wildlife including several white-tailed deer and armadillos. After riding bus after bus after bus for the past five years, this man was doing something different. He was doing his job, but it was more than that. He didn't have to spin tales and entertain us. He didn't have to tell us anything other than where we were going and when we arrived. But, he chose to go a step further and make the bus ride from Epcot to our campground like visiting an attraction and, in that way, he set himself apart from all of the other drivers.

Last week, a friend reminded me that magic lives outside of Walt Disney World, too. I was so caught up in the dreaminess and exclusivity of Disney magic that I forgot that each and every one of us has the opportunity to create that same feeling in our own circle of influence. Roger may be a cast member in Orlando, but it wasn't just his training that made him go above and beyond what was expected. That was his decision. It can be your decision, too. Disney magic is caring more than is necessary and giving more than is expected and it works just as well in a carpool as it does on a bus bound for the Magic Kingdom.

Vicariously Yours,
Traci

We celebrated Thanksgiving at "the world." It was our first major holiday away from our families. I decided to forego preparing an entire holiday meal in the bus. When Daniel called to get reservations, the only restaurant available was the Japanese steakhouse at Epcot. We weren't disappointed. The food was prepared with a dramatic flair and was scrumptious, but I walked away from the feast feeling like the anorexic Olson twin. Who knew using chopsticks could be so difficult? I thought about writing a book describing a revolutionary diet plan involving no drugs, no exercise, and no food restrictions. The key to the diet—you must eat everything with chopsticks. My working title is *Eat with Sticks and You'll Soon Be One*. What do you think?

We spent time at Universal Studios and its sister park, Islands of Adventure. So, how are Universal and Disney different? Walt Disney World focuses on the entire family, creating experiences for 4-year-olds, 8-year-olds, teenagers, parents, grandparents, and even Great-Aunt Hairy Chin and Uncle Smells Funny. Universal Studios has little to offer children under the age of seven; however, the parks are perfect for pre-teens, teens, and all of their tag-a-longs.

While Disney rides are tame, Universal's roller coasters, the Hulk and Dueling Dragons, would make you lose your lunch if a weak stomach is listed as one of your 2000 parts. However, Disney does focus more on "real" ride experiences rather than the simulated fun that Universal has to offer. I had to remember that Universal makes movies, Disney makes magic. Universal is expert at building sets and backdrops which left us in the realm of illusion. Disney is masterful at creating dreams and inspiration, leaving guests believing that we could be more—do more.

Christmas spirit was hard for me to find because without my friends, family, and even snow, it didn't feel like my favorite holiday. I assumed even Disney magic had its limits. That was, until we saw the Candlelight Processional at Epcot. It was the best show I had ever seen at any theme park, ever. There were no dancing animals and no colorful costumes, or flashy effects. It was Disney's Christmas show in the American Adventure pavilion. When we sat down, I expected to hear Jingle Bells, Frosty the Snowman, and Rockin' around the Christmas Tree. I thought I would see Mickey, Minnie and the gang dancing on stage with talented young men and women. That was what I expected because I thought that a politically correct company would never offend anyone with the real Christmas story.

We sat in the pavilion waiting for the show to begin and when the orchestra led with traditional holiday music, I thought maybe the spirit of Christmas would find me. The choir walked from the back of the theater to the front, each holding a candle, and a warm glow filled the entire room. Once on stage, the 400 performers began singing Christmas music—my Christmas music. It wasn't music about Santa Claus, but about the arrival of a baby on a night long ago.

The drama unfolded with Rita Moreno, the guest narrator, reading the Christmas story from the book of Luke and all of those voices joined together sounding like a heavenly host. And, they told the entire story, not just the "born in a manger" part. Four hundred voices joined to sing "The Hallelujah Chorus" and every person in the pavilion stood up. Tears streamed down my face as I realized that the spirit of Christmas had nothing to do with my friends, family, or any amount of snow. No, the spirit of Christmas was inside of me all of the time, each and every day of the year.

There was a festival going on at Epcot. It's called "Holidays Around the World" and it was a great learning opportunity for all of us. Several times a day, 13 countries had storytellers sharing how their country celebrates this time of the year. Mexico celebrates Posada (which means "inn") from December 16 until early February. We heard the tale of the Norwegian "Julenissen" who preferred porridge to cookies and milk. Canadians told a captivating adventure of mischievous Nalyuks that knocked on doors expecting treats and, if denied, would take your children. Thomas didn't like that story at all. I assured him that the Nalyuks would eventually bring the children back. No one wanted unexpected house guests at Christmas.

Vicariously Yours,
Traci

We started our Christmas shopping by visiting one of the largest malls I had ever seen, with a store that was the first of its kind. It had only been open for two weeks. It was M&M World and included 28,000 square feet dedicated to the candy-coated chocolate yummies. Every color and type was available from pink and blue peanut to chartreuse and white almond. There were colorful mixes for *Star Wars*, Florida Gator, and Jacksonville Jaguar fans. There were hundreds of logo emblazoned dispensers, shirts, towels, and ornaments. There was even a full-sized NASCAR. I wanted to stock up on a rainbow of candy products, but concluded that spending money on M&Ms would inevitably lead to spending money on new pants, so I passed. Instead, I dragged myself into a store where I could shop for a new swimsuit. Standing in the dressing room under the fluorescent lights crushed my obsession with the flashy chocolate morsels.

C.S. Lewis fans were excited that a film version of *The Chronicles of Narnia: The Lion, the Witch, and the Wardrobe* was being released on December 9. Thomas had read the seven-book series more than once and couldn't wait to see the novel brought to life. We worked hard to finish the first semester of school by December 8 so we could stay up late and attend the premiere just after midnight at Universal Studios. Other than the *Rocky Horror Picture Show*, I had not been to a midnight showing of a movie. When we arrived at the theater at 10:30 p.m., people were already in their seats. By 11:00 p.m., the theater was full with the exception of the break-your-neck rows down front. When the movie began at 12:01 a.m., the 500 seats were filled with fired up C.S. Lewis fans. I couldn't tell if they were electrified by the anticipation of the film or the 48 ounces of Mountain Dew they had sucked down while waiting.

The show was spectacular and we left Universal Studios at 2:45 a.m. on our way back to Fort Wilderness. Have you ever driven through a Disney property at that time of day? It was a unique experience. We saw hundreds of eyes on the roadside and quickly realized that the white-tailed deer were out gallivanting at the early morning hour. Based on our experience in Maine, we panicked. I just knew that one of those crazy hoofed animals was going to leap out in front of us and make us explain its untimely death to Disney security. It never happened.

The deer in Orlando were either trained or intelligent because, unlike their Maine cousins, they did not step onto the road. As we approached, they stood and watched us pass before continuing their nocturnal roaming. I was amazed and vowed to ask a cast member why they don't cross the roads. The answer we got was thought provoking. The staff person told us that their wildlife were smarter because their brains don't freeze in the winter. Could that be true? I had never heard anything like that before on Animal Planet. I weighed her answer and had to admit that since none of the 400 antlered-ones on Disney property had ever been hit by an automobile, it just might be correct.

My parents came to stay with us from December 11 to December 15. The weather wasn't perfect, but, as my mother said, "It wasn't eight inches of snow and 20 degrees, either." This was the third time we had visited Disney World with my parents and we thought we should show them things that they had never seen before. As they acquainted themselves with our bus and campsite, it occurred to me that they were already experiencing something new and different. I had forgotten that the life we live is not normal to most people. We could have stayed at the campground the entire time and they would have been entertained and thrilled.

I took my mom and dad all over the place by modes of transportation including car, bus, golf cart, boat, and monorail, to see the extravagant holiday decorations throughout the Disney properties and experience as much as possible in four days' time. I made a loose schedule. As much as I wanted to show them everything I could, I didn't want to send them home exhausted from their vacation.

At Epcot, my parents rode "Soarin'" (an attraction that simulates hang gliding) for the first time and they both commented that it didn't last long enough. I didn't even know they liked hang gliding. We also attended the Candlelight Processional; Eartha Kitt was the narrator that night—you know, Cat Woman—and she purred as she took to the podium. Thankfully, she refrained from using her feline accent while reading the Christmas story. I was most grateful. We stayed for "Illuminations," the fantastic firework and laser extravaganza that closes each day at Epcot, because it was Mom's favorite.

While Daniel worked, Thomas and I took my mom and dad to the Magic Kingdom. The crowds were minimal that morning and afternoon, so we had great opportunities to take in attractions rather than waiting in line. Grandma Lucy scored higher with her laser gun than anyone else on Buzz Lightyear, accumulating over 100,000 points and earning the title of Pilot 1st Class. My dad and I weren't sure how and when she became so proficient with a toy weapon but assumed it had something to do with working all of those years at public schools.

After picking up Daniel, we headed back to the Magic Kingdom for Mickey's Very Merry Christmas Party, a special event held several times during the holiday season. Because attendance was limited, it was an incredible chance to enjoy the park in a more intimate manner. Each family was photographed in front of a wintry background and sent on their way to enjoy complimentary hot chocolate and cookies along with special entertainment. My parents wanted to see the parade and, if we wanted to get a good viewing spot, we needed to claim our piece of sidewalk 90 minutes before kick-off.

Strolling down Main Street as we left for the night, the Christmas lights shone and faux snow fell from the rooftops. I stopped to watch my parents walking hand in hand. Thomas chased behind them, trying to catch the snowflakes on his fingertips. Daniel was taking pictures and, as he turned and looked at me, his eyes sparkled with delight. I couldn't have been happier at that very moment. We played together and laughed a lot. Mom even rode a roller coaster with me. It was just one more memory created by Disney that I would tuck away and cherish.

We went to MGM for a special treat—dinner at the '50s Prime Time Cafe. While waiting for a table, guests sat on what looked like my grandmother's furniture, watching clips of television shows old enough to be funny, again. The host yelled for the "whatever your name was" kids and you were ushered through a maze of kitchens to your Formica table. Our favorite server was sister Elizabeth, who wasn't my sister at all, but treated us like family, anyway. She called my mother Lulu, made Daniel set the table, and guilted us for making her return to the kitchen for drink refills. It was just like home except that my real sister would never have asked me what I wanted for dinner.

We grabbed our coats and walked to the "Spectacle of Lights" where the staff had adorned a mock New York street with glowing illumination. The work began in October and it took an entire month to ready the set for its unveiling. It was 5:40 p.m. and the streets were lined with hundreds of people saving their piece of sidewalk. I was surprised. It wasn't a parade. It was a holiday light display. What were they waiting on? A cast member selling spinning light-up toys passed and I asked why everyone was just sitting. He grinned and said, "I think they're waitin' on the 6:00 p.m. train." Really? I didn't know there was one. Appreciating his sarcasm, I walked away and wondered if Disney staff ever got sick of visitors. I imagined that costumed characters got tired of guests pulling their tails or pining for pictures. Hey, even a mouse could need some solitude.

We spent the last day of my parents' visit at Winter SummerLand, a Christmas-themed miniature golf venue with two courses, one summer and the other winter. Christmas music was played there year-round and Santa, Frosty, and the elves were prominently displayed. My mom didn't want to play golf. "It's been at least 100 years," she said as I dragged her to the first hole. Daniel, Thomas and I loved this course not only for its festive atmosphere, but because even a bad mini-golfer could score a hole in one.

As our game progressed, I saw my parents having the time of their lives—laughing at each other and themselves, as well as the rest of us. My mom sank six holes in one and Dad got five. I was thankful we didn't bet on the outcome of the game. It was the first time in my life that my parents had played miniature golf with me. I couldn't believe my good fortune. In just a handful of days, I had fulfilled two childhood dreams: hearing my mother scream on a lightning-fast ride and watching Mom beat Dad at putt-putt.

As we drove away from the airport after saying our goodbyes, there was a silence in the car. We were back to just the three of us. Yes, the sleeping arrangements would be easier. We would get to bed earlier and sleep later. But, the fun of sharing some Disney magic with George and Lucy made those days more precious to me than any amount of rest or comfort.

We left Disney on Sunday, December 18, and began our trip south. Daniel was sad. I didn't know how I felt yet. Our campsite had been so close to the Magic Kingdom that each night we heard every explosion over Cinderella's Castle. Every day we heard the blast of the horn on the train. We had heard all of the music for the various parades so many times that we could whistle every note. We were nearly run over by teenagers driving golf carts. The crowds had started wearing on all of us and yet, it was hard to leave. Mixed in with the annoyances were things like pixie dust, wishing on a star, and believing that dreams really could come true. I packed away my Mickey Mouse bag and Tinker Bell shirt, but I won't work so hard to put away the magic of Disney. Now more than ever, I wanted to hold on to the idea that anything could happen with a little faith, trust, and that special dust.

Our first night away from Orlando was spent in the parking lot of the Coral Springs Wal-Mart. There were no fireworks, no parade music, and no trains. Instead, we drifted off to sleep listening to the local traffic, clanking carts, and talkative shoppers. The trip would go on and, hopefully, the sweetness of that small world in Buena Vista, Florida would travel with us.

Vicariously Yours,
Traci

Sent: Tuesday, December 20, 2005
Subject: A Christmas Story

'Twas the night before Christmas and all through the bus,

Oh, the creatures were stirring, all around us.

The deer and the dogs, the lizards and bugs,

The neighbors were fighting. Who had my ear plugs?

One stocking was hung using duct tape and care,

And we hoped that Santa would know it was there.

With no house or chimney, no permanent address,

Would his sleigh be equipped with global GPS?

Our child was nestled in his sofa bed,

While sword fights and battles played out in his head.

His heroes would win as they always do,

I so missed the days of Winnie the Pooh.

We put on our jammies, kiss-kiss, said goodnight,

And soon fell asleep in our full hook-up campsite.

When outside our window arose such a clatter,

Only Daniel did wake to see what was the matter.

And what to his somewhat fuzzy eyes should appear,

But our neighbor inflating a Tampa Bay Buccaneer.

Yes, Christmas this year is a bit different, you see,

We live in a bus and we're parked in the Keys.

There's no snow, no family, no place to be,

Just a beach, a sunset, and our family of three.

As Daniel drifted into dreams and began to snore,

I wondered if this Christmas would mean much, much more.

For there were few gifts under our three foot tree,

In fact, there were none for Daniel and me.

No gift could mean more than being together,

And this trip and these memories would last forever.

Though we can't be with you, please know that we care,

And from all the way here to all the way there,

We wish you and yours the merriest day,

Time to go now, the beach called us to play!

Christmas 2005, on the road

Daniel, Traci, and Thomas Bray

We found the damage from 2005's Hurricane Wilma as we drove toward Key West. There was an entire neighborhood near Miami that had matching blue tarp roofing. Large trees had fallen down and boats were scattered on land. I began to wonder if Key Largo, our first destination, would be inhabitable. As we entered our campground, I was not convinced. The office doors were chained shut, from the inside. We checked in and were escorted to our site, but before parking, the staff had to move huge piles of debris. Daniel and I jumped out to hook up the bus and noticed that ours was the only RV whose wheels had turned in the last decade. I didn't want to stay, but we had paid in advance and had nowhere else to go.

We were befuddled at the condition of Key Largo because we had heard that it was beautiful. Not that we consulted a credible source for our information, but how could a Beach Boys song be so wrong? In researching Key Largo as a destination (something I didn't do until after we got there), I found that this northernmost key in Florida's paradise boasted a couple of activities that were foreign to me: scuba diving and sport fishing. Although Key Largo, the "Diving Capital of the World," had other area attractions, a state park being one of them, it appeared that to see the best of this vacation spot, visitors had to don a mask and get in the water. For me, a destination just wasn't worth it if I had to wear an oxygen tank to enjoy it.

After our nail-biting stay in Key Largo, we drove farther south on US 1 toward mile marker 20 where we would spend Christmas. Many people warned us about the drive. "The road will be difficult to travel in the bus." "That seven-mile bridge will be difficult with the bus." "That's going to be a long, hard drive in that bus." Guess what? I thought the drive was a piece of cake. Of course, Daniel did all of the driving. It was slower than we would have liked, but he never once swerved, slammed on his brakes, or yelled any inappropriate words.

The Florida Keys began with Key Largo and ended south, not with Key

West, but with a no name key—not to be confused with *the* No Name Key, located just north of Big Pine—but simply an island without a name. There were 800 land masses in total. Only 30 of those were inhabited. The rest were "nature preserves" and didn't have names. The number of keys will continue to grow because as the mangrove trees (those seen in the water with exposed roots), collect sediment from the ocean and solidify, an island is formed. Those islands become nature preserves as soon as the first weary bird sets down.

In the 16th century, Key West was discovered by our good friend, Ponce de Leon, formerly referred to as the vertically challenged discoverer of St. Augustine. When he discovered the island, he found many, many bones, likely the remains of Native Americans, so he named the place Cayo Hueso, the Island of Bones. In the 18th century, the Spanish name was anglicized (shocking, I know) and Key West was coined. It was probably a blessing for the future tourism business there because who would want to stay on the Island of Bones other than the contestants on *Survivor*.

The history of Key West is fascinating, beginning with the sale of the island in the early 1800s to two different parties. Both men tried to stake their claim, but the gentleman with the most political influence was given the deed. John Simonton divided his newly purchased land into plots and sold three of them to his friends, and together these four men became the founding fathers of Key West: John Simonton, John Whitehead, John Fleming, and Pardon C. Greene. Mr. Greene's quarter of land was first purchased by John Warner and John Mountain before it was sold to P.C., so for a short time in 1821, Key West was owned by five men named John. After the land arrangements were made, the next order of business was to rid the island of its pesky pirates which meant bringing in some muscle from the U.S. Navy, led by Commodore David Porter. While the scoundrels were indeed run off by the Commodore, one of the city's early industries, wrecking, was borne out of the piracy and helped many residents to gain wealth.

Wrecking involved the salvaging of sunken ships and was a dangerous business for those sailors who dared to venture into the rough seas; however, it was profitable. The first millionaire in Florida, William

Curry, made his money in that business, as did the rest of the entire community. In 1860, not only was Key West deemed the richest city in Florida, but also the wealthiest per capita in the entire country.

Salvaging was an incredible money maker, but sometimes the residents of Key West found more than furniture and household goods. They found survivors. Locals told us a tale about a sinking ship in 1831 where the townspeople saved all 250 passengers and crew onboard. That was an amazing feat when you consider that in that year, the residents numbered just over 500. Did any other town in history increase the population by 50 percent in one day? Talk about no room at the inn!

On one of our trips into town, I went sightseeing on my own. My destination for the day was the Curry Mansion, a white Victorian located on Caroline Street in Old Town. Millionaire William Curry's residence was built in 1855 for a mere $10,000 and included 7500 square feet of living space. I talked at length with the man sitting on the porch selling tickets. I was eager to learn about the home and its previous owners and besides, he looked bored. Inside, the first thing I noticed was the bird's eye maple paneling on the walls followed by a stunning set of Tiffany glass sliding doors. I meandered through the various rooms, studying the floor plan as I walked, paying close attention to the antiques filling the space. It was said that the first key lime pie was made in that kitchen by the cook, Aunt Sally. As I have learned on this trip, much of history is disputed when a story can't be confirmed. I doubted Aunt Sally would care much. It was just a pie.

Leaving the Curry kitchen (and my thoughts about eating a piece of pie), I made my way upstairs to climb the ladder to the Widow's Walk because the gentleman on the porch told me the view was stunning. The mansion was not a popular tourist attraction that day, which left me with the full run of the house for 30 minutes. I climbed the stairs and ladder to the Widow's Walk and took in the panoramic views of the town below me. The ticket-seller was right…it was beautiful.

I stood on the roof for some time, letting the sea breeze blow through my hair and the sunshine warm my skin. Suddenly, I noticed a figure out of the corner of my eye. I hadn't seen anyone else when I climbed the ladder and hadn't heard anyone moving around, so to say that I was startled and frightened to find someone next to me would be an understatement. I jumped back a few feet, grabbed my chest, and screamed, although, I have a hard time admitting to such a girly thing. After eyeballing the other guest on the roof, I realized this "person" was a dummy—a widow dressed in 19th century attire holding a telescope to her eye in hopes of spotting her long-lost husband. I should have felt better, but I didn't. Mannequins, dummies, and wax figures have always scared me and it was all I could do to compose myself enough to get out of the house. If I could have safely jumped from the roof to exit faster, I would have, but I had to settle for stumbling down the ladder and tripping down the stairs. When I hit the first floor, I sprinted out the front door. I blew past the man on the porch so fast, I'm sure he thought I either broke or stole something. I didn't care—I just wanted out of there. Thank goodness no one else saw me—except the dummy, and I'm not worried about her talking...her lips were sewn shut.

Another early industry and wealth maker in Key West was cigar-making—*fine* cigars. Cubans brought this money-making business as well as another to the island: cock fighting. Now, I didn't know much about cock fighting. I never learned the players, stats, or rules. I did know that it was eventually outlawed and the chickens were set free to roam the streets of the city. We were sitting at a stop light waiting for it to turn green when a rooster followed by three chicks and a hen crossed the road inside the pedestrian walk, heading toward a local restaurant. That surely answers the age old question, "Why did the chicken cross the road?" In Key West, they wanted to get to the key lime pie.

We heard that chickens were protected by law and that anyone caught performing malicious behavior against the poultry would be fined $500. On the other hand, it was perfectly okay to hit a pelican with your car and leave it dead in the street, which we saw a couple of times. We almost hit one twice. Pelicans, when stalking their prey, don't watch where they are flying and tend to collide with automobiles. I mean, I had hit my fair share of bugs, butterflies, and squirrels, but a pelican? That's a big bird. It would be like hitting a flying raccoon or cat.

Speaking of cats, they are almost as abundant as chickens in Key West. Ernest Hemingway, a famous member of the city's social scene, had special, six-toed felines. Descendants of these polydactyl animals continue to live in the Hemingway house for visitors to see. People paid money to see these oddities. Not me, but then I've never paid money to see a bearded lady or two-headed man, either. We were told by our tour guide that some Key West apartments come with a cat. So, if you rent an apartment and a cat had previously called it home, you get the pet. I would rather have a chicken.

In 1982, Key West seceded from the United States. It became known as The Conch Republic. It started when the people of Key West had had enough of a federal government roadblock that was hurting their tourism business. The government had a good excuse: something about illegal drugs and immigrants. In rebellion, the residents filed secession papers and declared war on the United States. A battle date was penciled in and the U.S. Navy showed up and waited. The residents of the Conch Republic gathered at the shoreline and threw stale Cuban bread and rotten tomatoes at the sailors. Thank goodness no one on the military vessels had itchy trigger fingers.

The republic then surrendered and filed for foreign aid in the amount of one billion dollars to help them rebuild after the war. Of course, the entire episode was perpetrated to produce enough publicity to force the government to remove the roadblock and restore the flow of tourists to the region. Because the secession papers were never challenged by the United States, the new foreign country, formerly known as Key West, remained intact. Their license plate said, "We seceded where others failed."

Why was it named the Conch Republic? Conch was something that the Bahamians brought to the Keys. When the British taxed certain food-stuffs in the Bahamas, the residents revolted and refused to eat those foods. Instead, they ate conch, which was edible, available, and free. The British couldn't tax the conch so the Bahamians continued to eat it and soon developed 28 ways to do so. The reasoning behind the name of the new republic varied, depending on who we asked. A common thread, though, was the belief that the conch shell represented a peaceful rebellion against unfair government practices.

Daniel and I tried the conch fritters at Jimmy Buffet's Margaritaville and didn't care for them, but the conch chowder from another local place was good. The natives of Key West identify themselves as "conchs." A person who has lived in the area for at least seven years is called a freshwater conch, while everyone else is a stranger. The school mascot is a conch, which makes the drill team members "Conchettes," football players "Fighting Conchs," and band members "Marching Conchs." Visitors to the area can purchase the republic's flags, exchange currency, and get their passport stamped. And I thought the only foreign countries we would see on this trip were Canada and Mexico.

We spent Christmas morning at the KOA before heading to Old Town, where we explored the harbor. As we were walking around the marina, Daniel caught sight of a beautiful old touring schooner. After talking to the ticket seller, we discovered that there was a special Christmas star-gazing cruise later that evening and we jumped at the chance to do it. We arrived just as the boat was about to leave dock and were each given a set of binoculars by our host for the evening, Joe Universe (a pseudonym, but one his wife gladly accepted because she then became Mrs. Universe.)

Joe was enthusiastic and knowledgeable about the night sky, which made us even happier with our decision to do something special on Christmas evening. We cruised around Key West for about an hour while Joe used a high-powered laser to point out stars, planets, and constellations. He told us a story about the star the Magi must have seen and followed in order to find the baby Jesus. The three of us sat huddled together under a starry canopy, listening to the water lapping at the sides of the boat, and imagined what it must have been like for the men who traveled so far to find the greatest gift the world had ever been given. Sure, next year we would again have a big tree with a heap of decorated boxes piled underneath, but the simplicity of this year would never be forgotten. Christmas at Mile Marker 20 would forever be etched in our memories as the one that forced us to do without, and yet, in years to come, I predicted it would be the one celebration we would look back on and long for once again.

Vicariously Yours,
Traci

None of us felt warm and fuzzy and there had been little family fun since leaving the southern tip of Florida. Why? I should start at the beginning, with Fleetwood RV. As you know, when you own a home there are myriad things that can go wrong and either you or someone more qualified will need to repair them. It was no different with a motorhome, except that our home was constantly on the move, making the repair of things tricky. We had been on the road for seven months and there had been broken things since early in the trip that we had yet to get fixed because our warranty from Fleetwood required us to do the following:

1.   Find a certified dealer in the area.
2.   Make an appointment.
3.   Take the bus in and leave it for the day.
4.   Come back and find out how long it would take to fix.
5.   Order whatever part was necessary.
6.   Wait days or weeks for the part to come in.
7.   Make another appointment with the dealer.
8.   Take the bus back in and leave it for the day.
9.   Get the bus fixed and go on our way.

That was how it should have worked. It didn't. We had a difficult time finding certified dealers who would work on our motorhome. Their logic was that if they didn't sell it to us, they wouldn't work on it. When we did find a shop willing to look at our bus, the appointment would be several weeks out. That didn't work because we never really knew where we would be and couldn't plan that far ahead. On the few occasions when we found a dealer and made an appointment that worked for us, something would still go wrong.

For example, one of our window treatments broke in August and I hadn't been able to open that window in five months. It wasn't a big deal, but we wanted to get it fixed, especially before the 12-month warranty expired in February. Also, one of our hubcaps disappeared, two more blinds stopped working, and the screen door wouldn't stay shut. We made an appointment with a shop outside of Orlando to get all of those things taken care of before the holidays. Fleetwood shipped the wrong parts. We lost a day while we waited and had to make a decision about what to do next. We could either have the correct parts shipped to the dealership near Orlando—meaning we would stop there on our way back from Key West—or we could start over with a new location somewhere in Texas.

We chose to come back to Orlando after Christmas, before heading west. We slept in three Sam's Club parking lots, a SuperTarget, and a hotel with few English-speaking employees. And, Fleetwood sent the wrong parts again. I wished that my normally push-over husband would have yelled at someone at Fleetwood, but he didn't. Once again we wasted our time at an RV dealership and were on our way to a different city with no resolution in sight for our repairs. Daniel and I couldn't understand why it had to be so difficult to service a motorhome. If the automobile industry worked as poorly as the recreational vehicle industry, I would think that consumer groups and 60-minute news programs would ruthlessly investigate and hound executives until they either improved the process or went into hiding on some Caribbean island. My rant, though, would go no further than our own bus because I avoid confrontation, too.

We spent New Year's Eve in Tampa, the third largest city in Florida. We had been in the state now for almost three months and loved every minute. Tampa would be our one stop on the west coast since we needed to be moving toward Texas soon. Why Tampa and not Fort Meyers, Sarasota, Naples, or Clearwater? We were all tired of beaches and sunsets and needed some time in an amusement park to yell and scream. Though I do love fast roller coasters, Daniel and Thomas particularly enjoy the kind that defy good sense and it just so happened that Busch Gardens in Tampa had a ride fitting the bill.

When we left Orlando, we neglected to make reservations for a campground our first night, which meant we would be sleeping in a parking lot. We pulled into town and found our asphalt landing pad, but realized that we shouldn't stay there. Many of the nearby businesses and buildings were abandoned and, although the Wal-Mart was open, the area was scary. We had to find somewhere else to sleep. We found a

Sam's Club that had a good sized parking lot and plenty of lighting—all the comforts a boondocker needs.

We woke up the next morning, peeked out the curtains, and discovered that this particular Sam's Club had a thriving early morning business. Taking up six prime parking spaces didn't endear us to the patrons of this store. As we ate our breakfast, I glanced out the window and noticed several customers shooting nasty looks and gesturing wildly toward our vehicle. I didn't want to face an angry mob before my morning coffee. Daniel maneuvered the bus through the narrow maze of shiny vehicles and, after a few moments of heated pantomiming by one man in particular, we left the parking lot and were on our way to our Tampa site where people didn't point, stare, or grumble at our presence. It is amazing how different things are when you pay to park somewhere.

We set up camp and took off for Busch Gardens' New Year's Eve celebration where the main attraction was a roller coaster called SheiKra. The ride's first hill was 200 feet high. When we reached the top, the cars stopped and dangled us over the edge, so we were looking straight down at the ground. When released, the sudden rush took my breath away and screaming became impossible. Thankfully, I went to the bathroom *before* getting in line. It was an exciting way to end 2005: facing down fear. It wasn't an important one, but a fear nonetheless.

January 1 was our last day in Tampa and it was spent doing chores: laundry, cleaning, shopping. We intended to drive to Atlanta on Monday, January 2. It would be a long one-day drive but would allow us the luxury of taking our time from Atlanta to Dallas, where we needed to be by January 20. The next three weeks included stops in Atlanta, Birmingham, Jackson, and finally, Dallas. The weather would be colder but in January, there wasn't any escape from winter unless we stayed in Florida, which wasn't an option for us. We had been there since October 20 and felt like we were becoming genuine Floridians; as soon as the temperature dipped below 70, we grabbed our jackets and long pants. Our tough Hoosier skin had begun to disappear. Yes, it was time to go.

Daniel performed a routine maintenance test on the fuel/water separator before leaving. A service guy in Myrtle Beach told him to check this contraption once a month and today was the day. I prepared the inside of the bus, making sure everything was put away. When Daniel finished, all that was left to do was start the engine, pull up the jacks and bring in the slides. The diesel roared and then sputtered before dying. Daniel tried to crank the engine. It wouldn't happen. I got out and walked around to see if anything was visibly wrong—as if I would know what to look for, anyway—and that's when I saw it: there was diesel fuel spewing from the back of the bus. When Daniel performed his test, something had gone wrong. He had turned the shut-off valve the wrong way so that all of the fuel had drained out of the lines feeding the engine and they were now full of air. Well, that couldn't be good.

Daniel called a repair shop to get advice and the service guy said, "You need to call a professional." While he was on the phone, a spokesperson from the crowd that had gathered to watch the mishap came over and offered the assistance of a fellow camper. He wasn't a professional, but he knew how to help. If I had had a red carpet, I would have rolled it out for him. Robert took charge. He gave each of us something to do and we obeyed without question. He became the professional we desperately needed.

After 90 minutes of searching for it, we gained access to the engine compartment. It was under our bed—not where Robert thought it would be. My bus was torn apart and there was a stranger in my bedroom. I was trying to be optimistic, but it was difficult. Daniel was still kicking himself. The once-stranger, now our good friend Robert, was trying to fix our home so we could leave. He sent Daniel to the gas station to get some diesel fuel while I held up our bed and watched him fiddle with the engine.

I asked Robert about himself and didn't get a lot of information. He did teach me about diesel engines. I now knew how to bleed air from the lines. I learned the difference between a diesel and gas engine. He taught me the importance of knowing how to work on your own motorhome and encouraged me to take some classes. I simply smiled and nodded at Robert a lot because I wanted to be polite, and my back was killing me from propping up my queen-sized Serta.

It took three hours for Robert to fix our engine. He had diesel fuel all over him and had even gotten some in his mouth. We offered to pay him, but he refused. Four and a half hours later, we drove away from the campground feeling humble and thankful for a man who didn't mind helping a stranger by sucking diesel fuel through a straw.

The lessons learned that day were many. Daniel discovered that "righty tighty" was not a hard and fast rule. Thomas found out that he can be patient when there are no other options. I understood that a primer on a diesel engine was a necessity. We all learned that when things don't work out exactly as you hope, God will provide. On that day, He sent us a man named Robert who was a nice person and good mechanic.

Vicariously Yours,
Traci

We drove across the Georgia state line and bid adieu to the "Sunshine State." We went north to Atlanta to pick up Interstate 20. Before Hurricane Katrina, we had planned on taking I-10 through the coastal regions of Alabama, Mississippi and Louisiana, but we thought avoiding those disaster areas would be best. One benefit to that decision was the ability to visit Atlanta, a city rich with diverse attractions for families, couples, and those not attached to anyone in particular.

The weather in Atlanta was not pleasant. Although the sun shone most of the time, we suffered through two nights of freezing temperatures. The electric heat pumps ran all through the night and the propane furnace kicked on and off, as well. Under fluffy comforters we were cozy in bed, but late-night trips to the bathroom were painfully frigid. It was the first time we had experienced these temperatures since our initial trial run in South Bend, Indiana. Our water supply iced over. We shouldn't have been surprised: a garden hose left outside in January could do nothing but freeze.

I read an article in *USA Today* about the new Georgia Aquarium, the nation's largest, which opened on November 23, 2005. Thomas and I had visited the other two huge fish zoos in Baltimore and Chicago, so we were interested to see how this one compared. The aquarium was worth visiting. Thomas loved that many of the exhibits were built allowing visitors to walk under the tanks. This perspective of the fish allowed us to see a side of them rarely seen, specifically, the bottom.

As I looked a small shark in the eyes, I wondered how thick the glass was between us. Thomas and I blended into a larger group of onlookers and moved slowly, as one unit, through the aquatic corridor. A booming voice from above called out, "Keep moving. Keep moving, please." I had no idea that fish-gazing had a time limit.

There was a retired shrimp boat turned children's play set, complete with climbing area, corkscrew slides, and touch pool. Although I love eating shrimp, the sight of 100 tiny hands petting the helpless crustaceans evoked a temporary sense of sympathy. Maybe the aquatic arthropods appreciated the extra attention. Or maybe they were just happy to not be lunch that day.

Daniel graced us with his presence on our second excursion in Atlanta. He did warn us that his phone would be ringing and he would be answering it. Thomas and I were accustomed to sight-seeing with Daniel on his phone not paying any attention to what we were doing. We would rather have him with us than not, if only to have him take pictures and occupy a seat so we could drive in the HOV (high occupancy vehicle) lane.

The World of Coca-Cola was an intoxicating destination for Thomas, but Daniel and I were curious, too. Over the years, I had heard about it, but had no expectations other than a free sample of my favorite Coca-Cola product. We bought our tickets, rode the elevator up to the third floor, and sat down just in time to see a 15-minute history about the famous carbonated beverage. The tour continued with exhibit after exhibit of ancient advertisements, merchandise, and collectibles, like walking through a 45-minute commercial.

On the second level, we hit the effervescent jackpot. National soda products spouted from fountains and international flavors were available for testing. I told Thomas that he could have as much soda as he wanted (it was free, and served in tiny paper cups) and his eyes popped out of his head. He began drinking and didn't stop until he had sampled 10 previously unknown soft drinks and only stopped when he sipped one that reminded him of cough syrup. Thomas zipped down the stairs like Ricochet Rabbit and stumbled into the gift shop where I found Sprite underwear, Tab shirts, Diet Coke hats, and Coca-Cola tees with "It's the Real Thing" printed across the chest. That one almost made me break our "no souvenir rule."

We left Atlanta and drove west to Alabama where we camped near Birmingham. There was a huge lake behind our bus that had mini mansions backing up to it. I wondered why anyone would build a starter castle near an RV resort. I suspected it had something to do with the good angling in that freshwater because a dozen fishing boats spent two days trolling from spot to spot.

Pell City, the town we called home for a couple of days, was charming and boasted 9600 residents. It looked and felt similar to many small communities around the country. The shops were minimal and the traffic was light, which made it easy to run errands in record time. It rained our first day there and we rented a movie to help pass the time. As we perused the selection at the local Blockbuster, Thomas noticed several games for an outdated system he received as a Christmas gift five years ago. He picked up each one and lovingly touched it as if it were a long lost friend. I watched him for a few minutes until I heard Daniel's familiar cackle in the other aisle. I tracked the sound and discovered him bent over, laughing at the vast selection of VHS tapes on the "New Release" wall. As cute as this municipality was, it had obviously not entered the technological future.

There wasn't a long list of attractions to see, but I did manage to find a science museum in downtown Birmingham which we visited on Sunday. The exhibits were engaging and, because the number of other guests was small, Thomas spent as much time as desired at each one. He loved manipulating the hands-on experiments, but his favorite was called the "Dream Station" and consisted of a blue background, television monitor, and camera that projected him and Daniel onto the movie screen, placing them in the middle of soccer, volleyball, and ping pong matches. There was even a fishing game called "Shark Bait" where they had to virtually swim away from man-eaters and electric eels. The McWane Science Center turned out to be more fun than academic. Thank goodness! After all, it *was* the weekend.

Our experience in Birmingham reminded me once again how important this trip has been for us. Our most precious and memorable moments occurred during the daily discovery of the unknown. Whether it was a new state or city, grocery store or restaurant, time spent learning something new had brought us closer as a family. Thomas had watched us grow from not knowing much about RV'ing to being comfortable with the lifestyle. He saw us get lost and heard us seek assistance. His parents had let down their guard nearly every day and shown him that it's okay to admit a weakness. We faced fears together and celebrated our conquests. Would that have ever happened if we had stayed at home? I couldn't say. What I do know is that my family now saw me for the person I really am, and they love me just the same. No year could have started out better than that.

Vicariously Yours,
Traci

Sent: Monday, January 16, 2006
Subject: The Mississippi Blues

Mississippi in January—there should be a blues song about it. The weather was gross and we had nothing to do over several days. Many famous people hailed from here and eagerly proclaimed their heritage. Faith Hill released a song about it and Jimmy Buffett's face graced tourism billboards, so something about this place was special, right?

We began our stay in one of the largest cities, Meridian, just over the eastern border. The town faced challenges long ago including a nasty visit in 1864 from General Sherman, whose troops destroyed the railroad and much of the town. Before he left, he said, "Meridian no longer exists." The town rebuilt the railroad tracks in 26 days, which paved the way for a period of extraordinary growth between 1890 and 1930, when it led the state in manufacturing. We spent three days there and found nothing to do.

I knew there were historic sites to see and landmarks, complete with national recognition, but these things did not entertain a 10-year-old boy. I read about 50 painted carousel horses, prominently placed around town; however, they did not move up and down, round and round, or at a high rate of speed. My boy had no interest. When searching for something interesting to do in Meridian, I checked out the town website and was impressed with it until I looked at the "fun facts" page. The people of Meridian considered guessing the correct number of fire stations, street lights, and city arrests as *fun*—seven fire stations, 6,300 street lights, and 16,000 arrests...just in case you were interested.

I thought it would be a "fun fact" to discover who planned the streets in Meridian. I was certain it was someone who received their advanced degree in traffic planning from a technical school based in Zimbabwe. Even if we saw the place we were looking for, we couldn't get there. We got lost so many times, that we began expecting it. The one place we were able to find twice was the O'Charley's restaurant. We had the same southern gentleman as our server both times. He wasn't the most observant guy. Daniel was dressed in head-to-toe Indianapolis Colts' gear and we talked with him about our trip, but when we ordered unsweetened tea on our second visit, Columbo said, "Ya'll aren't from around here, are you?" Our drink choice gave us away—only Yankees drink unsweetened tea.

We crossed the state of Mississippi to Vicksburg, where we camped for the first time at a casino. The Isle of Capri RV Resort was a step above a Wal-Mart parking lot, but not a big one. The first day in Vicksburg, we drove through town just to see what was there. We saw three large casinos sitting on the Mississippi River, a small and dilapidated historic downtown district, and the Vicksburg Battlefield National Park. We cruised for miles in all directions, but couldn't find much more than rural areas and run-down neighborhoods. It took us two days to find a Wal-Mart—now you know *that's* saying something. Daniel didn't need to worry about me spending money in this town.

On Friday, we hit the casino. My dad, who wins nearly every time he walks into one, gave Daniel some pointers. I was only interested in the food. I don't know why, but I thought that the casinos must have good grub—buffet-style, all-you-can-eat—and I wanted it. Daniel sauntered up to the gal at the hospitality desk and slyly asked for a "player's card." She smiled wide, probably thinking that my husband should hand over his money now and save the misery of standing at a slot machine all night.

We went to the restaurant for dinner. We must have stood out like an Amish couple at a car show. Our server came up to the table and said, "Whatchu sittin' down for? You think I'm gonna bring it to ya?" I felt like I'd been chastised by Aunt Jemima. She instructed us to help ourselves and we obeyed, quickly. We studied the buffet selections before making any commitments. To make healthy food choices, I would have to identify the most lethal offenders and create a sliding scale from there.

We circled the food lines two or three times. Everything was fried or swimming in an inch of butter. No wonder the other patrons at the restaurant had a nice glossy coat. Daniel couldn't identify the purplish/black soup, and asked the employee standing there what it was.

She sneered and said, "Gumbo," and I swear she added "stupid" under her breath. I approached the area labeled "Cooked to Order." The chef—I use that term loosely because other than the big poofy hat, nothing about him screamed "trust me with your stomach"—smiled a gummy grin and said that all he had at that time was crab meat. I was perplexed. Did he mean that I could have anything I wanted as long as it was crab meat? Or, did he mean that I could have crab meat cooked any way I wanted? I settled on a salad and a small slice of pizza while Daniel bravely chose fried grouper, fried catfish, beef round, and a salad. He needed the sustenance to maintain his strength at the slots. I decided to forego that experience.

Saturday was the mildest day in Vicksburg, so we spent it at the national park surveying the 16-mile battlefield used during the Civil War. After catching the informational film at the Visitor Center, we purchased the audio tour so we could guide ourselves while listening to some guy with a nice voice regale us with the significance of each area. Within the national park, there were over 1,300 monuments to the soldiers who fought and died in battle. It was fascinating for us to compare Gettysburg to Vicksburg.

While Generals Lee and Meade clashed in Pennsylvania, Pemberton and Grant were duking it out in Mississippi. Gettysburg lasted only three days, while the battle at Vicksburg began in December of 1862 and went on until July of 1863. Both battles ended on July 4, 1863. I thought that was incredible. The Confederate Army suffered two decisive defeats on one day. The largest difference between the two battles, other than the length and renown, was the number of casualties. Gettysburg claimed three times as many lives as Vicksburg.

General Pemberton was told to protect Vicksburg at all costs from falling into Union hands. Lincoln knew that if Grant won there, control of the Mississippi would be his. The campaign was not going well and the Union suffered terrible losses, but Grant was determined to carry out his mission and succeed. Toward the end of the battle, Grant blasted the people of Vicksburg from land and sea, causing them to hide underground in caves. In a journal written by a citizen of Vicksburg during the attack, a comment was made that the only time the explosives didn't fall were when the Union troops took their meals. Another resident wrote that if General Grant thought that the women and children would be weakened by constant bombardment, he was wrong. Maybe this woman should have been in charge of the Confederate Army because General Pemberton gladly surrendered Vicksburg. By Grant's sheer will, President Lincoln gained control of the Mississippi River and the tide began to turn in the Civil War.

My will was to vacate Vicksburg as soon as possible. I wanted to leave behind the 30-foot-tall brightly lit Ameristar Casino sign that shone through my bedroom window and a town that struggled to be family-friendly. The people were kind, but I expected them to be. They did live in "The Hospitality State."

Vicariously Yours,
Traci

Last Sunday, as we crossed the bridge over the Mississippi River entering Louisiana, we all cheered. We were one state closer to Texas and hoped that this place would be more exciting than all of Mississippi. It wasn't. Other than the Sci-Port Discovery Center, a 67,000 square foot interactive museum downtown, there was nothing for Thomas to do. Shreveport looked like a cheap imitation of Vegas. Casinos and neon lights filled the sky with flashing advertisements for B-list entertainers and worse.

Though Shreveport and its sister city, Bossier, boasted sites and landmarks on the National Register, the prevalence of monstrous casinos obscured any glimpse into these gems as we drove through both communities. I heard nice things about this part of the country, but as a first-time visitor, I didn't feel any southern hospitality. We didn't choose this stop though because of area attractions or historical significance. We stayed for one reason—it was approximately two and one half inches west of Vicksburg and east of Dallas. We discovered that this distance on our atlas equaled three hours of travel time—a comfortable amount for Daniel to drive and still get some work done. It wasn't the best way to ensure lovely surroundings, quality accommodations, or family-friendly activities; however, we figured that planning this way allowed us the rare opportunity to live in cities and towns that were large and small, beautiful and ugly, fun and boring, safe and scary. Now, doesn't that sound like fun?

We stayed in another Isle of Capri Casino campground because...I don't know why. It was nothing more than a parking lot next to a large casino/hotel. The location was also remarkably close to a train yard which we didn't see, but heard. In the middle of our first night, we awoke to a horrific sound of metal slamming into metal. We jumped out of bed and threw open the blinds to see the terrible accident that just happened, but through the black night saw nothing. Just as we fell asleep again, another crash jolted us from our bed. It wasn't until morning that we saw just how close the tracks were to our site. We realized that we would not be sleeping much in Shreveport, Louisiana.

We saw a Texas Roadhouse restaurant from the highway and wanted to eat dinner there—a pre-celebration for being one state closer to the Lone Star state. The sign for the establishment was in a very visible location right off the highway. Despite the prominent placement, it took us almost an hour to find it. We drove around the same one mile area for 45 minutes and it was only when Daniel stopped at a third gas station to ask for directions (yes, he does do that) that the restaurant appeared before our very eyes. I don't know how we missed it that many times. Could it be because it wasn't on a real road? There was no street name and the building was blocked from view by a large hotel.

Daniel was hungry before we left the bus, and he doesn't behave well when he needs to eat. As a matter of fact, his normally pleasant attitude and jovial mannerisms transform into something more primitive. The hostess wasn't listening when Daniel began complaining to her about how long it took to find their establishment and how annoyed he was. She ignored him and began talking about something else while ushering us to our table. I thought Daniel would pinch her tiny head off of her body. She was carrying a basket of rolls, though—that probably saved her life.

We ordered our food and when I turned to talk to Thomas, he was gone. Daniel pointed under the table and I bent over to ask him what he was doing, but he shushed me. I sat up and saw the cause of the commotion: Andy Armadillo. The restaurant mascot was moseying toward our table. I guess Thomas didn't want his autograph. The costumed character got the message because he passed our table and bothered some other child. I had to admit that a giant armadillo wearing a cowboy hat, chaps, and a sneery smile was a far cry from something cute like a mouse or dog. Armadillo-man passed our table on several occasions and each time Thomas dove for cover. After the tenth walk-by, I wanted to tackle the nocturnal annoyance, hog tie him, and take him outside where he could play "Who wants to be road kill?" on I-20.

People in Louisiana call crayfish "mudbugs." They set traps on their property to catch them and then eat them. Yuck! That would be like me catching worms in my yard and then cooking them up for dinner, but only after I had consulted my *How to Eat Fried Worms* book.

Yeah—I'd better just leave Shreveport. For now, I'll let you drift off to sleep and remember...don't let the mudbugs bite.

Vicariously yours,
Traci

Texas, the Lone Star State, where cowboys wrangle cattle and play football, rangers round up criminals and hit homeruns, and mavericks not only play basketball, but also throw out the unofficial state motto "Don't mess with Texas." We crossed the state line from Louisiana and could almost hear a big round of "Yeehaw" somewhere—or maybe it was the three of us. As we drove along I-20 toward the Dallas/Fort Worth area, we noticed several overhead flashing signs announcing a statewide arson/fire ban which I found interesting. Wouldn't it be obvious that arson would be banned *all* of the time? It was our first indication that life in this part of the country was going to be different.

We stayed in Arlington, a suburb south of Dallas, a perfect launching point for the many activities we had planned. The difficulty would be in choosing just a few. If we had come here during football season, we would have taken Thomas to see the Cowboys, but it was January and the boys in blue were vacationing. It didn't matter too much because in this part of the state, athletic spectacles are readily available and varied. Families could take in a sporting event of their choice: football, basketball, baseball, hockey, racing, and rodeo...real rodeo. It wasn't the kind we had seen at the Indiana State Fairgrounds, but the genuine show where the cowboys and cowgirls are Texans. If we wanted roller coasters and bumper cars, we could visit the original Six Flags over Texas. The amusement chain took its name from the various colors—Spain, France, Mexico, Republic of Texas, Confederate States of America, and U.S.A.—that have flown over the state. The initial park began here with little more than a Native American village and train, stagecoach, and gondola rides. Fort Worth was a possible excursion, too. Named for the Sundance Kidd, the town's square celebrates the ranch hands and gunslingers of the Wild West who frequented the area during cattle drives of the 1800s.

We first visited Dallas a couple of years ago, so we ventured into areas we had never been. Since Daniel and Thomas were both involved in Scouts, we drove to Irving, Texas, where the National Scouting

Museum is located. Thomas's favorite activities were the pinewood derby track (with test cars to play with), a laser shooting gallery, and a virtual-reality game. I loved the Norman Rockwell gallery, which included his largest collection of original works relating to the organization. The artist began his career illustrating for *Boys' Life* in 1913 and went on to work as the art director for the magazine until 1916. He loved the Scouts and what they represented so he painted his first calendar cover in 1924—free of charge—and continued for another 52 years.

Daniel enjoyed an exhibit highlighting famous members throughout the years including presidents, CEOs, and professional athletes. I have a hard time visualizing Michael Jordan wearing a Cub Scout uniform and selling popcorn. The Chicago Bulls jersey and expensive athletic shoes I see, but the little blue shirt with gold neckerchief...no, definitely not. For many boys growing up, the very seeds of leadership are planted and cultivated through scouting activities. Hank Aaron, Neil Armstrong, William Bennett, Bill Bradley, James Brady, George W. Bush, Bill Clinton, Walter Cronkite, Dwight Eisenhower, Bill Gates, Harrison Ford, Henry Fonda, and John Glenn are just a few of the many men who at one point in their lives decided to become a part of this organization. What father or mother wouldn't want their son involved in a group that focuses on being trustworthy, loyal, helpful, friendly, courteous, kind, obedient, cheerful, thrifty, brave, clean, and reverent? In a world where tolerance reigns and relativism rules as the philosophy of the day, the Boy Scouts of America hold fast to the values and morals that our country was founded on and for that reason alone, they demand respect. At the very least, when a Scout shows up on your doorstep selling popcorn or pizza, think of Michael Jordan and just buy some.

Get out your wallet and look at your bills. If you find a small FW somewhere on the front, it was printed in Fort Worth, Texas, at the newest Bureau of Printing and Engraving. It sits in the middle of nowhere. As we stepped out of the car, an authoritative voice announced the things we could not bring into the building: cameras, backpacks, cell phones, weapons, explosive devices. The necessity of telling visitors not to bring in explosive devices or weapons harkens back to the arson ban, but I'm sure they have good reasons for being specific. The security was tight, but one guard told us that they get more curious cattle than people out there.

The tour began with a short film on the history and making of the notes. We were then led into a room where we watched a man use a Spyder Press to make a circa 1800 five-dollar bill. Though he used authentic methods, he said that the process would have involved two people, a man and woman, who worked together. Even before women's liberation, we helped make the money!

Printing has developed into an incredible process where machines are capable of producing millions of notes per day. Because our money is printed on a paper that is 75 percent cotton and 25 percent linen, you can wash, dry, and iron it. Keep in mind that the life cycle of a one-dollar bill is only 22 months; a ten-dollar bill 18 months; and laundering cash will only decrease the shelf life. Interestingly, the one-hundred-dollar bill has the longest life cycle of 60 months. Really? In whose hands does a C-Note last five years? In mine, it would be more like *Gone in 60 Seconds*.

Ninety-five percent of all notes made replace worn-out currency. Of those notes, 45 percent of them are the one-dollar denomination. I also learned that the Bureau of Printing and Engraving makes notes, not currency. A note only becomes monetized, or spendable, when its possession passes from the printers to the Federal Reserve, which occurs when the completed notes cross a threshold in the basement of the building. The quality assurance specialists watch stacks of money on a conveyer belt and intermittently choose a bundle to thumb through for imperfections. One woman in particular, who we were told was highly skilled, looked 100 years old and had been watching money pass her by for decades. She reminded me of an elderly Laverne or Shirley watching beer bottles go by before grabbing one and taking a swig.

Some Texans eat armadillo. I did not know that. You can't just go killing them, but if you find one that died of natural causes—or on a well-placed automobile bumper—you are welcome to take it home and grill, bake, stew, or fry it. We also learned that authentic Texas chili has little more than beef and peppers in it. The food experiences alone were worth the drive across Alabama, Mississippi, and Louisiana. We found Tex-Mex heaven! Our first week in Texas was everything we hoped it would be—spicy food, fun activities, and people who say "howdy." There's a reason Texans are so proud. You should make it a point to find out why.

Vicariously yours,
Traci

After a quick trip to Indianapolis for a sales meeting, we picked up the bus at a storage facility in Dallas only to find that the batteries were almost dead. The bus started, but weak auxiliary batteries eliminated the possibility of spending the night in a nearby parking lot. We would need to either drive for at least an hour or run the generator. After four hours' sleep on Saturday night and an early morning flight, driving was not what we wanted to do, but it was the best option. Since Austin was our destination on Monday, we headed south. A couple of hours later, just after midnight, we found ourselves in Waco, Texas. We spied an empty Sam's Club parking lot where we pulled in, killed the engine, and fell into bed.

We made it to Austin and into the campground without incident, which always made for a good day. Our new home was well advertised as the "highest rated in Austin" and one of the "best parks in America." When we entered the office, the gal at the front desk told us about a free pancake breakfast offered to all guests. I love pancakes, but my experience with free meals at RV parks was limited. My initial thought was to say, "No thank you." It wasn't until she added, "Nine times out of 10, they'll fill you up." I was hooked. We would now have to eat the pancakes just to find out why the one person couldn't get full.

If you have never been to Austin, be prepared for a city filled with diversity and college students. While we were there the Longhorns of UT (University of Texas) celebrated a Rose Bowl victory and you can just imagine the partying that was going on. The only time I've ever seen more people painted orange was watching the Oompa Loompas dance for Willy Wonka. Along with 50,000 enthusiastic college students live 1.5 million Mexican free-tailed bats. These residents put on a show of their own each night from April to October as they leave the shelter of the Congress Avenue Bridge in search of an all-you-can-eat bug buffet. Of course, since we visited Austin in February, we missed the entire thing.

We didn't get to do a lot of sightseeing or exploring in Austin because of the days spent in Indianapolis the previous week. Daniel was playing catch-up with work and Thomas and I had numerous school lessons to labor through. It was frustrating to be in a phenomenal city and not visit the area attractions and landmarks. Our trip didn't always work out the way we wanted, but that is the way it is on the road.

There were a couple of evenings that we got out of the bus and, on one of those occasions, we stopped by a local restaurant called Taco Xpress based on the recommendation of Rachel Ray and her "$40 a Day" program. The tacos were scrumptious and spicy and went down perfectly with an icy cold Dos Equis. I learned that Mexi tacos—a mixture of egg, jalapenos, onions, and tomatoes—are my new favorite food and Thomas discovered a salsa that challenged his love of all things hot.

After dinner, we drove through downtown to get a quick glance of the eclectic night scene. We saw more orange people. The 100+ live music venues in Austin have earned the city the nickname of "Live Music Capital of the World." With all of the entertainment, the vibe on the streets was electric. It was also too adult for our young man, which was why we didn't take him clubbing.

There were marvelous things for us to do in Austin and we wanted to do them, but we didn't. We didn't go to the Bob Bullock Texas State Museum to experience the three floors of interactive exhibits, including the exploration and settling of the land, the characters that participated in the building of an independent republic, and how Texans have lived off the land and continue to do so. I would have loved to take Thomas to the Austin Children's Museum where he could have explored his musical genius in the Kiddie Limits exhibit. It would have been wonderful to tour the Texas State Capitol and see up close the unique pink granite used to build the largest state capitol building in the country. Daniel wanted to spend an afternoon drinking tea and taking pictures in the historic Driskill Hotel where Lyndon B. Johnson in 1964 and George W. Bush in 2000 waited for election returns. We missed a lot in this special city, but…if we felt like we had to do everything in every city we visited, this trip would have become an impossible undertaking not so different from our lives before we left Indiana. We would have to schedule, plan, and commit weeks or months in advance instead of taking the journey one day at a time. I preferred to risk missing a few landmarks than sacrifice the lifestyle we had come to treasure.

Vicariously yours,
Traci

After settling in near downtown San Antonio, we grabbed the camera and headed out for an afternoon of sightseeing. The first place on our agenda was the Alamo, located just across the street from the Hyatt Regency—an interesting juxtaposition of old and new, soaring and diminutive, sleek and rough. The hotel towers over the tiny old building and yet the beauty of that historical shrine draws a visitor's gaze in such a way that you almost don't notice the hotel at all. At first glance, I was perplexed at the size and wondered how the events of so long ago could have happened in such a small space. It was only after entering the building that I realized this singular structure, along with remnants of a wall outside, was all that was left of the original fort. The signs posted near the carved wooden doors set the tone for what was within: all hats were to be removed, no pictures were to be taken, and talking was limited to a whisper.

The only building left standing after the assault is the church, which served primarily as the powder magazine, artillery position, and soldiers' quarters. Inside the shrine were large plaques inscribed with the names of all who fought and died for Texas's freedom. I didn't know much about what happened in those thirteen days in 1836. It didn't matter. Although historians disagree on the specifics, what is known are the names and the reason for the bloodshed. We saw a movie called *The Alamo: The Price of Freedom* at the local IMAX theater and, although it was not of the same cinematic quality as *The Patriot* or *Braveheart*, the movie was able to convey the intense sense of duty those men possessed.

The leader, Colonel William Travis, was a man who believed that God was on the side of the defenders of Texas and he would rather die than surrender. He wrote these words before the siege began in earnest, "To the People of Texas and All Americans in the World—I am besieged by a thousand or more of the Mexicans under Santa Anna. The enemy has demanded surrender at discretion; otherwise, the garrison is to be put to the sword if the fort is taken. I have answered the demand with a cannon shot and our flag still waves proudly from the walls. I shall never surrender or retreat! Victory or Death!" His number was a meager 189 men compared to the more than 2,500 Mexicans standing at the ready to decimate all who opposed General Santa Anna. It is said that Travis drew a line in the sand and asked that any man willing to die along his side should cross the line. All but one did—and in the early morning of March 6, 1836, the Mexican soldiers attacked the Alamo and killed everyone inside.

The battle was not without a cost to the Mexican army. More than 2,000 men died at the hands of those 189. Amazing! Also, the siege allowed Sam Houston and his men enough time to prepare a strategy for the time when the opposition would come for them, and when it happened, the Mexicans were obliterated. Why? Because those who sacrificed their lives at the Alamo gave Houston's men not only time to ready themselves, but also the inspiration to fight with courage beyond anything they might have known before. It was Houston's men who cried "Remember the Alamo!"

If you visit San Antonio between February 25 and March 6, re-enactors enable you to relive some of the scenes that might have happened during those dark days. Freedom—Americans still live and die for it, and yet there are those who think that we should not be involved in spreading democracy throughout the world. I disagree. Of the 189 men who died at the Alamo, there were only 11 who claimed Texas as their home, while 29 men were from other parts of the world. Why were they fighting for freedom in Texas? I don't know, but I know that they crossed the line Colonel Travis drew in the sand. They were well aware of what they were fighting for and against.

The River Walk, the heart of the downtown area, is a haven for tourists and locals alike. The footpath meanders along the water where restaurants and shops lure passersby to stop and have a margarita or purchase a sombrero. The restaurants were varied, but the theme was Mexican. A local tour guide encouraged us to try the assortment of dining options: German Mexican, Chinese Mexican, Italian Mexican, Tex-Mexican, and Mexican Mexican.

Near the Rivercenter is the ticket office for Rio San Antonio Cruises. We jumped on a tour boat for a 30-minute narrated cruise. Our guide told us the history of the city and pedestrian walk and showed us unique landmarks. We were told that each Valentine's Day hundreds of amorous couples line up on Marriage Proposal Island to get hitched by the Justice of the Peace. The island isn't particularly pretty or romantic. It is just a big tree surrounded by grass and a concrete wall.

We ventured outside of downtown to visit Max Lucado's church, Oak Hills. Since he is a well-known author and speaker, we assumed his congregation would be big...it was *huge*. On a typical weekend, attendance peaks at 5,000. Imagine if Colonel Travis would have had those numbers at the Alamo! We chose a Saturday evening service because we were leaving for New Mexico the next morning. I couldn't tell you the name of the minister who spoke, but I remember the message clearly. He unbuttoned his jacket to reveal a t-shirt that boldly said, "I HAVE ISSUES!" It was amazing to me that a minister in a gargantuan congregation would be vulnerable enough to admit something like that. His issues weren't earth-shattering. He didn't know all 66 books of the Bible. So what? He was addicted to caffeine. Who isn't? What I appreciated was his willingness to come clean about personal weaknesses—large and small. It reassured me. Maybe my insufficiencies, too, can be used for some greater good. And maybe, I *don't* have to fix everything in one year.

We left San Antonio, but know without a doubt that we will be back. With so much to do, this city is a mecca for family vacationers. Besides the Alamo and River Walk, Fiesta Six Flags and Sea World entertain visitors of all ages. Sporting events are held year-round. Shoppers can flex their retail muscles both downtown and in the suburbs. Fabulous food, exceptional festivals, and friendly people made *this* Texas destination one of the best yet.

Vicariously Yours,
Traci

Sent: Friday, February 10, 2006
Subject: The State of Nothing

In need of somewhere to hook-up, we rolled into a roadside campground in Fort Stockton, Texas, boasting "el cheapo" rates. There was no one in the office, just a note with the rates and instructions on securing a site. We grabbed an envelope, chose a random number, and slipped $13.00 through a slot in the door. And I thought customer service was dead.

It was Superbowl Sunday and several campers were roaming, beer cans in hand. Too exhausted to socialize, we set up camp, unhooked the car, and left before anyone could talk to us. We needed supplies. As we entered Wal-Mart, we noticed that we were a minority there. Inside the store were real Texas cowboys and not one of them was taller than five and a half feet. I teased Daniel that he looked like the "Jolly White Giant". I don't think the gauchos appreciated my husband's jovial personality. Daniel smiled a warm hello to several of them and, while most sneered in return, one growled at him. I was relieved we weren't spending the night in that parking lot.

We finished the remainder of our trek to Carlsbad, New Mexico, the next day. It wasn't a difficult drive—the two-lane highway was as flat as a twice-steamrolled squirrel—but the lack of interesting scenery caused the minutes to feel like hours. Daniel was driving faster than normal at 70 mph, but tedium punctuated the vacant landscape. It was 160 miles of barren dirt, brown bushes, prickly pear cactus, and deteriorating buildings. We passed the Texas state line, entering New Mexico, and only knew it because there was a small sign no larger than a piece of paper to the right of the road.

We had a singular purpose for visiting Carlsbad, New Mexico. Jim White, a curious teenage cowboy, discovered 100 years ago that some of the most striking things in the world were right beneath his feet. Daniel called the national park to arrange for a guided tour through the famous caverns. The tour was to take place at 10:00 a.m. on Tuesday morning and since our campground was 45 minutes from the park, the alarm was set appropriately. What we didn't know was that when we entered New Mexico, we also entered a different time zone. Oops! Along with the startling discovery of a time change, we awoke to find our water hose had frozen overnight. We jumped in the car and stopped at the local fast food joint to grab a bite and wash up. Thankfully, morning rush hour was non-existent in Carlsbad and we entered the park with 30 minutes to spare before our tour.

The Visitors' Center was 15 miles from the entrance and was reachable only by a winding, steep road. Minutes before our assigned group departure, we stepped out of the car and heard the announcement that our tour would be leaving soon. We sprinted to get our tickets to join the tour. We were escorted into an elevator with a shaft equal to one and a half times the height of the Washington Monument. As soon as the doors closed, the smiling ranger became grim as she recited the rules of the cave. "Don't touch anything. Spit out your gum. No going off the path. Speak in whispers, and watch your children." As her tone grew more forbidding, Thomas looked away from her gaze and mouthed, "Jeesh." I thought this had better be really impressive or at least an incredible story.

We exited the elevator and joined the rest of the group. It took two seconds to notice that we were several decades younger than everyone else in our assemblage. Thomas tugged my arm and whispered, "Mom, why is everyone so old?" Our guide was Ranger Smith—a man as exciting to listen to as Al Gore or Dan Quayle—and his assistant was Judy. We weren't told her last name, but we made one up for her. She had a persistent cough that echoed in the bowels of the underground wonderland, so we dubbed her Judy Coughs-a-lot. Her malady coupled with the monotone narrative of "Smithy" made paying attention difficult, if not impossible.

The further we walked, the more our AARP friends had difficulty negotiating the path. Some were struggling with breathing while others maneuvered slowly because of bad hips and knees. Daniel and I were ready at any moment to assist with a careful nudge, push, or CPR. The tour went on and on and Ranger Smith went on and on and soon I was mentally checking out. I did perk up and pay attention when our leader mentioned that the cave had not collapsed for more than 250,000 years and said, "We were due for one." He added the sarcastic remark that if a cave-in occurred, it would be a nice gift from the government because burials usually cost more than $14.00. No one laughed. Not even Ranger Smith. Some of the elderly folks started keeping an eye on him, I think. Though the cavern was stunning, the best part was sitting atop a mountain and looking across the land all the way to Texas.

Our time in New Mexico was over, but we had seen everything we wanted: a curious roadrunner outside our window, an uncommon national park, and a whole lot of nothing. I started thinking about the nothing and realized that sometimes it is a wonderful thing to see. In this world where so many of us are inundated with information, advertisements, and programs—manmade stimuli—it was nice to look out over miles and miles of God-made stuff and see nothing more than the beauty in that.

The sapphire blue sky, sandy brown desert, and Granny-Smith-green cacti came alive when there were no distractions. In that entire nothingness, there was something to see and enjoy. No wonder people are drawn to remote areas. As we drove toward El Paso, Texas, we passed the Guadalupe Mountains along the Texas Mountain Trail and were in awe of the panorama. We stopped for a roadside lunch at Salt Flats where the vivid colors of nature contrasted with the white salt desert. Approaching El Paso, the roads became dotted with houses and stores, the cars became more numerous and stoplights halted our easy progress west. In the city, there would be development and busyness and that would be okay, but I will always remember the beauty of those miles spent looking out the windshield of the bus, seeing nothing, and loving every minute of it.

Vicariously yours,
Traci

El Paso is the sixth largest city in Texas and our last stop before leaving the Lone Star State. As we arrived, we noticed a stunning view of mountains to the north, a road sign pointing the way to Mexico, and a highway filled with cars speeding off to somewhere. *We would not be bored here*, I thought. Our campground gave us stacks of tourism information to pore over—something I thoroughly enjoyed. It was in these complimentary brochures that we discovered key historical facts, what to see and do and the all-important, where to eat.

Part of the city's history was portrayed in the film *Glory Road*. The story of Don Haskins, the basketball coach who in 1964 recruited young black men to play at Texas Western University, took place in El Paso. Although he faced much criticism, he led his team to victory in the 1966 NCAA Men's Basketball Championship. The school changed its name in 1967 to the University of Texas at El Paso (UTEP), but the pride of that barrier-breaking team is obvious in the community. We were in town soon after the film's release and the streets were marked with billboards and banners celebrating the accomplishment.

After setting up camp and finishing work and school, we visited a working ranch just east of the city for dinner. Cattleman's Steakhouse was located on Indian Cliffs Ranch, a quirky place offering hay rides, animal encounters, and lots of meat. I have a family that loves steak so when I read that this place received an award from *People* for "Best Steak in the Country," we made plans to go. On the way there, I read a different article about the restaurant—one which also talked about the award from *People*...given in 1983...over 20 years ago! I didn't tell Daniel. I let him keep driving. We were almost there anyway, and both he and Thomas were excited to eat award-winning steak and I figured that if it was good 23 years ago, surely it was still good, right? Besides, I had chosen the place and admitting I might have made a mistake seemed premature.

On the way there, we turned onto a rather curvy road and Daniel was dying to test his Formula One skills. I commented that the posted speed was 45 mph. Daniel pouted because he *really* wanted to drive fast and furious on that challenging road in the middle of nowhere. The three of us were discussing why the speed limit might be so restricted way out there when we happened upon a white car laying on its side. The police had just arrived and the two girls inside the car at the time of the accident were sitting intact on the side of the road, crying. They looked unharmed, but visibly shaken by what had happened and I fought my strong desire to use their misfortune to further prove my case for driving sensibly. Daniel, however, knew exactly what I was thinking because he looked at me, squeezed my knee, and slowed down.

The ranch was not far from the overturned automobile, but we were stuck behind a motorhome driving painfully slow up a steep hill. The RV could only go so fast, which challenged Daniel's ability to remain calm. Normally, he loved our fellow travelers and would smile and wave to each one, but his stomach rumble caused him to lose patience and he began gesturing and vocalizing in his frustration. Just as he was certain he would starve, we crested the hill and there it was. Outside the entrance were a frail horse, slobbery dog, and two pesky peacocks that comprised the "animal encounters" portion of the ranch. At this point in the evening, the only animal encounter Daniel was interested in was with a big slab of meat, so we passed on the oddball petting zoo and headed inside.

The restaurant was huge (large enough to house a world-record buffet), but the menu selections were limited. Ninety percent of the items were beef products and 10 percent belonged in the "other" category (seafood & chicken). If I had been a staunch vegetarian, I would have been hard-pressed to find anything to eat. Of course, the décor would have turned my stomach *before* the menu. I suspect that this place had put several taxidermists' kids through college.

There were several sizes and cuts of steak on the menu including something called "the cowgirl," a 24 oz. porterhouse steak that Daniel and Thomas split, "the ladies' filet," a 7 oz. cut that I ordered, and several other steaks that were so big, I don't know who could eat them and walk out of the dining room unassisted. Accompaniments were baked beans, cole slaw, and rolls. I asked the server if they had any vegetables and he looked at me and said, "Just mushrooms." Not what I had in mind, but okay. Even the appetizers were beef. The food was good, and the servings were hearty enough to challenge even the most defenseless contestants on *The Biggest Loser*.

On Thursday, we finished school and work so that we could venture into Juarez, Mexico, the sister city of El Paso. Juarez could be reached either on foot or by car from four bridges in the downtown area. We walked in order to avoid what looked like a long, inconvenient line of cars on the other side of the bridge awaiting entrance into the United States. The pedestrian path crossed the Rio Grande and we thought this would be an incredible photo opportunity. It wasn't. The river barely existed there anymore due to forced irrigation and the re-routing that took place in 1968 because of boundary disputes between Mexico and the United States. We didn't even stop...who would want to see a picture of a river that used to be there?

Our path crossed a toll bridge with a fee of 35 cents each direction. We paid, entered Juarez and were immediately accosted to purchase prescription medicines, eyeglasses, and alcohol. I had been to Mexico before and was used to this behavior, but Daniel and Thomas were taken aback by the barrage of sales pitches. We walked with purpose down the main street and found the historic "Mision de Guadalupe," a white adobe building that has been standing since 1668, and the Cathedral of Juarez.

Our entrance and presence were not accepted warmly. We were met with many stares and scowls. We have toured several churches throughout our travels and have always acted appropriately. We don't talk, run through the aisles, blow out the candles, or play with the holy water. We generally just walk in, take a picture, ooh and aahh to ourselves about the pretty church, and walk out. Not one to be deterred, Daniel whipped out his camera and began taking pictures when a young girl turned around and threw eye daggers at him. Yikes! Was there a rule in Mexico prohibiting photography in church? We took the hint and left. Our reception there made us appreciate the bothersome street peddlers and we darted back onto Main Street.

Standing in the middle of the pedestrian plaza, we were discussing our options when a man approached us who spoke perfect English. He invited us to his restaurant. I asked if it came with a reasonably clean restroom and when he said "si," we agreed to follow him. The café was charming with colorful décor and lively music. Our "hombre on the street" was also our host and server, and, after pointing to the restrooms, he offered to take our drink orders. Now, what do you know about the water in Mexico? Right. Don't drink it. Imagine my surprise when my intelligent husband ordered water to drink. "But it's bottled," he said. Of course, when the bottle was brought to him, the label read (in Spanish) "Bottled in Mexico." I asked if the name of the water was "El Tap-o." Behind that full-on frown, I think he tried to find the humor, but was genuinely concerned for his intestines. We left Mexico with full bellies and valuable information: when leaving Juarez on foot, you must have exact change in pesos. You won't make it back if you don't.

On Friday, we drove to Alamogordo, New Mexico, to the White Sands National Monument, a fabulous sea of white gypsum that covers almost 300 square miles. The trip from El Paso should have taken 90 minutes. For us, it was longer. We detoured and ended up on a military base. Our clues that we were in the wrong place were many including several rocket launchers, a sign written in Arabic, a funny green smoke in the distance, and a mock Iraqi town. I knew we should have taken that left at Albuquerque.

Turning around, it didn't take long to find our destination. We stopped at the Visitors' Center and spent a few minutes chatting up the ranger inside before renting three sleds and setting out for the biggest hill we could find. Our purpose today was to experience sand sledding. As we drove through the dunes, the gypsum was so white that it was difficult to believe it wasn't snow. The drifts piled high along the roadside added to the illusion and Daniel had to remind himself that he needn't drive like a nervous granny after an inch of the white stuff.

We climbed our first dune and, with a running start, threw ourselves onto the sleds and screamed with reckless abandon down the hill. Because Thomas was the lightest, he zipped past us and hit the bottom before turning around and running back up the hill to do it again. I don't know how many times we raced up and down the sandy slope, but we were all sweating in the 50-degree weather. There was only one other family out there laughing, screaming, and sledding with us. It felt like we had found a hidden gem in the desert. And we had. It struck me that if we had never left Indiana, we might never have known about Alamogordo, New Mexico, and it would have been our loss. Surrounded by white sand in the desert Southwest, we learned yet one more time that the best experiences require little more than the great outdoors and each other.

We pulled up camp on Saturday morning and drove west toward Tucson. Leaving Texas was not easy, but then neither was leaving many of the other places we visited. Did we get to see everything? No, but the wonderful thing about this trip was the opportunity to see as much as we could before we needed to move on. The Lone Star State provided us with incredible memories of nice people, wonderful cities, historic landmarks, fabulous culture, and a sense of pride born into Texans—or maybe it's branded into them. I understand a little more of the "Don't Mess with Texas" saying and the idea that everything in Texas is bigger. It just is.

Vicariously yours,
Traci

For the entire 350-miles to Tucson, we looked at brown shrubs, brown grass, brown dirt, and brown mountains, all from our brown bus. And I love brown...brown coffee, brown chocolate, brown(ies), but after a few hours I longed for color, wanting to see a spark of green or yellow or red. But, January in the southwest is brown.

We looked for other things to pass the time. By mile number 200, Daniel and I had listened to and sung with all of the music in our abbreviated collection, including Thomas's Radio Disney CDs, which tested our memory of MC Hammer lyrics. By mile number 280, we had talked about subjects previously not covered in the first twelve years of our marriage—you know, important stuff like the first time we drank soda or our favorite flavor of Kool-Aid. Mile number 300 brought about a game called "Spot the Saguaro." I think it was somewhere between mile number 349 and 350 that I finally found one.

While Daniel and I became one with our seats, Thomas played on his computer, read a book, and killed an imaginary foe with his plastic sword. For Thomas, it was 350 miles of quality time spent doing whatever he wanted. He doesn't ask where we are, where we are going or if we're there yet. That is the beauty of owning a motorhome. While our son was surrounded by his favorite things, Daniel and I were surrounded by brown. There's a commercial on television that asks, "What can brown do for you?" In our bus, brown gets us from where we were to where we wanted to be, in comfort. As I said before, I love brown...even in the middle of nowhere.

We took in a stagecoach tour of Tombstone. I spoke to the driver as I handed him the tickets and he assured me that he would show us key sights and tell us fascinating tales. His voice was soothing and I was eager to sit back and listen for the 45 minutes we would be his guests. As we pulled away, something happened to our guide—he developed an accent that I'm sure he thought sounded like John Wayne, but more closely resembled Jon Lovitz. Scooby Doo did a better impression.

We bounced around the streets of Tombstone listening to this thespian recount stories of years gone by, all while trying to muffle our laughter.

During the tour, we saw several places that looked promising. Daniel wanted to see the O.K. Corral re-enactment. I knew next to nothing about the historical event other than someone got shot. That was an understatement. What happened there was a gunfight of such epic proportion that a legend was born. The characters were the Earp brothers, McLaury brothers, Doc Holliday and Ike Clanton. The story behind the fight had something to do with a law prohibiting firearms in town. That was where things got a little gray for me. On October 26, 1881, behind the O.K. Corral, the four cowboys and lawmen met. As they stood facing each other, at a distance of no more than a handshake or a thrown punch, words were exchanged followed by 30 seconds of gunfire and 30 gunshots, the story tells. Considering the town ordinance about guns, I was confused that so many of the men had them. That must be why the cowboys died.

It was exciting to watch the show if only because one of the actors looked like Sam Elliott. After a quick bite to eat and a stroll down Main Street, Thomas and I were ready to go, but Daniel wanted to shop for a souvenir. In this Wild West town, there were countless places to spend your money and even more people eager to take it from you. Shops should have sold T-shirts that said "I was robbed in Tombstone!" I must admit that when Daniel mentioned visiting this place, I didn't want to go. However, after a long day of walking along dusty roads, hearing tales of dirty deeds, and seeing men in spurs, chaps, and hats, I enjoyed the place and I think you would, too.

On Monday, we wanted to spend some time in Saguaro National Park, a unique landscape near Tucson. The namesake cacti were an impressive sight from the car, but we wanted to hike alongside the giant prickly succulents. I read that the saguaros grow only in the Sonoran Desert and need a "nurse" plant as young cacti to shade and protect them. In the right environment, the plant has a life span of 150 years and can grow as tall as 50 feet and weigh up to 10 tons. We found a parking area and hit the trails. I was worried about encountering a snake or mountain lion, but in the hour we spent in the park, all I saw was one bird. We stopped several times on the way up the path to sit on rocks and enjoy the complete peace and natural beauty of our environment. It was a Monday afternoon and we were alone on the side of a small mountain surrounded by cacti that were older than most of the people back at the campground. Amazing.

We made it back to the car and drove to the Arizona-Sonora Desert Museum. We arrived late in the afternoon with only an hour to explore before closing time. We sped through the small animal exhibits making note of the numerous snakes. No wonder we didn't see any on the trails: they were all here. We lingered in front of the prairie dogs long enough to admire the large and detailed system of tunnels that could rival those in New York City. We also checked out the roadrunner. I had never seen a real one and I was flabbergasted that it didn't resemble the cartoon character. It was feeding time for the birds and our feathered friend was eating a mouse, not bird seed. Did Wile E. Coyote not know that his prey preferred meat over grain? Stupid coyote.

If I had to describe Tucson and its surrounding area in a phrase it would be "authentic Arizona." Though the city is growing, wide open spaces remain untouched. That might have something to do with the commanding presence of the mighty saguaro cacti that stand guard in the desert. While Phoenix has become the Los Angeles of the Southwest, Tucson remains true to its cultural heritage and celebrates the Native Americans who have lived there for eons. My hope is that this part of the state doesn't try so hard to develop into a city of mega office buildings and contemporary skyscrapers, redundant retail and gourmet restaurants. I like it just the way it is...Sonoran hot dogs and all.

Vicariously yours,
Traci

Sent: Wednesday, February 22, 2006
Subject: A Week of Highs and Lows

Phoenix—I almost hate to tell you what happened there. You may have been there for business or pleasure and you probably enjoyed it. And you should have...the city works hard to lure tourists to its golf courses, shopping, and resorts, but the climate is the state's largest industry. My experience there was not positive. It wasn't even nice. It was the first time in the past eight months that we almost had a throw-down at the campground. Our neighbors were grumpy and the staff tried to make us leave because they had us confused with someone else.

I was walking to the laundry room with a load of dirty clothes in my arms when an older lady said, "Check out is 11:00 a.m., you know." I assured her that I did, but added that we weren't checking out until the next day. Her eyes narrowed and she said, "No, you are leaving today." She ordered me to follow her to the office. "Can I at least put my clothes in the laundry room first?" As if I were being sent to the principal's office, she told me to follow her *now* before I did anything. I obeyed. Once inside, she pulled out a registration card and said, "You only paid through today and you need to leave." "But my husband paid through the 17th." "No, you are supposed to check out today." Trying to maintain my civility, I took a deep breath and said, "No, I am not checking out until tomorrow." Another staff member joined the conversation and pointed out that we had checked in on the ninth and were due to check out today. My face grew hot. Not only had I not been there during that time, but I couldn't even remember where I had been. Crabby Connie got within inches of my face and said, "Look, you have been here a week. You paid for a week and you need to check out today." I lost it. I was hormonal and had been standing there with my dirty socks and underwear in my arms while these two women harassed me for no reason. Trying hard to control the escalation in my voice, I said, "You're both crazy. I have only been here a couple of days and I am not leaving until tomorrow." Eyes wide and mouths agape, they looked at me and then at the registration card. "Are you in site 14?" "No, I am in site 12." Their eyes hit the ground and one of them uttered, "Oh. Never mind then." Never mind? I wanted to wring both of their necks, but I had laundry to do. *Welcome to Phoenix*, I thought as I walked out the door, slammed it, and mumbled a few indecent things.

We visited Indian ruins and went grocery shopping. We saw a movie and went hiking. I asked several locals what we should see and do in *their* town and they sent us to an outlet mall. We weren't impressed. We spent hours in horrendous traffic to visit suburbs and community events, but everything was forgettable. Phoenix had failed to "wow" us with family attractions and friendly residents. As the sixth largest city in the country and a hot tourist destination, I have to believe that something draws people there. We just didn't see it.

With such an abysmal stop in Phoenix, we eagerly drove west to California. Our destination was a town called Indio. Daniel read a magazine article about Joshua Tree National Park and mentioned he would like to go. In my travel guide, there was one sentence about a festival that took place at the exact time we would be there. All we needed was a campground; now *that* was a bother. A big event meant that all of the conveniently located parks would be sold out. After 20 phone calls, Daniel found one in Palm Springs that accepted our reservation. The only hitch was the age restriction—campers had to be 55 years or older. We hoped they wouldn't notice our youth. In fact, we were surprised when we checked in that no one said anything to us about not meeting the requirement. We don't look 55—or even a day over 40.

As we drove the 20 minutes to Indio on Saturday morning, I felt like we were cruising on one of the country's dream drives. I hadn't seen that much flora since shopping for landscaping last spring. Every home was gated and could have graced the cover of *Architectural Digest*. Even the bus stops were artistic and sculptural—which I found interesting. Surely no one in Palm Springs rode the bus when they had Land Rovers and Jaguars in their garages. We stopped at a bank in the area and, as I waited in line behind a lady at the ATM, I checked out her cashmere sweater, designer jeans, and Gucci loafers and then looked at myself— North Face hiking shoes, jeans, sweatshirt, and hat. It was like comparing Neiman Marcus to Wal-Mart. The thought made me laugh out loud, which prompted Ms. Fancy Pants to turn around and look at me. That was awkward. I started to explain to her why I laughed but knew she wouldn't think it was funny. She just rolled her eyes and walked away.

Cash in hand, we made it to the National Date Festival where we watched the main attraction: a series of animal races between camels, llamas, and ostriches. This year marked the 60th anniversary of the festival and excitement was in the air. We sat in amazement as jockeys raced around the track on animals that obviously didn't want to be ridden. Llamas refused to run, ostriches swerved and kicked, and camels bucked and threw men from their backs. It was riveting! Along with the captivating entertainment, we learned that dromedary camels are so plentiful in Australia that they are free for the taking. Of course, you have to catch one first. We were told that you can hire a camel cowboy to wrangle a beast of burden for you for a mere $500, but the transport fees back to the United States are as high as $100,000. I doubt your investment would be returned, regardless of weekly kiddie carnival rides and annual live nativity scenes.

After the race was over, Thomas and I took a quick ride on Ivan the Great, a fuzzy and stinky adolescent dromedary. And then, it was time to go. We had some special trees to see. Joshua Tree National Park encompasses almost 558,000 acres and includes two desert ecosystems, the Mohave and the Colorado. Jumbo rocks sit in the shadow of majestic mountains and shelter the most interesting vegetation I had ever seen. We spent several hours exploring the park by car and on foot and were completely enchanted by the Joshua trees. I read that they were the ugliest tree in the world. I disagree. If you have never seen one, it bears a remarkable resemblance to the truffula tree in Dr. Seuss's environmental commentary, *The Lorax*. My husband loved that book and read it to Thomas often when he was young. As we drove through a long stretch in the park, Daniel caught sight of a distant silhouette and recognized it immediately. A chief character in the story that inspired him to take up the cause of our planet's resources was standing in front of him. I doubt a lone tree had ever been so admired.

Along with the likeness of the Joshua trees to those in the children's story, the preservation of the land itself mimics the book. Like the

Lorax, one person recognized the horrible destruction of important plants and decided to do something about it. Minerva Hoyt took responsibility for the desert and pressured President Roosevelt to proclaim the area Joshua Tree National Monument in 1936. In 1994, Congress renamed the monument as a national park. The day we spent there was magical for us. We hiked through an area called Cholla Cactus Garden and climbed huge granite boulders. The temperature began to drop, but there was one more place we wanted to go before heading back to the bus: Keys View. We parked the car and sat on a bench to watch the sun go down. Below us, the rock formations on the desert floor looked like building blocks that children had forgotten to put away. The sky was deepening from azure to periwinkle and indigo. There was a ray of light pointing to one Joshua tree far below us and, although I can't be certain, it looked like the one that Daniel had befriended. Our eyes strained to see the flock of bright white birds that tumbled and turned like a kite caught in a gust. I have never been a nature girl. I don't enjoy getting dirty. I don't appreciate bugs. But over the past several months, the most extraordinary moments have been spent in the great outdoors—in the very place I thought I didn't like.

I celebrated my 36th birthday by dropping my bus off at an RV dealership in southern California and hoping while I spent the day playing with my family, my home on wheels would be fixed. I was amazed at what a difference one year made. Last year, I was in Indiana for my 35th birthday and my husband and I spent the day buying our new motorhome. There was no special dinner, movie, or significant gift, but signing that purchase agreement was the true beginning of this journey. This year we spent the day in Malibu, California, walking on the beach, skipping stones, and watching the tide chase away the sandpipers. After the beach, we drove a few miles up the road to the Santa Monica Mountains and hiked a six-mile trail to a peak where we saw mountains studded with golden rocks and deep green trees against a turquoise sky with a few wisps of white cloud. Back in the car, we stopped to buy fresh strawberries from a farmer and headed back to Van Nuys to pick up the bus. When we arrived, my two window shades had been replaced, the jack system was working and the rest of the parts had been ordered. An appointment was made for February 27, when the remainder of service items on the motorhome would be fixed. Yes, the answer to the riddle, "How many RV dealerships does it take to fix our bus?" had been answered: six. I walked the beach in Malibu, climbed a mountain trail, and picked up my "like new" motorhome. What could have been better than that?

Vicariously yours,
Traci

Sent: Monday, February 27, 2006
Subject: A Purpose Driven Week

After getting the bus back, we settled in at our campground in Anaheim, California. It was a nice place where we were encouraged to pick fruit from the abundant orange trees. Located within minutes of Disneyland, Angel Stadium and the Anaheim Pond, our new home for the week was perfect for enjoying the area attractions. The only difficulty we had experienced since arriving in southern California was negotiating the roads. The closer Daniel and I got to Los Angeles, the more lost we felt—much more so than in any other area of the country, so far. The road conditions were horrible and the directional signage was minuscule or non-existent. I wondered if Governor Schwarzenegger had seen the condition of his state's roads outside of Hollywood from anything other than a helicopter. The drivers weren't much better. We were either being passed on all sides like we were idling, or were surrounded by hundreds of cars revving their engines in hopes that a lane would open up. No wonder road rage is a problem there.

What were you doing in 1952? Maybe you were nothing more than a thought in your parents' minds or maybe you were well on your way to adulthood. Our servicemen and women were just leaving Japan after the end of World War II. Also, the British tested their first atomic bomb while the Americans tested one of the hydrogen varieties. The world was in turmoil and chaos; leadership was changing around the globe and yet, Walt Disney was dreaming of a wonderful place where parents and children could play together.

Amidst the aftermath of the war, Walt Disney announced his intention to build Disneyland, the happiest place on earth, on a plot of land covering about 100 acres. He had a plan—Main Street, Frontierland, Adventureland, Fantasyland, and Tomorrowland—and he saw these places in his mind before they were ever put on paper. Did he know how he was going to make it work? No. But he never thought for a minute that it wouldn't and when the theme park opened on July 17, 1955, Walt's dream became real.

Opening day was challenging. A record heat wave hit the area and few water fountains were operable. The heat also affected the asphalt on the streets and sidewalks, causing it to soften and mire the high heels worn by female guests. Someone printed counterfeit tickets that brought a crowd more than four times what was expected. Do you think Walt sat down on that first day and thought he had made a mistake? He could have, but he didn't. He could have agonized over the weather, the plumbers' strike, and the phony tickets, but he didn't. His wife may have, but then who could blame her? Walt was the kind of man who focused on what went right instead of what didn't. How can I be so sure? Because he was the one who, during one of the greatest wars in the history of this world, thought not about the tragedy of it all, but rather about building a place where families could escape and ride an elephant through the air, visit a fairytale castle, and take a trip on a spaceship.

Over 50 years later, Disneyland still offers a place for families to get away from the everyday—away from the pressures of our fast-paced lives—and play. Sure, the rides and attractions have grown and changed over the years, but the purpose and vision have not. We visited Disneyland and its sister park, California Adventures, on three occasions and had a good time, but not a great or "magical time." From the moment we drove onto the property, we spent most of our stay waiting in lines and were exhausted when we stepped inside the gates. What disappointed me was the scaled-down size of everything. Cinderella's castle looked more like a townhouse. The Astro Orbiter sat at street level rather than high atop the Tomorrowland Transit Authority as it does in Florida. Splash Mountain was more of a molehill and the "It's a Small World" ride was…smaller. I walked around thinking it was a waste of time to have come here. But then I remembered that this was Walt's first effort and it was a monumental accomplishment, and I shouldn't be so judgmental. I realized that before you can build a world, it's a good idea to start with a land.

My aunt told me that the *Queen Mary* was docked in Long Beach. As we perused the internet looking for information about visiting hours and tour options, Daniel discovered that on February 23, something would happen that had never happened before—the *Queen Mary 2* would be sailing into town to meet up and exchange whistle blows with its namesake. We hopped in the car and made our way to this historic event. I didn't know much about the famous ship, so I did some research on the way and learned that her maiden voyage was in 1936. She was used in war service between 1940–1946 carrying troops and wounded along with Winston Churchill on three different occasions. In 1947, the *Queen Mary* was returned to peace-time service and continued to cross the Atlantic for another 20 years until she was retired in December 1967 and given to Long Beach, California.

The main road to the pier was closed so we grabbed the closest parking spot we could find. As we walked toward the water, we noticed that a large crowd of locals had taken their lunch hour to see this event and were gathered on a bridge overlooking the bay. We joined them. Within a few minutes, a formation of planes began skywriting the message "Hail to the Queens" and the crowd roared and applauded. The crowd was still watching the tight formation when the *Queen Mary 2* glided in—sort of. At least her smoke stacks were visible. At 12:30 p.m., the ships whistled in greeting to each other and then we waited to see the full profile of the new arrival. The crowd cheered and readied their cameras, but the rest of the ship never came into view. After several minutes, the grumbling workers headed back toward their office buildings and we were left with just a few others on the bridge. Having nothing else to do, we made our way down to the dock. As soon as we arrived and could see the full size of the cruise liner, she turned around and left. The historical event was over. We stood there and looked at each other in amazement. *That* was it? Hundreds of people lined the pier and boardwalk, commemorative t-shirts and photos filled the shops, an author was signing books written about the *Queen Mary*, lunch specials honoring the historic meeting had been planned and the ship was gone. The *Queen Mary 2* had to get on her way to Mexico so it came, it whistled, and then it bid us all "adios."

We considered attending church at Robert Schuller's Crystal Cathedral, but then I had a thought. I checked one of Daniel's favorite books, did some research and found the perfect thing for us to do on a Saturday night: attend Saddleback. I don't know if you have read *The Purpose Driven Life*, by Rick Warren, but my husband had, several times. We cleaned up, jumped in the car, and drove to Lake Forest, California, where the Saddleback Church is located and offers six mega-services each weekend. We arrived early, which was a good thing, because the parking was similar to a sold-out sporting event. The property more closely resembled a college campus than any church I had ever seen. We entered the Worship Center and found a seat in the nosebleed section—Thomas's choice. The music was spectacular and the message was poignant, but it reminded me of just how much I miss my worship service back home, especially teaching my fifth grade class. Could I really be longing for home? Surely not. There was still so much more to see.

Vicariously yours,
Traci

We had to be out of our bus for a week during repairs, so we bought tickets to Hawaii. The flights were inexpensive, the hotel was reasonable, and we had our luggage with us—so why not? Daniel and I had visited Maui and Kauai several years ago, but this was our first trip to Oahu. When we told people of our Hawaiian vacation, the first question was always, "Which island?" followed quickly by "Oh, you should really try Maui or Kauai." Even the service representative at the RV dealership expressed his condolences when we mentioned Oahu. We were miffed by the apparent bias toward what appeared to be an incredible vacation spot—I mean, how could millions of Japanese vacationers be wrong? We weren't sure what we were going to find on the island other than sunshine and pineapple, but we were determined to discover the best that Oahu had to offer and have a great time doing it. After all, no one recommended Birmingham, Alabama, or Vicksburg, Mississippi, and those places were fine—well, compared to sitting at home and doing nothing.

The flight was only five hours and, after we landed, we picked up our rental car and headed for Honolulu and our home for the week. Although the traffic was thick, the roads were easy to follow once we figured out that island directions are based on the ocean, mountains, and wind. Our hotel was just a block from Waikiki Beach and well within walking distance of Diamond Head, upscale shopping, and hundreds of restaurants. The main drag there resembled Beverly Hills with well-guarded boutiques including Chanel, Gucci, and Tiffany & Co. Within the past few years, retailers have invested millions in a renovation and escalation of shopping opportunities for tourists—or more specifically, Japanese tourists—who flock to the area and spend hard-earned yen on extravagant items. Better them than me, I say.

While we were in Hawaii, Oahu had record precipitation which could have ruined our vacation, but it didn't. After spending the afternoon at the beach, we wanted to go for a walk. The concierge told us that Diamond Head was only a couple of miles up the road and the hike up to the rim was an easy one. Just as we hit the sidewalk, it started to pour. If I had been in Indiana, I would have gone back inside, turned on the television, and grabbed a snack; however, I was not about to let a dribble of rain dampen my desire to climb the inactive volcano. Thomas and Daniel were the unfortunate victims of my enthusiasm to get outside and see something. I sang every song I knew that had rain in the title: "Raindrops Keep Fallin' on My Head," "Singin' in the Rain," "Blame It on the Rain," " Don't Rain on My Parade," and "Cryin' in the Rain." My ride down memory lane wasn't exactly lifting my family's spirits. The entrance to Diamond Head State Monument did.

As we stood at the trailhead, the rain stopped and the sun came out, revealing the phenomenal beauty of the crater. I understood why it was the most photographed place on the island. Built in 1908, the path begins 200 feet above sea level on the floor of the basin and climbs for only a mile to the summit, 761 feet above sea level. I was enamored with the colorful birds and striking flowers, but not more so than the breathtaking view of the ocean from the lighthouse, where we could just make out the heads of surfers waiting for the perfect wave. We had to admit, the wet walk was more than worth it.

The most important thing that Daniel wanted to do while in Oahu was visit the USS Arizona Memorial. At 6:00 a.m., we rolled out of bed and drove to Pearl Harbor—in the rain. We were told by the concierge at the hotel that we needed to be there no later than 7:00 a.m. so we could stand in line and get "good" tickets for the exhibits. So we did. For 30 minutes, we stood in a downpour that drenched us to the point of saturation—dripping hair, dripping clothes, and dripping eyelashes. Did I mention that this was Daniel's idea? Thankfully, we entered the museum at 7:30 a.m. and were given tickets allowing us to be with the first group to view the film and take the boat out to the *USS Arizona*. We filed into the theater at 7:45 a.m. and it was then that I became emotionally involved in being there. Why? Because the film was made up of actual footage from the day of the attack on Pearl Harbor; it was not a re-enactment and there were no actors.

I was transfixed by what I saw and heard. As the film progressed, the juxtaposition of the Hawaiian paradise and the horror of the attack struck me and I began to think about the night before it happened. There had been a party with a band, great food, and good friends. While they danced and ate, the enemy was plotting their destruction. Almost 2,400 personnel were killed on December 7, 1941, many of those deaths happening within the first few minutes. At 8:06 a.m., the *USS Arizona* suffered a direct hit and quickly sank to the bottom of the harbor, taking the entire crew with her—brothers, friends, fathers and sons. Those men had been going about their day, eating breakfast, shaving, talking to friends and then there was a big boom and it was over. The oil still rises from the sunken ship. A flag was raised during a small ceremony and everyone stood silent and honored those who had perished. It wasn't my idea to visit Pearl Harbor, but I gained a greater appreciation for those who lived and died as a part of what Tom Brokaw calls "The Greatest Generation."

With such an early morning start, we were left with lots of time to do "touristy" things. Trying to lighten the mood, we jumped in the car and drove to the Dole Plantation. In Colonial days, the pineapple was so prized a fruit that some women would rent one for the day to use as a centerpiece and, when it was returned, the same pineapple would be sold to a more affluent family who then got to eat it. True, the pineapple is a symbol of hospitality, but long ago, it was more a symbol of wealth and position. The plantation, still actively growing pineapple, papaya, coffee, chocolate, bananas, and flowers, sits near the famous North Shore of Oahu, where only the most experienced surfers dare to try their skills. My skills, on the other hand, were more suited for family-friendly, fun places with pineapple trains, gardens, and mazes. We had an excellent time running through the Guinness World Record maze and sharing pineapple whips afterwards. And, it only rained twice.

On a tropical island, the obvious choices of recreation include snorkeling, fishing, boating, and scuba diving. When we heard about a ride on a submarine, we were sold. The boat ride out to the pick-up spot was lovely, but when our underwater chariot popped up out of the ocean, it was just about the coolest thing I had ever seen. After boarding, we were told necessary information about the vessel, including the number of passengers it held, how thick the viewing portals were, and where the barf bags could be found.

The sub dove from 50 feet to 107 feet, in and around the artificial reefs where the creatures of the ocean spend their days and nights. I found great irony in seeing the fish in their environment while I was peering through a giant viewing glass. I imagined them talking to each other saying things like, "Hey, what's that looking at us?" "Man, those things are ugly" and "What do you think they'll do if we tap on the glass?" We saw turtles swimming close enough to reach out and touch and a shark that made me thankful for the four inches of glass between us. As we descended deeper in the ocean, the colors disappeared and everything became black, white, or gray. As we surfaced, I wished we could have stayed longer. I enjoyed feeling like a mermaid for a while.

We drove to the western point on Oahu and on the way there found the slums. It amazes me how easily Daniel and I can find ghettos; at least we weren't camping there. We passed through several public beaches where squatters were living in tents and cars. Someone had strung a long clothesline between two palm trees and hung their wash on it. I was shocked to see that in Hawaii. We learned that beaches where tourists venture are kept clear of the homeless, but on the part of the island that includes the power plant and pig and cattle farms, the police let the unfortunate enjoy a beachfront address.

The state park that was our destination sat at the very end of the road, so we got to drive through many areas of Oahu that the average tourist would never see. I assure you that the drive was worth it because Kaena Point was one of the most attractive places on the island to hike. We walked about two and half miles through mud before coming to a sign that said "Trail Closed, Dangerous Conditions." I wanted to turn back and we did until Daniel noticed that other hikers were going on. When we returned to the warning sign, we saw a plank of wood placed across the chasm where the trail had washed out. Obviously, the other folks had crossed the makeshift bridge and continued on. Daniel looked at me and asked what I thought. Was he serious? The trail was closed and there was a danger sign. He asked if I thought we should continue on the footpath. "The other people did it." My common sense told me we should turn around and go back, but I started thinking about this trip and how we were supposed to be seeking adventure. I did the only thing I could think of doing—I asked Thomas what he wanted to do. The three of us decided to risk our lives based solely on what my 10-year-old son wanted and the fact that we had seen other people doing it. Wouldn't that fall into the category of "Bad Parenting 101?"

We were 30 feet above the ocean and the only thing between us and the sharp, unforgiving lava rocks was a rotting piece of two by four. Of course, I made Daniel go first—he does have the most life insurance. We all made it across without incident and as we neared the tip of the point, we saw an albatross breeding area. There were at least 50 nests filled with giant eggs. We never left the trail but must have spooked one of the birds, because she buzzed us. I was thankful she didn't relieve herself on me. We walked farther and discovered a monk seal napping on the sand near the water's edge. He barely lifted his head as we stood taking pictures. The hike had been muddy and wet, humid and sweaty, and just a bit hazardous, but we loved it all. I can assure you, Waikiki would never be as interesting.

After a week in Honolulu, we were sunburned and tired and ready to go back to California, but not before we walked one more time along the beach at Waikiki. We grabbed a salad at Wolfgang Puck's and sat down at a beachside table to watch the waves crashing in the ocean. We talked about all that we had done, what our favorite thing was and what we would never do again. We talked about "the next time." We topped dinner off with ice cream and chose a spot on the sand to watch the sun dive into the Pacific and the nightly ritual of lighting the torches on the walk. I let out a huge exhale and basked in not only that moment, but all of the moments over the past week: climbing Diamond Head, visiting Pearl Harbor, swimming with the fishes in the sub, standing next to an albatross nest, and watching my boys parasail. Some say Oahu is overdeveloped—and it is in some areas, but the incredible thing about Oahu is the opportunity to be in a big city and in the middle of nowhere, all on one tiny island. Sure Honolulu is congested, but it is the largest city in Hawaii and the state capital. Is Oahu too commercial? In Waikiki, yes, but then tourism is the number one industry for the state and tourists love retail development. They even have four Wal-Mart stores.   If you are planning a trip to Hawaii, don't rule out Oahu as a destination, especially if you have children.   Choose a hotel close to Waikiki Beach and get a rental car so you can travel outside of the overpopulated areas.   Try to find something off the beaten path and when you find it and there's a "Trail Closed: Danger" sign, don't turn back. It might just be the place you're looking for.

Vicariously Yours,
Traci

After returning from Oahu, we picked up the bus only to discover that not everything had been fixed—BIG surprise. While in Hawaii, we decided to be optimistic and plan ahead. What would be the harm in a little forethought? The three of us talked about where we might go upon returning to California. With all of the rain on Oahu, we wanted to dry out and thought the California desert would be perfect. However, while we were planning and plotting in Hawaii, the Fleetwood parts department and service folks were arranging an extended stay for us in Los Angeles.

After getting this news and taking a very deep breath, Daniel looked for a campsite where we could spend an indefinite waiting period. Another week or so in Los Angeles was not what either of us wanted or expected, but on this trip we learned the value of patience. Off we went to Anaheim for four nights, waiting. Daniel caught up on work, Thomas caught up on school, and I caught up on cleaning, laundry, and *Law & Order* reruns on TNT.

Within a few days, the dealership called. Two of the three parts were in. Without hesitation, we decided to forego the third part and live with a squawky bathroom fan. When we arrived for our appointment at 9:30 a.m., we found that our previous service guy had taken the day off (coward!) which left us with a new guy who needed to be caught up on who we were, why we were there, and what needed to be done. We walked the new guy through the vehicle, discussed the repairs, and told him we needed to pick it up at 3:00 p.m. We had reservations in Barstow, and wanted to get out of town before the infamous Los Angeles gridlock. He nodded and said, "I'll see what I can do." We left our home in the hands of the new guy and drove the car to a local mall where we needed to kill five hours. By myself, I could easily spend that time just trying on jeans and shoes, but with Thomas and Daniel, shopping was out of the question. We found a restaurant open for breakfast and sat down to a mediocre meal served by my grand-mother—or at least she looked like my grandmother. After lingering at Granny's diner for as long as she would tolerate, we moseyed over to the bookstore in hopes of finding a spot to occupy for a few hours. I love big box bookstores. We drank coffee, snacked on scones, perused magazines and books, and surfed the internet for three hours before realizing we should probably vacate the premises before security was called.

At 2:30 p.m. we pulled into the parking lot of the service shop and I offered to find our contact to check on the progress of the bus. After all of the bad experiences with dealerships before, I think Daniel didn't mind sitting this one out. "Hey, New Guy, when will my bus be done?" I said behind a hopeful smile. The response wasn't good. "Oh, I don't know—maybe another hour or hour and a half." I lost it. If my head hadn't been attached, I know it would have spun off. Tired of getting the run around by service people, I bellowed, "No! You don't have that long—I want my bus done now." I think I even stomped my foot and put my hands on my hips. My pseudo-tantrum didn't work, but I couldn't help myself. He looked at me and silently listened to my ranting. He never held my eye contact or changed his expression. To him, I sounded like Charlie Brown's teacher. I was still verbally assaulting him when he turned around and walked away from me. I was stunned. Slowly, I walked over to the car and told Daniel what had just happened. There was nothing either of us could do to make the situation any different or better than it was, so we sat in the car and waited.

We waited for two and a half hours before the bus was finally done. Daniel and Thomas got out of the car after about an hour or so and stood watching them work in hopes that it would speed up the process. It didn't. I tried to call someone to vent to, but no one was home; lucky for them. The only thing that made me happy that day was the knowledge that no one, not the technicians or the new guy, was leaving until we did, which was well after closing time. *Good*, I thought, *I hope their dinner gets cold.*

It was 6:00 p.m. before we were able to pull out of the parking lot. We were exhausted, emotionally and physically, but thrilled to be leaving Los Angeles with its bright lights, countless people, and heavy traffic. Driving into Barstow at night left us wondering what the area looked like. There were no lights to give us even a hint at our new home. When we woke up the next morning, we looked out the window to find the magnificent mountains just a few miles from us and the word "Calico" written on the side of one. While doing laundry, an employee from the campground asked if we were planning on visiting "Calico" and when we said, "Sure," she gave us a complimentary family ticket. We were committed.

We finished work and school for the day and loaded into the car bound for a town that 117 years ago was a booming mining community. The Calico Mining District was one of the richest in the state of California, producing $86 million in silver and $45 million in borax. In 1887, the town's population reached 1200—today that number is nine. On the day we visited, we discovered that we were in the off, off, off season. The employees far outnumbered the visitors, which should have allowed for a more welcoming visit, but it didn't. I think we were more of a nuisance than anything. For example, as we entered "Maggie Mine," one of the original mining tunnels, the guy selling tickets was reading a book that must have been difficult to put down. We stood for a few awkward moments before he reluctantly stood up and stared at us. I said, "We'd like to tour the mine, please." He stared at us for a while longer and then slowly said, "That'll be $3.00 then." Daniel asked him how often the train, a narrow gauge diesel, left the station for its eight-minute tour of the old town and he replied, "As soon as someone pays their money." He was a man of few words, but then maybe it was better that way.

We entered the tunnel, which was well lit and kind of cozy, but Thomas didn't like it. I think the mannequins creeped him out and I have to say that they did catch me by surprise the first time I saw them "posed" back in a hole "working"; however, unlike Key West, I held my ground. The mine wasn't big at all, but what it lacked in size, it made up for in productivity. Inside was one of the most profitable mineral deposits, the "Glory Hole," where a significant amount of silver had been excavated. Thomas urged us on to the exit. I assumed he would never be a miner or even a spelunker.

Again, as we approached the ticket booth, we interrupted the employee's non-work–related activity. We jumped onboard and realized that we would be the only passengers. Wow, a private tour! We sat back in our seats, ready to be amazed and educated with historical Western lore. The stories told by the pre-recorded narrator were interesting, but the only thing I remembered from the tour was a story about a hill surveyed recently and found to be quite lucrative. It was covered in over $6,000,000 of silver ore. Now before you start planning your trip to Barstow, I need to tell you that the processing fee for that much silver ore would run you in the neighborhood of $10,000,000. Better cross becoming a silver tycoon off that "to do" list. The best part of Calico for me was watching Thomas saunter into the "Li'l Saloon," pushing both of the swinging doors open like a real cowboy and letting them fly back, nearly knocking me off of my feet. He smiled wide at the bar maiden and ordered himself a sarsasparilla and then took it outside where he challenged his dad to a "shoot out" on the street.

As boring as it was, Calico was thought-provoking for me. I appreciated that what happened in Calico could happen anywhere in the United States. Ghost towns came about because industry changed—livelihoods were lost, people moved on, and a town that was once growing and full of life died. What's the difference between Calico and any other town across America that suffers thousands of industry cutbacks? People are left with little hope of making a living so they do what they can: they pick up their household and move somewhere else, leaving a once-thriving area with empty homes, restaurants, and local businesses. What prevents a city that loses its primary industry from becoming a ghost town? I like to think that the difference lies in the people of our modern communities—residents with a fierce loyalty and enthusiasm for creating and re-creating vitality where they live. I wonder if the townspeople of Calico tried to find new industries or did they just walk away, settling for a place where people come, pay a few dollars, and look at what used to be there. Thomas used to think that ghost towns were scary places full of spooky skeletons, dark doorways, and substantial spiderwebs. Since leaving Calico, he knows that they contain nothing more than a shadow of what used to be there—along with some tacky gift shops, overpriced restaurants, and costumed characters.

Having been to many historic places all over the country, we were excited to visit a place with pre-historic significance. We were going hiking in Rainbow Basin, an area where many large fossils have been found, including those of the oldest North American mastodon and pronghorn, camels, and three-toed horses. The map we had was incorrect so we ended up once again driving onto a military base and only figured it out when we saw a "tank crossing" sign. It was at this point that Daniel turned around and sped in the opposite direction, but not before getting out to take a picture of a tank.

We found the correct direction and bumped our way over what were the worst roads we had encountered yet. Daniel was going 5 mph and the car was still struggling. By the time we parked and found the trailhead, it was 3:30 p.m. It was a bit late to start a hike, but the trail was only a couple of miles and we thought, confidently, that we'd be back in an hour or so. I led the way down the path into what looked like a dry creek bed surrounded on either side by rock walls. Thomas followed closely, but Daniel was busy taking pictures. The trail disappeared for a few minutes when we were faced with large rocks to climb and then picked up again on the other side. I started getting the feeling that we were in a place few people visited. As we climbed over more and more rocks, I began thinking about the possible wildlife out there—snakes, bobcats, and other desert animals—that I am not necessarily afraid of, but not interested in having face-to-face meetings with, either. My mind took over and soon I was checking all of the cracks and crevices before putting my hands and feet in them. An hour or so passed and the sun was beginning to go down. We came around a bend and saw a coyote in our path. Hmmm...was it sleeping or dead? We approached and found that it was dead—which should have made us feel better, but all I could think about was what had killed the coyote.

At 5:00 p.m., we realized we didn't know where we were and the sun was fading fast. So what did these two college-educated parents do? We left the path to climb a nearby hill in order to figure out where we were. Bad idea. I had read in the information given to us by the campground that the hills weren't solid, which meant that climbing could be hazardous, with a potential for slides. We did it anyway. We climbed and slid and climbed and slid. We weren't getting anywhere. Daniel and I knew we needed to turn around and go back the way we came...and quickly.

We ran as much of the trail as possible, only stopping to climb the boulders in our way. My mind again told me that we were approaching a time in the evening when any wildlife would leave their hiding place in search of food and I didn't want to be it. Just as darkness covered the park, we found the car and sprinted to it. Suddenly, I missed the bright lights of L.A.

Our last days in Barstow were very quiet. We ventured to the outlet mall to get a couple of things for Daniel and drove by an old "Harvey House," something that became a generic term for a hotel/restaurant serving weary travelers in the Old West. We also found a stretch of Route 66 running through the middle of town. Thomas had been asking when we would drive on Route 66 and when I told him we were on it, he looked out the window and said, "Oh, I thought it would look different." I don't think he was impressed. We visited Barstow Station, an old train-station-turned-rest-stop with fast-food, gift shops, and ample parking for big buses. The significance of Barstow now is apparently its location—halfway between Los Angeles and Las Vegas. A rest stop…that was the reason we came to Barstow. We needed a break from the big city and a place to figure out the next few weeks. When we left Barstow, we were bound for Vegas, a place that was not somewhere I wanted to see, at least not with Thomas in tow. But, the weather was supposed to be good there and the location was perfect…two and a half inches from where we were. Just the way we liked it.

Vicariously Yours,
Traci

Sent: Thursday, March 23, 2006

Subject: What Happens Here Doesn't Have to Stay Here

Vegas. When we began planning our journey over a year ago, it was not one of the cities I longed to visit. Why? I would be traveling with a 10-year-old boy and even though I had heard rumors that the town was trying to become an all-ages destination—I had my doubts. Daniel loves poker with the guys, but real gambling? I couldn't imagine him playing anything high stakes. He doesn't have the heart of a risk-taker. I was told by friends that the shopping was fantastic (stores like Prada, Chanel, and Louis Vuitton) but those shops were for the moneyed. Besides, when living in a 40-foot motorhome and hopping from KOA to KOA, I had little room for anything other than "campground couture." We could see a show, but Thomas wouldn't be interested unless someone was sword fighting, jousting or throwing axes—in other words, unless someone's life was being threatened. We could walk along the Strip and see the spectacular lights, but what else would we see? I imagined lots of skin belonging to girls barely old enough to vote that would either require us to blindfold Thomas for several city blocks or, worse yet, discuss things with him that we weren't ready to tackle.

These were the thoughts running around in my mind as we drove to "Sin City". Who would voluntarily take their impressionable child there? Well, we did put his life in danger on a trail in Hawaii...but Vegas? Imagine my surprise when I discovered how much I love Las Vegas. I don't know that I would call it a family destination just yet, but it was a great place for the three of us to spend some quality time.

We had two campground choices—right in the middle of the casinos or somewhere 10 minutes north. With nine months of campground experiences, I found it difficult to camp in a place called Circus Circus. I pictured tents filled with clowns, loud music, and crowds. Trust me, we have seen this carnival activity in several facilities across the country and none of them were so boldly named. Why would we volunteer for a bad night's sleep?

In the end, we chose the Hitchin' Post because it sounded like a quiet place to park our rig and relax with other weary travelers. And it was, until F16s performed an extended fly-by. The sound was so deafening that we gave up talking to each other and resorted to charades. We left the bus to escape the roar of the jets and to visit a towering hotel with much more than just a view at the top.

The Stratosphere wasn't hard to find. At over 1100 feet tall, it was as easy as locating Yao Ming in a crowd of kindergartners. We parked the car and went inside to buy tickets for the elevator ride to the top. Daniel tried to convince Thomas and me that we should also purchase tickets for the hair-raising attractions that dangle thrill-seekers 100 stories above the street. We weren't ready to commit to that. As we left the elevator and walked out onto the interior observation deck, I was stunned at how high we were. There were visitors leaning against the floor-to-ceiling windows, watching the sun begin its descent in the desert. We stepped outside an exterior deck and as I held onto the rail and looked down to the street below, my knees buckled. The wind whipped furiously at that height and the tower felt like it was swaying. I stood there long enough for a white-knuckled sunset with my family before diving back inside to the relative safety. Daniel and Thomas remained outside to watch the gradual illumination of the strip far below.

If it were politically correct to leave Christmas lights up all year, I'd do it. I would also decorate in the style of Clark Griswold—go big or don't bother. For me, one of the best things about Las Vegas is the incredible electronic display. There are 15,000 miles of brilliant neon tubing on the main drags. I assume the people in Vegas believe in going big. What other city has the Eiffel Tower, Statue of Liberty, and Wayne Newton? Only in Vegas, baby. I couldn't help but smile as we passed Treasure Island, the Venetian, Bellagio, and Caesar's Palace, places I had only seen on television or in movies. While casinos may have birthed what Las Vegas is today, 75 years after the first one was licensed, the city had become more than a gamblers' paradise.

Only five percent of visitors said their primary reason for coming to town was gambling. Maybe they aren't being truthful, or maybe the casinos have become adept at seducing those "non-gambling" types to just give it a try. After all, *anyone* could be the next big winner. This professional enticement leads to an astounding 87 percent of visitors eventually gambling somewhere—and we worry about peer pressure with our children.

There are almost as many slot machines as hotel rooms in Vegas—over 120,000. We didn't gamble at all, although I did have to discourage Daniel from dropping a few coins in the slots at the grocery store. Seeing the machines at Von's didn't surprise me as much as seeing people playing them, did. Why would someone waste time plunking money into a noisy contraption when they could stand outside the Bellagio watching an enchanting fountain dance to Elton John's serenade or taking in the roadside spectacular at Treasure Island? There was so much entertainment available from the sidewalk that it hardly made sense to go inside. A volcano erupted outside the Mirage, a roller coaster sped along its track at New York - New York, and the Eiffel Tower soared diminutively at Paris Las Vegas.

What inspired me most were the lights on Fremont Street. Five city blocks, 1400 feet of illumination, delights passersby with short shows several times a night. The avenue glows with 12,500,000 synchronized bulbs along with one-of-a-kind vintage signs including 1966 Aladdin's Lamp and The Hacienda horse and rider from 1967. In Vegas, there's no need to wait for December to see extravagant displays and you don't even need to drive. Just walk down the streets past any number of buildings and soak in the warmth that only neon can offer.

Would you believe me if I told you that passing a convenience store with a drive-thru inspired one of our activities in Vegas? It did. After showering, primping and donning our best campground clothes, the three of us were on our way to The Little White Chapel. We entered the parking lot where a canopy of cherubs provided just the right amount of romance and privacy for our ceremony. Potted trees lined both sides of the drive-thru lane. Considering what it was, I found it charming. With our car idling, a young man leaned out the building's window, as if to take our order. Daniel told him we wanted a renewal and the employee popped back inside to get the minister. We gave Thomas the camera and designated him the official wedding photographer at which point he jumped out of the car and began shooting pictures of everything—some even of us.

While Daniel and I giggled in the car, Thomas was busy taking photos of the landscaping around the chapel. Soon a tiny lady appeared and leaned her entire upper body out of the window. She introduced herself and then began the ceremony. Thomas got back in the car to witness the festivities. The minister was kind, and her words were eloquent, but looking at her hanging from the side of the building was distracting. She was in midair and I kept hoping she didn't fall on the asphalt below. When it came time to say our vows, Daniel and I held hands and looked deeply into each other's eyes. Thomas couldn't take it. Moving in slow motion and as quietly as possible, he opened up his door and left. His door didn't close tightly, though, and as I promised to love, honor, and cherish, again, the dome lights flickered on and off. Within minutes, we were married again—Vegas style.

There were numerous things to do in Las Vegas, but if your visit doesn't include Red Rock Canyon, a National Conservation Area, you've really missed something. West of town, the park encompasses 196,000 acres of pristine land and welcomes over a million people every year. The day we visited was cold, but we were dressed for it and couldn't wait to find a trail. The three-mile hike we chose was considered difficult and led back through a rocky canyon with a stunning waterfall at the end. We read that it only appears during January, February and March when the mountain snow melts. We were cold at the trailhead but warmed up as we rock-scrambled to our destination.

Mountains rose up on either side of us and then it started to snow. You would think that the snow would upset us, but we were ecstatic. We hadn't seen snow since last winter and it reminded us of home. The further we hiked into the canyon, the more secluded the area became and the bigger the challenges that confronted us. We discovered that the three of us were pretty good "monkeys" when it came to climbing. Thomas never complained once during the two hours we spent there. As we approached the waterfall, we stood in awe of this little-known treasure that few visitors to Las Vegas get to see. There were no bright lights illuminating it. No neon. No flashy billboard. And yet, this feature impressed us with its marvelous simplicity.

My appreciation for the great outdoors had grown tremendously on this trip. Despite the bugs and creepy, crawly things, I have learned to enjoy nature in a way that I never did before. Red Rock Canyon offers a 13-mile scenic drive, and that's okay, but in my experience, if you don't get out of the car and follow a trail, you'll never find the hidden gems waiting at the end. Our hike was hard and we were exhausted, but we limped away from that trail sharing a special experience. We conquered our most difficult hike yet, we got snowed on in the desert, and we saw a waterfall with a limited engagement.

If you would have told me how much Vegas would impress me, I would have called you crazy—silently, of course. I was concerned about finding activities we could enjoy as a family and how the city might look and feel to Thomas. I was wrong to be worried. In Vegas, there's the great indoors and the great outdoors. There are bright lights, neon lights, and synchronized lights. There's fine dining, buffet dining, and 24-hour dining. There's a small Eiffel Tower and huge Stratosphere. There are gondola rides, roller coaster rides, and Circus Circus rides. It is an oasis in the desert with a long history of entertaining people from all walks of life—young, old, male, female, rich, and the soon-to-be poor—with not only legalized gambling, but with quality shows, signature dining, and high-end shopping. The city has worked hard to make every visitor feel welcome and safe, whether they come to gamble or not, and while I wouldn't begin to recommend Vegas over Disney for a family vacation, I would suggest that some day, when the Cinderella dresses, Buzz Lightyear costumes, and Mickey ears are long put away, take a look at what Las Vegas has to offer. And if you feel the need to do something crazy—the drive-thru at The Little White Wedding Chapel is open until 1:00 a.m.

Vicariously Yours,
Traci

Needles, California, was a good stopping point on our way to Arizona. Our original plan was to leave Nevada and drive north into Death Valley, but Mother Nature wasn't playing nice with us. When we checked with the campground in Lone Pine, California, the weather was very cold—"freeze your water hose" cold—so we checked around and found that Arizona was warmer. Also, we wanted to get to the South Rim of the Grand Canyon and unless we took the time to drive there from Vegas, we would find ourselves too far away once we began traveling north again.

We found the KOA and set up camp. Since it was a weekday, we did the usual routine of work and school. It wasn't terribly interesting or fun, but it paid the bills and kept us out of trouble with the State of Indiana. Afterwards, we ventured out to see what Needles had to offer. It wasn't much. Founded in 1883, the town was once a bustling community due to the Sante Fe Railroad and some years later, Route 66. The trains and cars these days simply pass through the sleepy desert town without stopping even for fuel. We were surprised to see the lack of development in the historic district, or anywhere, for that matter. There was one grocery store, one pizza place, and not much else. There wasn't a Wal-Mart within 20 miles of Needles. I asked the lady at the campground where everyone shopped and she told me they drive to cities some 30 to 40 minutes away in Nevada where, of course, you find not only better product selection and pricing, but also slot machines to help pass the time. She also said that one family pretty much owns the town and intends on discouraging any improvement or growth; however, she assured me that one day, the town would be revitalized. By the look on her face, I assumed that would be after one particular local family had gone either missing or extinct. I wouldn't consider her bitter, although she did call this nowhere town a backwater which led me to believe she wasn't a member of the Needles Chamber of Commerce. Trying to change the subject, I asked her if she ever got tired of looking at the mountains surrounding her desert campground. Did she ever stop noticing them? She smiled wide and looked out the window toward the nearby peaks before answering, "Nope, I find myself looking at them all the time." Ah, so it was a backwater, with a view.

I had purchased three books by an author named Tracie Peterson. The genre was historical fiction with settings in the Southwest, primarily New Mexico and Arizona. I loved them! As I read, I was caught up in the incredible history and pioneering spirit of those who dared to develop the desert into a place where tourists would travel by train into a virtual no-man's land in hopes of experiencing the exotic—riding a mule to the bottom of the Grand Canyon, perusing archeological dig sites for fossils and artifacts, and learning the customs and cultures of different Indian peoples. The details described made me want to go back in time and hop aboard a passenger train bound for Williams, Arizona, or the Grand Canyon. Imagine my surprise when the opportunity to do just that happened.

The first steam train traveled between Williams, Arizona and the South Rim of the Grand Canyon in 1901, carrying passengers and supplies, as well as a vision of hospitality driven by none other than Fred Harvey, the "Civilizer of the West." Even though he died that same year, his sons knew that developing an elegant and comfortable place where tourists could eat, sleep, and be entertained was a foregone conclusion for the Harvey Company. In 1905, a luxury hotel called El Tovar opened 20 feet from the South Rim and began the makings of an entrepreneurial legacy at what is now one of the nation's most popular national parks. Not only did the hoteliers build the first accommodations on the rim, but also the only lodge on the floor of the canyon, Phantom Ranch, which opened in 1922, allowing tourists to rest overnight after a long mule ride into the gorge.

The campground we stayed in wasn't historically significant. It was brand new. The family that revitalized the railroad, depots, and trains between Williams and Grand Canyon also built a brand new hotel, restaurant, RV Park, pet resort, and gas station. Anything a tourist might need, Max and Thelma Biegert supplied. The story of this couple and their desire to rejuvenate a small town in Arizona inspired me. Would you like to hear their story? Of course you would....

Though the railroad opened in 1901 and carried thousands of tourists from Williams to Grand Canyon, time took a toll. The Great Depression and world wars, along with the proliferation of the automobile, caused the trains to fall out of use. In 1968, the last diesel left the station carrying three passengers, pulling one coach and baggage car. There was no fanfare, no send-off, nothing. As the last whistle blew on Engine 14, only those onboard and the canyon itself heard the signal of a passing era.

The tracks sat silent for 20 years until some investors began looking at the feasibility of reopening the line. Though many looked, none could see past the financial and mechanical obstacles. The town struggled through those years without the railroad providing jobs and tourists. However, in the late 1980s, the Biegerts became involved in the project and, using their fortune, began rebuilding what was once the preferred way to travel for the important and unknown, elite and laborer, soldier and civilian. Over 30,000 railroad ties were replaced along with countless rails, bridge beams and spikes. Sixty-five miles of weather-beaten, time-worn track had to be painstakingly reconstructed, but on September 17, 1989—88 years to the day from the first train leaving the station—a locomotive filled with eager passengers left, bound for the national park. The Grand Canyon Railway now transports more than 200,000 passengers each year, more than two million since reopening in 1989, and has breathed life into what could have easily become a ghost town. Thankfully, the people who lived there refused to let that happen.

We boarded a shuttle bus to the depot where we watched a quick 15-minute skit sure to entertain even the grouchiest customer. The cowboys were discussing the possibility of robbing a train later in the day...should we be concerned? The whistle blew and the conductor called, "All aboard," which was our cue to find our railcar and take our seats. The cars were old with steam heat and heavy wooden windows that could take off a finger if caught between the frame and the sill. Thomas and I sat together while Daniel took a seat in front of us. We were all under the weather which, when coupled with the noise of the train, kept our conversation to a minimum. Thomas read his book, I read the paper, and Daniel laid his head against the window and slept.

The rhythmic "click click, click click" of the train on the tracks lulled him into a comfortable snooze, or maybe he was just trying to ignore the screaming children across the aisle. At 40 mph, the train traveled the 65 miles in. . .well, you tell me. Come on mathematicians, what's the answer to the story problem? It's a trick question, really, because it took us two hours and 15 minutes to travel those 65 miles—for what reason, I could only guess. During the trip, there were entertainers to help pass the time—characters dressed in their best Western wear play-ing instruments, and a three-year-old boy trying to see how many times he could jump on his seat and smack his sister before his mom stopped him.

Feeding the wildlife in the canyon is illegal. There are signs posted all over the place stating just that—with pictures, too, for those who can't grasp the written word. The number of people we saw feeding the squirrels was incredible. I lost count. Do you know what happens to the fuzzy rats that are caught being fed by naughty visitors? They (the squirrels) are captured by the rangers and relocated elsewhere where statistics say they will soon die—80 percent of them do. The signs all along the rim path talk about the laws and the consequences: "Feed a squirrel, kill a squirrel." Feeding wildlife causes it to become dependent on humans for survival, but one family kept enticing a chattering critter with marshmallows just to get a picture with their child. I was bewildered and almost angry. I wanted to walk over there and point to the sign over their heads. Save an animal's life—don't feed the squirrels.

I read a book written by a popular personality on Food Network and in it, she described her first thought as she gazed upon the Grand Canyon. "Nice, can we go now?" Mine couldn't have been further from hers. As I stood and gazed at one of the most indescribable natural wonders in the world, I was awestruck by the intricate and delicate details carved into each rock and the richness of colors.

My first look at the gorge reminded me of something I had seen on tel-evision. Thomas was watching Nickelodeon early one morning and, as I turned to see what was on, I watched a group of children talking about atheism. In the next five minutes, the discussion touched on why God's name shouldn't be used in the Pledge of Allegiance, what being an atheist meant, and the importance of the separation of Church and State. I was flabbergasted. It made me both sad and angry that a children's television channel had chosen to run a story teaching freedom from God. Looking at the Grand Canyon, I thought to myself that though weather and time were the politically correct, scientifically sound explanations for its development, there was something else to be considered...the Creator of wind, rain, water—and even time.

In our society, it is easy to look at a striking painting and value the giftedness of the one who put color to canvas, creating an image of such loveliness that we stand in awe. We don't question the existence of the artist. We see his work. And yet, some people look at the magnificence of the Grand Canyon and believe that the creator was nothing more than nature and time. The glorious artistry in that formation for them is nothing more than a coincidence of natural elements. Personally, I could not gaze at the most beautiful living, breathing picture I had ever seen and deny the artist or His creation.

As I was surfing the internet, looking for things to do in and around Williams, I came across an article called "Quirky Arizona" where I was able to find something, well, quirky to do. We drove north up Arizona 64, on our way to the national park, but stopped at one of Arizona's lesser-known amusements, Bedrock City. The miniature amusement park was located in a small community called Valle and was built in 1972. It didn't look like it had changed much since then. We paid our $12.00 entrance fee, and passed through the gate to Fred and Wilma's hometown. Inside, we found Bedrock had fallen into disrepair. Ramshackle versions of Fred and Barney's houses sat across a dirty make-shift street from long-out-of-business city services. The town's jail, theater, and beauty salon had spiderwebs large enough to catch elephants. The petting zoo was sad, with two depressed "goatasauruses." The highlight of the 30 minutes we spent there was watching Daniel and Thomas slide down the Brontosaurus's back, yelling, "Yabba dabba doo!"

Daniel wanted to check out the IMAX movie about the canyon, so we stopped just south of the park and bought tickets for the 30-minute film dubbed "the ultimate sensory experience." It wasn't what we had expected, which I suppose was our problem. We thought it would simulate a helicopter ride through the canyon, giving us the experience of being daring without having to actually do it. What we saw was the history and exploration of the gorge, which was interesting but caused shrieks of horror from small children when two mountain lions jumped out and attacked a surveyor. After the film, a father sitting next to me was attempting to explain the incident to his little girl. Thomas leaned over and said, "It wasn't exactly a Disney movie, huh?"

When we visited the canyon on Friday, the train ride was fun but allowed only three hours to hike, shop, and eat. We knew we had to go back, and we did. We walked as far as we could and were fortunate to find a pseudo-observation deck where we climbed down to view the South Rim from a different vantage point. As we came around a bend, two mountain goats appeared on our left and lay down on the jutting rocks near the edge. They looked at us as if to say, "Oh great, another tourist." I looked down to where they came from and couldn't imagine how they managed to not plummet to the river below. From where we were, we could see Bright Angel Trail winding down into the canyon, we smelled the fir trees surrounding the path, and felt the crisp late-spring breeze. I didn't want to leave. It was the first experience that rivaled Niagara Falls. The temperature began to drop and we hiked back to the village for a quick ice cream and one more look at the brilliant vista in front of us. It was time to leave.

We were told that at night, after the people have gone, the animals come up over the rim to investigate. I wanted to see that. Already, my mind dreamt of coming back and staying at El Tovar Lodge and then hiking down to the Phantom Ranch where we would eat a steak dinner, sit by a campfire, and listen to the Colorado River rumbling by. We would watch the sun rise and set over one of the most stunning natural monuments in the world and then we would get an ice cream and walk the path along the rim, hoping to see a goat or two. Can you see it? I hope you do. The Grand Canyon…there's really nothing else quite like it.

Vicariously Yours,
Traci

Daniel had a vivid childhood memory of visiting the Petrified Forest and Painted Desert, so when deciding where to go after the Grand Canyon, it seemed only natural to head east to Holbrook, Arizona. We set up camp and went out in search of the area's main attractions. The Petrified Forest was officially protected by the government in December 1906 by President Theodore Roosevelt, which meant that this year marked their centennial celebration. Funny, no one mentioned it at the Visitors' Center. I read it on the National Park Service website. Wouldn't you think there would have been a sign or something—maybe some balloons or streamers?

What the rangers lacked in promoting the centennial celebration they compensated for in talking up the highlights of the park. The particular ranger we spoke with regarding where we should go and what we should do was especially enthused about our hiking into the "Wilderness Area." Though I appreciated her confidence in our survival skills, I was looking for more of a "drive and look" experience with the possibility of a hike or two along the way. No need to flashback to Barstow, California, where we got lost in the desert and nearly fell over a dead coyote. As she continued to hand us more and more information, we smiled and nodded before darting out to the car and beginning our trek through prehistoric land.

There are more than 700 archeological sites in the Petrified Forest and only half of the preserve has been studied. Thousands of fossils and artifacts have been found within the park and in order to protect these valuable glimpses into our past, simple rules have been put in place such as, "Please stay on trails and behind any barricades," and "Do not remove any natural or cultural object from the park." As we parked at various points along the way, I was amazed how many times I saw people leave the trails and handle the natural landscape. One entire family was posing for a picture while standing on top of a petrified piece of wood 20 feet off the marked trail. I don't understand why people neglect to follow regulations put in place to protect a fragile environment (not that the petrified wood was delicate, but the plant life surrounding it was), just to take a stupid souvenir photo. Visitors act as if they don't understand that stepping off the trails and onto delicate soil kills things that aren't even seen by the naked eye. A sign in the park says, "Plants in this environment grow by the inch and are destroyed by the foot." This means that by the time you have taken your photo, had it processed, shown it to all your friends, and put it away in a scrapbook, the living things that your foot killed have still not reproduced. I hope the picture was worth it.

We spent a few hours tooling around the Petrified Forest and Painted Desert and, with the exception of one hike, we were bored. Daniel's vivid childhood memory must have been more fantasized than he recalled because even he was surprised at the blandness of color in the Painted Desert. Maybe my expectations were just off. We had just been to the Grand Canyon. I didn't think I would see a Monet landscape, but most of the desert was gray. Is that even a color? I read that the coloration changes at sunset and sunrise, neither of which we saw, so maybe the lighting was bad on the day we visited. For whatever reason, the park didn't hold an allure with us like other parks had. We *were* impressed by the bold colors in the petrified wood—the first 10 times— but after looking at log after log and wood chunk after wood chunk, even petrified wood lost its appeal. Not that it wasn't stunning and a wonder to behold, but 45 minutes of "oohing" and "aahing" over wood was long enough.

There were other things to see within the park, including the remains of the ancestral Puebloan people said to have lived within the forest between 1200 and 700 years ago. One site in particular, Puerco Pueblo, was a one-story community with approximately 100 to 125 rooms surrounding a plaza. No one knows what happened to this group. Some say they moved on, or migrated because of drought, while others say aliens must have taken them. I think they got tired of all the petrified wood. (I know I did.)

Holbrook, Arizona, was founded in 1881 when the railroad arrived and was named after the chief engineer, Henry Holbrook. In the frontier days, cowboys, ranchers, and railroad men made the town an exciting place to be unless you were a "proper woman," and those were few and far between. Lawlessness was rampant and the local saloon, Bucket of Blood, offered everything these wild Western men needed: gambling, liquor, and painted ladies. It was said that in 1886, Holbrook, boasting only 250 residents, lost 26 people to shoot-outs in the street. And I thought crime was bad in my hometown.

The year 1887 brought a lawman by the name of Commodore Perry Owens and his two six-shooters to town. He was credited with the city's most renowned gunfight with the Blevins family. In 60 seconds, three bad guys died and one woke up wounded. The historic site of the Blevins gunfight still stands as well as the gnarly saloon. Time passed and the community continued to flourish in spite of fire and more trouble with cowboys. By the time Route 66, the Mother Road, appeared and World War II ended, Holbrook finally became much more than a frontier town.

One of the most unique features in Holbrook is the Wigwam Village, built in 1950 by Chester Lewis. The original was located in Cave City, Kentucky. When Mr. Lewis saw the place, he fell in love with it and bought the rights to build his own. This motel in Holbrook was the sixth operation of Lewis's to open, which explains the name Wigwam Village #6 on the National Register of Historic Places, a designation it earned in 2002. In 1974, Interstate 40 bypassed downtown, bringing about the eventual closing of the eccentric inn until it was reopened by his family, two years after his death, in 1988. The Wigwam attracts people from all over the world because of its authenticity—no phones, no internet, no ice machines—and location on historic Route 66. Though we didn't stay there, we did stop by to take a picture and closer look at the 16 steel and concrete structures, each 32 feet high and 14 feet in diameter. The '50s never looked so good.

Taking a cruise on old Route 66 sounded adventurous and romantic so we jumped in the car one evening and took off. It wasn't our first drive on the Mother Road—we drove on it in Barstow, California—but this was an intentional trip in search of the unexpected, which we found within just a few minutes. We ran out of road. Well, that was a letdown. Feeling rather defeated after only 15 minutes of cruising, we pulled into a restaurant, sat at a table, and quizzed our server about the famous road. He said that to drive on the famous highway, we would have to spend much of our time entering and exiting I-40. There was no romance in that.

When constructed in 1974, Interstate 40 completely sidestepped Holbrook and as time went on many of the long stretches fell into disrepair. That is the price of progress and development for our communities and environment. Route 66 used to be Main Street in towns across America, but as bigger, smoother, and faster interstates were constructed, those places lost thousands of would-be visitors and revenue. Consequently, many of them are now struggling just to get by. An area that once served as an appealing rest stop along our country's greatest road now survives on the nostalgia of a few and the curiosity of far fewer. Native American wares and petrified wood can be purchased at a number of trading posts and souvenir shops, but I doubt anyone is getting rich, or making ends meet. As we shopped at the grocery, I noticed that the people looked tired and dazed. Maybe it was the weather or just the circumstances of the day...or maybe in the town of Holbrook, Arizona, a slow and painful process began in 1974 when Interstate 40 bypassed the people living there, leaving them petrified along with the wood.

Vicariously Yours,
Traci

A drive that should have been two and a half inches of scenery enjoyment turned into a test of Daniel's ability and nerves. Maneuvering a 40-foot motorhome can be complicated, especially if there are poor weather conditions or road hazards. In RV travel, things like wind, snow, rain, construction, traffic, hills, and valleys turn a leisurely drive into an "edge of your seat" experience. The wind was strong as we left Holbrook. It was so gusty that many tractor trailers and motorhomes pulled off the side of the road and were waiting out the weather. Not us. It was a work day for Daniel and it was the end of the month again. He needed to get to Sedona as soon as possible to wrap up his sales for the month of March. We would have to risk getting blown off the road.

The wind died down just as we approached Flagstaff, but an energetic sign flashed over the highway alerting us to a new problem: "Winter Driving Conditions, Please Drive Carefully." That couldn't be good. Referring back to my list of hazards for motorhome driving, you'll notice that snow, rain, hills, and valleys all made the list and we were about to experience all of them in the next 30 miles. The bus made it up the hills only to find that rain became hail and then snow. As Daniel held fast to the steering wheel, I spotted other road signs that we had come to dislike: "Check Brakes" and "8 Percent Grade Over Next 10 Miles." A big hill was coming, the snow was accumulating, and we were not even close to our destination. I watched Daniel's knuckles turn white and recalled something he said before we began this trip: "I never want to drive this thing in the snow." I think it is never a good idea to say never.

The road became whiter with snow, traffic continued to thicken, and accidents dotted the interstate like mile markers. Through it all, Daniel maintained an adrenaline-charged focus and weathered his first brush with Mother Nature's fury. Ten miles from our exit to Sedona, the sun shone high in the clear blue sky and all traces of winter evaporated. For the next 40 minutes, the drive became what it should have been from the beginning, leisurely and beautiful.

Several people back home had told us about the stunning landscape in Sedona. I was skeptical, but I was wrong. The colors were so bold they startled me. Emerald green trees were clustered atop fiery red rocks with a brilliant turquoise blue sky serving as the backdrop. I was speechless. I felt like this place was an amalgam of Vermont, Hawaii, and Grand Canyon—all in an area no larger than 19 square miles. I couldn't wait to go exploring.

The scenery in Sedona was distinctive, and the communities in the area had built churches, businesses, restaurants, and hotels in the same color values, allowing your eye to focus always on the beauty of nature and not the necessity of development. Our campground was tucked away in a valley and had easy access to many hiking trails and rock formations. We explored a trail to a bridge that crossed Oak Creek, a long flowing waterway cutting through the middle of town. It was only seven miles, but the day was warm and the rocks reflected the heat so much that 70 degrees felt much hotter. The hard work was worth it when we reached a summit and looked out over the city below. We stood for several minutes trying to record the image in our brains. The colors were so saturated that the panorama didn't look real and yet, it was. We found a bench on the trail and stopped to rest and bask in the richness of the setting. The sun was beginning to go down and the red rocks began to glow and glisten like rubies. We spied on a few lizards toasting their skin in the late afternoon warmth and then we had to go. I didn't want to. I could have stayed there forever.

There was another colorful characteristic of Sedona. The residents appeared to be a displaced group of hippies who rejected society and built their own community. Those we met seemed enlightened, touting the benefits of crystals, magnetic vortexes, and green tea. Even with the obvious New Age feel to the town, there were numerous mainstream churches intermingled with alternative establishments where a very different sort of "religion" was being sold. A fascinating juxtaposition in a shared parking lot was a Methodist Church and Center for Enlightenment. Sedona was an ecumenical soup of belief systems; a peaceful place where relativism ruled.

It was said that there are four vortexes, or swirling centers emitting energy from the Earth's surface, that positively affect either your "feminine side," "masculine side," or "balance." We didn't visit them. It wasn't that I doubted their existence; I only questioned their power. I also don't believe in the power of crystals other than their ability to make Swarovski wealthy. Regardless of my personal biases, I did find that the people there were some of the nicest and most easy-going folks I had ever met. Could the relaxed attitude in Sedona have something to do with the alternative teachings available on nearly every corner? Or could it be that living in an awe-inspiring environment with no morning or afternoon rush hour, overcrowded high rise buildings, or suburban materialistic competitions left residents stress-free? I would guess that in Sedona, neighbors wouldn't think to compete over who has the nicest crystal, knows the correct colors of the chakras, or has the most Feng Shui home.

Whatever the reason, the people there were the picture of contentment—driving a Subaru and wearing Birkenstocks, a gray ponytail and a relaxed smile defined true peace and success. For me, the natural beauty of Sedona was enough to make me want to stay longer and return as often as possible. There were many art galleries, fabulous boutiques, and eclectic restaurants—none of which interested anyone in the bus but me. It would be a perfect getaway for adults who enjoy the outdoors and something off the beaten path. The next time I stop there, I'll be sure to visit Cathedral Rock so I can get more in touch with my "feminine side."

After three short nights in Sedona, we took a detour in our trek around the country. We pointed our noses south once again to Phoenix where we could escape the cool temperatures and precipitation that had caught up to us. Who knew that California would have a late winter this year? Besides, nearly all of Daniel's customers and co-workers were vacating the Hoosier state for Spring Break fun in the sun. We thought we'd do the same.

We spent a full week in Phoenix where we lay by the pool each day and read. Sure, Thomas and I did our school lessons and Daniel worked, but by early afternoon, we were outside enjoying the baking sun. Each day was more relaxing than the one before and we loved the time away from all the hustle and bustle of traveling around the country. The campground was fabulous—family-friendly, full of amenities, and incredibly quiet. It was a week of heaven for us, except for Thursday. That was the day we climbed Camelback Mountain.

We left the campground not knowing where the mountain was, which might sound crazy, but we figured if we drove toward the mountainous area near Scottsdale, one of the peaks would stand out. Traffic was heavy, but then it always is in the greater Phoenix area, so we drove slowly, making certain that we checked every landform for a camel likeness. Finally, as we looked off in the distance, Daniel and I both said, "There it is." It looked exactly like a resting camel—head, hump, and rear end. I read that parking could be difficult there because of its popularity but had no idea just how many people climb Camelback daily.

We parked, grabbed our water, and noticed that most of the people entering and exiting the trail were in jogging clothes. We hadn't seen joggers on a hiking trail before and thought surely they weren't running up the mountain. That was *exactly* what they were doing. Daniel and I were shocked to see 20 to 30 fitness freaks running up the steep trail and jumping from rock to rock like mountain goats. How did they do that? The climb itself consisted of a 1.2 mile footpath over a 1200-foot vertical climb. In some places, the trail was so steep that the rangers installed handrails so hikers didn't fall. But did the super athletes use them? No, they just ran up the big slabs of rock as if they were on a treadmill.

Daniel and I were stopping every so often to catch our breath—using Thomas as our excuse, of course—and these folks were running past us both on the way up and the way down. One woman climbed the mountain twice before we reached the top. I already didn't like her because she was tall, blonde, and thin, but then she passed me three times on the trail. I wanted to trip her or shove a Twinkie in her mouth. When we chose this trail, the literature described it as "difficult and strenuous" and "for experienced hikers only." We had hiked quite a lot before Camelback so we believed we were experienced hikers. It wasn't the "difficulty" as much as it was the "strenuous" that got us. Climbing the towering, steep rock walls was great fun—it was the breathing while doing it that was hard.

The trail itself was tamer than previous experiences only because of the "iron men" and "iron women" zipping past us. We never got lost, wandered off the path or tripped over a dead animal and, just between you and me, things like that add just the right touch of adventure to a hike. Nope, the only adventure on Camelback was in making it to the top, where we sat for a good long while and enjoyed the vast view of the city below. Climbing down the mountain was not much easier than climbing up, with the exception of being able to breathe normally, a wonderful benefit not to be taken for granted. Again, we scooted and skidded our way down the massive granite, distressing our pants in ways not intended by the manufacturers, but we made it down in half the time and would have sprinted to the car if we had any energy left. We learned a lot on our hike up Camelback. For example, staring in exhaustion at yet another steep incline doesn't make it go away or get you any closer to the top. Also, avoid asking those on the way down, "How much further?" because it only leads to additional frustration. They will all say, "Just a little more," when what they mean is, "You're not even close." Finally, we learned the most important lesson of all, one we kept seeing over and over again on this trip, serving as an essential life lesson for the three of us: anything worth doing would be difficult, strenuous, or hard. Camelback Mountain was all three.

I used to wonder how people from Minnesota, Illinois, or New Jersey could relocate and retire to Arizona. Wouldn't they miss the changing of the seasons? What about those 100-plus temperatures in the summer? How could you feel at home in the desert? After spending another two weeks in Arizona, I understood why people moved there and lived happily in this climate. The desert is more than dry heat, prickly cacti, and unbearable temperatures. It can be a lush landscape full of beauty and comfort for all who are willing to adapt to its unique environment. In Arizona, there is something for everyone. The northern region boasts national forests, parks, landmarks, lakes, rivers, and snow in the winter. Sedona, Flagstaff, Williams, and Grand Canyon offer rich history, beautiful landscapes, and invigorating activities. Southern Arizona introduces visitors to the Old West where legends and cowboys intermingled. Spanish and Mexican cultural influences abound in the south, allowing you to feel as if you've entered another country. The landscape is unique with saguaro cactuses standing guard over the Sonoran Desert and a ski resort, of all things, located in one of the five surrounding mountain ranges. Central Arizona—the Valley of the Sun—encompasses Phoenix, Scottsdale, Tempe, Mesa, Peoria, Paradise Valley, Glendale, and much, much more; however, Phoenix rises above them all. As the sixth most populated city in the country, it offers professional sports, outdoor sports, and my personal favorite, retail and dining sports. If a big city experience is what you desire, Phoenix fits the bill. Posh resorts, eclectic restaurants, and boutique shopping fill the "Camelback Corridor" and offer even the pickiest of travelers something to meet their needs.

Tired of the traffic and crowds in the big city? Head to Arizona's west coast where a fair lady can stand on the real "London Bridge" and know that it won't fall down. Yes, the actual London Bridge was purchased by the state of Arizona in 1968 and moved to Lake Havasu City where it was rebuilt and made into a centerpiece for a festival commemorating the "world's largest antique." If you like water sports, Lake Havasu City is said to be the "Personal Watercraft Capital of the World." With 450 miles of shoreline, Lake Havasu offers water enthusiasts 45 miles of track to exercise their most gnarly moves. Arizona *does* have more than the Grand Canyon. Whether we retire here someday or not, I do know that we will return to this southwestern state as often as possible because the sun shines brighter, the mountains are more than molehills, and the burritos are "mas deliciosos."

Vicariously Yours,
Traci

As spring began in earnest in Indianapolis, I imagined my parents' magnolia tree in the front yard and remembered how magnificent the blooms looked and smelled. I pictured the many trees in our old neighborhood blossoming and leafing out and wondered if the dwarf lilac bushes at our old house smelled as good this year as the last. I thought about the excitement building in town with the Speedway opening, bringing with it the racing teams, visitors, and events that marked the nearing of the "Greatest Spectacle in Racing." I watched from my computer what was going on in my hometown and I had to admit that there were times when I wished more than anything that I could transport myself back there for just a day or two. Spring in Indianapolis is one of my favorite seasons and this year I would miss it. And for what? Some might say that I was missing my favorite season for a once-in-a-lifetime experience—traveling the United States and living in a motorhome. Some might say that missing spring at home for just one year allowed us to see things that other people wait until retirement to see, and sometimes...they wait too long. I suspect most people would agree that missing one spring in Indianapolis is nothing compared to the opportunity of visiting places that some see only in pictures, and I would have to nod my head and admit that even though I miss the beauty and excitement of spring in Indianapolis, trading one season of nostalgia for an entire year of adventure would be a "No Deal" for me. So here I am in California again, experiencing what spring looks like on the left coast and hoping that days, months, or years from now I will look back on the spring of 2006 and think fondly of blooming cholla, leafy yuccas, and terrible traffic.... It is after all, southern California.

We took a day to drive and hike through Joshua Tree and I can't imagine spending that time doing anything else. Since we had just climbed Camelback in Scottsdale, Thomas asked the park ranger where the most challenging hike was and our destination and task became clear: climb Ryan Mountain. Although we stopped to rest once or twice, the path wasn't particularly difficult or strenuous; the view took our breath away more than the hiking. Clusters of granite formations stood as a background to the park's charming namesake trees. Continuing up the path to the summit, we discovered a handful of desert flowers in bright shades of orange, purple and pink sprinkled in among the rocks and cacti. It amazed me how something so beautiful could grow and flourish in such an adverse environment. People are like that, too, adapting to the most difficult of conditions, growing amid the many hardships, and succeeding where others dare to even try.

Sitting on a pile of rocks at the top of Ryan Mountain, we talked about many things—the weather, the park, and going home. Home had become something we thought more and more about and looked forward to with mixed feelings. From my rocky perch, I must admit that the joshua trees looked more appealing to me than any old bradford pear or crimson maple. For as far as I could see, spring in the desert was showing just how lovely cactus blossoms, statuesque mountains, and jumbo rocks could be, if given the chance by my Midwestern mentality. Several minutes later, we reluctantly began our descent. Thomas and I were trying to mimic the amateur athletes running down the mountain in Scottsdale when the unthinkable happened...oh come on, what do you think happened when we were running down the trail? No, I didn't fall, but Thomas did. He was able to catch himself before hitting a cactus or tumbling over the side, but his knees paid the price and bled impressively for the entire trip down the footpath.

Because he does have a flair for the dramatic, he showcased his "war wounds" to all passersby including a couple of 20-something guys who assured him that they, too, had taken spills like his and lived to tell the tale. Besides, chicks dig scars, right? We returned to the car and Scoutmaster Daniel performed the appropriate amount of first aid to the knees and Thomas miraculously healed after a few chicken tenders and a frozen Coke from Burger King. I urge you to keep this treatment in mind if and when you or a loved one falls down a mountain trail and skins both knees. A minor disclaimer: it does not work if your fall down a mountain lands you on a barrel cactus or turns into a full-on plummet over the side. On second thought...you had better not run.

With work and school on Monday, we had only a few precious hours to try something new in the Palm Springs area and we wanted it to be a memorable choice. While driving across I-10 several times, we saw signs for the Palm Springs Aerial Tramway and, after reading about it in my *Frommer's* guide and checking out their website, we gave it a go. Since Daniel had to work most of the day, we took the tram up the mountain for sunset and possibly a dinner atop Mt. San Jacinto. Sounds romantic, doesn't it?

As we stepped aboard the world's largest rotating tram cars, the operator explained that while traveling the two and a half miles up the mountain in just over 10 minutes, we would pass through five distinct "zones," including the Sonoran Desert, upper Sonoran, a couple of transitional levels, and finally, the arctic or alpine zone. When we left our campground in Indio, it was 80 degrees and now we were traveling to the arctic? There was an entire group with us wearing shorts and sandals and, as the staff member spoke about the snow and freezing temperatures at the top, you could literally see the mothers in their summer Lilly Pulitzer outfits shiver with dread while their children roared with excitement at the prospect of playing in the snow in shorts and t-shirts.

The ride up the mountain was magnificent as we watched the topography change like a turning page in a book. When we stopped at the uppermost station, at over 8500 feet elevation, the only thing Daniel and Thomas wanted to do was eat. It was dinnertime so I followed them through the building, past the gargantuan picture windows, and into an eatery. Not since the casino in Mississippi had I seen food that looked that unappealing. There were two restaurants at the Mountain Station, a fine dining establishment and a moderately priced cafeteria. Looking for something quick and light, we searched the food line at the "Top of the Tram" and couldn't make a decision. Even Thomas commented that his school cafeteria fare looked better than anything there. Still, people were stuffing themselves with plates full of this odd-colored, mushy cuisine.

Feeling nauseous and light-headed, we settled on soup that bore a remarkable resemblance to the gruel Orphan Annie ate before being saved by Daddy Warbucks. Thomas was disgusted and limited his dinner to saltines. A crowd of newcomers sauntered across the restaurant floor dressed in their finest attire, looking very much like Mr. and Mrs.

Thurston Howell III and company. One of the ladies surveyed the "Top of the Tram" and said (with her pinky and nose high in the air), "I thought there was an exclusive restaurant up here somewhere." The members of her party all looked around and then nodded like bobble-heads. I caught the attention of one of them and pointed the way to the fancy-schmancy place. They all sprinted—in a dignified manner, of course. Thomas looked up, held out his hands, and said, "Alms for the poor, my lady, alms." It was time to go. There would be no sunset or romance atop that California peak. At least we scored a dazzling view.

We left early for our last stop in southern California, Chula Vista, a town just south of San Diego and north of Tijuana. I would love to tell you about all of the fabulous things we did while there, but I can't. Instead, we spent our days trying to buy a house in Indiana for our return to Hoosier civilization in June. Daniel also had customers who needed long-distance attention. Life got in the way of our "vacation" that week and forced us to stay at the campground. Under those cir-cumstances, I was thankful for the fair weather and premium location of our temporary home. Our site was on the South Bay in Chula Vista and afforded us the opportunity to walk along a meandering path between the ocean and a recreation area where many locals took daily advantage of the perfect temperatures. I had never seen so many peo-ple utilizing a public park unless there was a soccer game going on. Families flew kites, walked dogs, and grilled lunch in the middle of the afternoon. I watched the happy and relaxed faces of those people and wondered how they had found the time to spend a few hours outdoors. Why weren't they home running from dance class to karate or Scout meetings to soccer practice?

Every day in Chula Vista, I walked along the bay and studied the peo-ple gathered there and it reminded me of how important this trip had been for us. Over the past several months, we had invested countless hours in doing nothing extraordinary, taking every opportunity to spend time together roasting marshmallows, walking in the woods, or reading books. One afternoon, we flagged down an ice cream vendor, took our goodies over to a bench, and sat for 45 minutes, watching the water chase birds off of the beach. The breeze blew softly against our faces and the smell of the sea filled our noses as we sat there enjoying nothing more than being together. For most families across America, that kind of quiet, stationary family time is non-existent. I think it shouldn't be. Some might think it is easy for us to have those family moments—we live in a motorhome and travel from city to city and state to state—and it is, but only because we chose this lifestyle. For you, it isn't necessary to drive all the way to Chula Vista, California, to spend quality time with your loved ones…all you need to do is cancel your morning golf or tennis game or evening out with the guys or gals. Carve out some time to do nothing extraordinary with your family and see how important "nothing" can really be.

The morning of Good Friday arrived and, as Daniel sat at his computer working, I noticed the sky becoming dark and the waters foamy. A storm was coming and we needed to break camp and leave. I wished someone had been timing us because I was certain we did it with record speed. Just as we hooked up the car and jumped back in the bus, it began to pour. A drive that was supposed to last three hours doubled due to thundershowers and gridlock. Southern California traffic began to wear on me and I fell into a funk. Rush hour was terrible, the rain continued to fall, and my spirits tumbled into a pit called "I want to go home, now." I became teary-eyed for many miles along the highway. I was sick of California. I was tired of campgrounds. I no longer wanted to be lost, cramped, and isolated.

We pulled into the KOA in Barstow, unhooked the car in the rain, plugged in the electricity, and got ready to settle down and watch television. Daniel turned on the satellite and it spun for a minute and then ground to a stop. That was the last straw for me. All I wanted to do that night was crawl into bed and lose myself and my bad mood in some mindless TV drama. I wanted to watch someone else be more miserable than me. Was that too much to ask? For whatever reason, I wanted to go home. I wanted to forget about the rest of the trip and go back to Indiana. I cried for an hour about things that just yesterday were nothing more than minor inconveniences. I cried for all of the broken things on the bus and the things I thought might break. Something snapped in me on Good Friday and I decided that 10 months was long enough for this crazy trip and life in a motorhome. Daniel was a smart man—he looked at me and said, "If you want to go home tomorrow morning, we'll cancel our reservations and start driving." Thomas had never seen me cry and didn't know what to do. I felt emotionally crushed. In the morning, we were supposed to drive to Lone Pine, California, where we would visit Death Valley and Mt. Whitney.

Daniel and Thomas walked on eggshells the next morning, not knowing whether we were going north or going home. Needless to say, we went north. Even though I wasn't certain yet that I didn't want to go home, I knew that I didn't want to be the girl who said she'd be gone a year and quit with two months to go because it got hard. The drive to Lone Pine was magnificent. Sunshine, mild temperatures, and no traffic—it was perfect. As we pulled into the campground in Lone Pine and set up camp, something remarkable happened...the satellite started working again. For me, it was a miracle. Things in a motorhome didn't fix themselves.

We settled in around a campfire and under a starry night roasted marshmallows. Suddenly, I remembered why I loved this trip. There had been special moments over the past 10 months I would never forget, moments when I recalled how hectic and disconnected our lives were *before* the trip. I realized that if we hadn't left—if we hadn't walked away from all that was comfortable, known, and normal—Thomas would never have learned how to skip a rock on the shores in Bar Harbor, Maine; I would never have been inspired to write a book while listening to Jiminy Cricket and watching fireworks light the sky over Cinderella's Castle; and Daniel would never have realized that his sales ability had nothing to do with how many appointments he made or how many miles he drove. How could I come home now and miss what might happen in Salt Lake City or Yellowstone National Park? The short answer was that I couldn't. Sure, I longed for closet space, a dishwasher, multiple bathrooms, and an address, but to come this far and leave without finishing...how could I do that?

Vicariously Yours,
Traci

Lone Pine, California, a small town dotting the landscape of Highway 395, served as a haven from all things "big city." There were no sky-scrapers, no towering hotels...not even a Starbucks. People who came here weren't looking for retail therapy or fancy attractions. In fact, there were few reasons why folks came here at all. The first required hiking boots, physical prowess, and an iron will—because standing more than 14,000 feet above Main Street was a large rock by the name of Mt. Whitney, the highest point in the continental United States. While we weren't going to climb Mt. Whitney, we could buy a t-shirt that said "I stood there and watched while other people climbed Mt. Whitney," and we could put that particular activity on our list of things to do before we get too old to either do it or remember that we wanted to.

Another reason people came to the middle of nowhere: a film festival. You mean you didn't know that Lone Pine, California, was home to more than 400 movies? We didn't either. Apparently in October each year the town celebrates its heritage in the movie industry—one that includes films such as *Gunga Din, High Sierra, How the West Was Won,* and *Charge of the Light Brigade.* Over the years, actors named John Wayne, Errol Flynn, Gary Cooper, Gregory Peck, Cary Grant, and Humphrey Bogart spent time in the very same hills, deserts, and diners that we did. Even contemporary films, *Maverick* and *Tremors,* had used the backdrop of this little California town.

The community's location also draws many visitors. It is a town "on the way" to many places including Carson City, Los Angeles, Yosemite National Park, and Death Valley. If a vacation where the drive itself holds a special allure for you, then I challenge you to find a more beautiful and diverse highway anywhere in this country. Bordered by the Sierra Nevadas and high desert, the route offers a diverse moving portrait of snow-capped mountains, dry lake beds, and colorful rock formations, as well as quaint towns—each with its own personality and claim to fame. Lone Pine may have its film festival, but Bishop has Mule

Days, Big Pine boasts the oldest living tree, Ridgecrest has China Lake, Boron has *the* Borax Visitor Center, and Kramer Junction has a solar energy plant. You could spend weeks stopping in each town, exhausting the area attractions and never see the same thing twice.

But even with all of the landmarks, festivals, and diversions, I believe that the biggest reason folks visit Lone Pine, California, has less to do with entertainment and more to do with the lack of it. People come here to get away from their hectic lifestyles and whether they drive from Los Angeles or Mammoth Lakes, it is the natural beauty and the sheer nothingness that entices them. Here, in the middle of the mountains and the desert, lies a piece of land almost untouched by commercialism and development—a place where there are no bright lights to compete with the starry sky and few roads to carry noisy vehicles within your range of hearing. Lone Pine, California, offers a refuge to anyone trying to get away from it all—a place where the sky is bigger, the air is cleaner, and the nearest Wal-Mart is hundreds of miles away.

On our first day in town, we asked the campground office manager for recommendations on what to do and she immediately checked the clock and directed us to the Alabama Hills. Now I know what you're thinking...*Alabama Hills in California?* I asked the same thing and learned that some of the early prospectors in the area were sympathetic to the Southern cause during the Civil War and named many of their mines, and eventually the entire area, after a Confederate warship, the *Alabama.* It was in those rounded hills of weathered stone that hundreds of movies were filmed and where the three of us would hike and climb in search of one thing...the nipple. Though our destination was Arch Rock, we had to use the womanly formation as our directional guide. Just as sailors used the North Star, we kept our eyes on the nipple. It wasn't hard to distinguish from the other rocks—it was appropriately named, leaving no doubt as to its identity. We came upon the granite arch and I climbed to the top. I hadn't thought much about getting down when I encouraged Thomas to join me. That was a mistake. It wasn't so much that the rock was high, but the nubby surface drew blood quickly from whatever body parts glided across it. What had made climbing the rock easy—the sticky, bumpy texture—made getting down painful. Mental note: climbing smooth rocks in Sedona, Las

Vegas, and Phoenix is fun, but climbing coarse rocks in California requires first aid.

Another afternoon in the Alabama Hills, we tried to follow a map given to us at the campground depicting "Picture Rocks." Someone discovered that many of the groupings in the hills resembled other things and had identified, named, and mapped them for visitors to find on a self-guided tour. Out of the 30 geological formations noted on the neon pink map, we found three. We are fairly intelligent and had traveled most of the country for the past 10 months and I assure you we had used maps of all sorts to find our way. We sat and stared at rocks. Did we see the baboon? No. We stared longer. We closed our eyes and opened them quickly. Did we see the rhino feet? No. We used one eye and then the other. We even tried to "magic eye" the rocks thinking that not focusing on anything must be the key. Did we see the fishman? No. Now, I won't say that the rock pictures don't exist (I wouldn't want to be labeled a rocktheist), but I will say that the mysterious person who discovered the pictures and drew the map might be Keith Richards or Ozzy Osbourne. I just didn't see their rock fantasy.

Having little luck with the Alabama Hills, we ventured up Mt. Whitney...by car. Daniel drove up the mountain to a place where we could park and climb an abbreviated three-mile trail to the top, but the road was closed due to snow. I was willing to get out, take a few pictures, and head back to the bus; however, Daniel wanted to walk up the closed road to see how far we could go. Hmmm...a closed road...in an active bear area? Okay. And so the three of us began climbing the Whitney Portal Road and soon found that it wasn't snow that had caused the closure, but huge rock slides. It wasn't a drivable path, but it was a stupendous footpath to walk. The Alabama Hills shrank into nothing more than pebbles beneath our gaze. The desert below looked so small, like a child's sand box. I was amazed at the many trees clinging by nothing more than a root or two to the side of this wondrous mountain. The walk wasn't difficult, but the uphill climbing did get our hearts pumping. While Daniel and I were breathing normally, Thomas was, in his mind at least, near death and said, "I just...can't...make...it...any...more..." In my caring motherly way, I replied, "Gut it up, little man." At one of our rest stops, we met a couple of women from the area—one was a park ranger in the Mojave and the other a Bed & Breakfast owner in town—and we talked about California national parks, including Death Valley and Joshua Tree. Thomas loved talking to park rangers, especially pretty ones, which, not surprisingly, were hard to find in the middle of nowhere. We learned a great deal from them and got some ideas on things to do during our trip to Death Valley the next day. After saying goodbye, we walked farther up the road and each time Thomas would say, "How...much...farther?" I would say, "Just to that tree up there." After a half dozen different trees, Thomas caught on to my devious ways and refused to go any higher. As Daniel and I turned around and followed Thomas down the mountain road, we talked about our next trip to Lone Pine—a trip that would include a long walk and a big mountain.

The picture I had in my mind of Death Valley was one of narrow, unmarked roads cutting through hundreds of miles of sand with tumbleweeds blowing through the arid terrain and large black birds sitting...waiting...watching for their next meal to stumble into view. There was no color, just brown sand, rocks, and vegetation, all blending into one another, causing visitors to lose their way. And there would be skulls and skeletons. That was what I expected to see in Death Valley. What would you expect? Imagine my surprise when we entered the park and found lush vegetation, colorful canyons, and snow-capped, green mountains. Sure, there was a desert there, but the diversity of surroundings took my breath away and changed my view of that place forever.

From Lone Pine, the drive was far, but it didn't feel long or boring. We stopped at Stovepipe Wells, an oasis in the desert complete with a campground, motel, restaurant, and gift shop, where we bought a map that was very helpful in finding our way around the park. The ranger we met at Mt. Whitney suggested we climb Telescope Peak, so we found it on the map and sped away. If only she had shared *all* of the pertinent information regarding tackling such a feat. The trailhead was 30 miles from Stovepipe, at the end of a road marked "limited use." I didn't know what that meant, but I would soon find out. Fortunately, we had plenty of fuel, water, and enthusiasm to help us on our way.

We drove in and out around mountains on winding roads surrounded by rocky formations and tall trees. We watched jack rabbits darting through the desert vegetation and, occasionally, bravely cross the roads while "Hitchcockian" crows anticipated having rabbit for dinner.

As we neared our destination, we came across an interesting landmark of eight large charcoal kilns built back in the late 1800s by Chinese workers. The ovens looked like giant beehives made out of rocks and mortar with a wee little door in the front and a few ventilation holes around the top and bottom. We read that the structures were used to burn the local wood, turning it into charcoal, and then hauled by horse and wagon some 30 miles to a factory for utilization. The operation was shut down after only three years, for what reason, I don't know, but my guess would be that the distance to transfer the charcoal became problematic. After the three of us thoroughly inspected the area, we debated whether to continue our drive to Telescope Peak. I had discovered vital information that the friendly locals forgot to mention. For example, the "limited use" road that would take us there was recommended for four-wheel drive vehicles only, not luxury sedans. I was aghast when Daniel started driving his Infiniti up that road. We had heard bad noises in the bus, but let me tell you...the Infiniti was making such a raucous that I assumed the vehicle didn't want to go. Daniel loved his car so I was mystified that he kept driving over the rough terrain. He had his windows down, listening—for what I don't know—but the loud banging and kerplunking persisted. I said, "Daniel, please turn around. If the wheels fall off out here, what do we do? We *are* in Death Valley, you know." Another 10 grueling minutes passed and finally, he relented and turned the car around, putting us all out of our misery. We did hike another trail, Wildrose Peak, or at least part of it. It was heavenly. The mountain was covered in pine trees and cacti and the smell of fresh trees was intoxicating. Lined by colorful rocks and vegetation, the path led us up a winding trail to a summit that we never saw. The sun started to go down and a chill was in the air. It was time to go. As we left Death Valley, it occurred to me that the name seemed all wrong. I had seen nothing that brought to mind an untimely demise or unfortunate event...well, except for those crows.

The drive to San Francisco would take us three days with stops in

Bakersfield and Chowchilla. As always, we were glad to leave where we were and go somewhere new, but this place had been a quiet respite from the craziness of southern California. I would miss the starry sky, the Alabama Hills, and the mountains. I would also miss the people of Lone Pine…relaxed, friendly and carefree, like those in Maine and Sedona. Would there be anything I wouldn't miss? Sure. Lone Pine was a one-grocery-store town offering milk at $5.00 a gallon and bread at $3.69 a loaf. We didn't pay that much for groceries in Hawaii. I started thinking that going from a town like Lone Pine to one as busy as San Francisco might leave us feeling schizophrenic, but with only one more week in California, we would need to plan on a busy, touristy time. Of all the places we had been and were planning to see before coming home in June, I looked forward to San Francisco the most. Maybe I watched too many Rice-A-Roni commercials as a child, but I always dreamed of riding on one of those street cars and leaving part of my heart in that famous town.

In retrospect, I can't tell you how happy I was that we drove north instead of east, toward home, when we left Barstow. I still struggled with a desire to get off the bus and live a normal life, but I'm glad we hadn't done it just yet. We hadn't been to Utah or Colorado. And there was still Wyoming, Montana, and the Dakotas. What about the Mall of America? Doesn't every girl need to flex her retail muscles there? If we had gone home when I asked to, we might have missed our one opportunity to see all of those places, and for what? Besides, who would want to read a book about a family who traveled 75 percent of the country for ten months? I know I wouldn't.

Vicariously Yours,
Traci

Spending a week in the San Francisco area was one of the highlights of this trip for me—not that I expected anything different. I simply couldn't imagine being in the middle of so many famous places and not having a fantastic time. If I ever moved to California, I would live just north of San Francisco, minutes from the Golden Gate Bridge, Muir Woods, Sausalito and a short drive from the country's most beautiful wine region. Sure, some folks think California dreams only come true in places like Los Angeles, while still others would rather drive for a Tiger's life in Palm Springs, but for me, San Francisco and the area surrounding it holds an allure beyond any hopes of running into celebrities while grabbing my daily cup of energy at Starbucks or look-ing for a lost golf ball at the nineteenth hole.

If you have never been to San Francisco, you need to put it on your list of 100 things to do before you die. Why? Because in and around that city are things that just don't exist anywhere else and, since we all only live once, isn't it imperative to see and experience as much wonder and beauty as possible before we reach the point in our lives when we start regretting all that we didn't do?

In the City by the Bay, architecture and engineering—coupled with one man's vision in the 1930s—created one of the most striking American landmarks to date: the Golden Gate Bridge. Miraculously surviving the great earthquake of 1906, 14,000 magnificent Victorian homes line the streets of this old city, bringing not only exceptional beauty, but also a determination to restore and protect the past. Civil War history meets modern retail therapy at Union Square, where pro-Union rallies have been exchanged for high- end shopping and dining. And only in San Francisco can a person take a boat to an island that offers no palm trees, sandy beaches, or fruity drinks with cute mini umbrellas. No, Alcatraz offers something that guests would never want to experience themselves: a glimpse into an inmate's life where freedom was only a mile away. If you long for the great outdoors, head north of the city to one of the most beautiful places a tree would ever want to live, Muir

Woods, or drive a little farther and take in the lush landscape of Napa Valley and the many wineries there. Having spent seven days in this wonderful city, I can assure you that whatever it is that you like to do while on vacation—you can do it in the San Francisco area. And while you're there, you might as well try some new things, too, because that city is indeed a treat.

On our first day in town, we drove without a specific agenda. Sometimes, this free-spirited activity takes us to the middle of nowhere or even just to Wal-Mart; however, by venturing out absent of a specific plan or direction, we often found ourselves seeing incredible things. On that day, we came upon one of our nation's most famous landmarks and as we drove over it, we marked the momentous occasion by chanting, "We're going over the Golden Gate Bridge, we're going over the Golden Gate Bridge." I've never seen any statistics on this, but I would guess it is as recognizable an American landmark as the White House or the St. Louis Arch. And I can tell you that it isn't the most beautiful bridge in the country; we've seen more stunning ones in Boston and Charleston, but then both of those structures were built just a handful of years ago, not exactly a period of time when our country's future was under scrutiny. Consider this: the final design for the Golden Gate Bridge was submitted by Joseph Strauss on August 27, 1930, and included two pedestrian walkways and six lanes for northbound and southbound traffic at a cost of $35 million.

What was going on in California in 1930? The state was, along with the rest of the nation, struggling through the Great Depression. Businesses and banks closed their doors while individual investors lost everything. Thousands of people lost jobs, property, and all hope...or did they? At the same time that Californians were facing their most challenging economic situation in history, the state managed to host the 1932 Olympic Games and build two amazing bridges that would in time bring the world to see what this part of the Golden State had to offer. Although the Bay Bridge connecting Oakland and San Francisco was completed first and opened with much fanfare, the Golden Gate Bridge demanded awe from all who saw it with its incredible design and striking color, being called "a curve of soaring steel, graceful and confident."

While building the Golden Gate, it was expected that at least 35 men would die; however, a much smaller number took that prediction literally and fell to their deaths. Although 11 men perished, 19 were saved due to the rigging of a safety net strung below the construction site and in the true spirit of camaraderie, these men became known as the "Halfway to Hell Club." Just imagine the t-shirts for that group: "If you fell, join Halfway to Hell." I might buy one.

The opening day of the bridge took place on May 27, 1937, for pedestrians, and the following day for autos. In the first year of operation, more than 30 million crossings were counted. Imagine that: in 1937, the automobile was not owned by every Brad, Jack, and George on the street and *definitely* not by Linda, Kelly or Karen, and yet still millions of people crossed that bridge, utilizing each of those six lanes. I have to wonder if Joseph Strauss had a sort of "Field of Dreams" vision (the "if you build it, they will come" principle), and come they did by numbers that continue to increase yearly. The bridge serves not only as a landmark, but as a destination in and of itself. Every day hundreds if not thousands of people walk, jog, and bike across, always stopping to take in the views of the bay.

There are a couple of different places to park your car and explore the structure on foot, and I encourage you to do just that at least once during a visit because only at a close proximity can you see some of the more intricate design elements on the bridge. For those emotionally distressed folks who might try to jump to their death from the railings, there are signs that say, "There is hope. Make the call. The consequences of jumping from this bridge are fatal and tragic." There are also telephones with a direct connection to a grief counselor. Not that any part of someone jumping to their doom from the bridge is funny, but I thought it especially interesting that they call the consequence of jumping both fatal and tragic—like it would actually make an emotionally distressed person stop and think, "Hmmm...I knew this was fatal, but I had no idea jumping to my death would be tragic. I had better reconsider this." There were also signs above the pedestrian walkway on the supports stating "No Trespassing" for the truly stupid who might find it an extreme sport to climb onto the main cables and grind, climb, or base jump.

Daniel's favorite sign was the one noting that shooting a missile off of the bridge is a misdemeanor. A misdemeanor? I would think that shooting a missile from anywhere would bring in the FBI, Homeland Security, and many other agents of authority seeking to charge the offender with something more than a petty offense. But here's the thing: if we hadn't gotten out of our car and walked across the Golden Gate, we would never have seen any of that stuff. We would never have stood exchanging greetings with the crew of a barge passing below us or watched windsurfers ride the wake of that very same vessel, leveraging wind, water, and body weight to fly above the bay, if only for a few moments. If we hadn't taken the time to explore the bridge, we would not have been able to stand in the middle of the pedestrian walk listening to the hundreds of cars zooming past us and marvel at the foresight of a small group of people who in 1933, decades before President Bill Clinton would ever utter his re-election campaign mantra, physically began building a bridge to the future and in doing so, gave the rest of the country a golden opportunity to visit their incredible city.

Our first destination in San Francisco was Fisherman's Wharf, a historic area where generations of fishermen have made their living since the days of the Gold Rush, and one that still offers an array of activity including a variety of shopping and dining experiences, tours of the city by boat, trolley, bike, or Segway (those stand-up people scooters), and my personal favorite: a live show with hundreds of sea lions at Pier 39. After parking the car, we walked to the far end of the wharf to visit the Ghirardelli Chocolate Factory, a company established in 1852 to test the willpower of everyone who walks within a mile of the sweet-smelling place. The factory still offers a view into the making of their famous chocolate, except this was much less Willy Wonka and his chocolate river and more like a few vats of soon-to-be chocolate squares getting pushed around by large granite rollers and mixers. Even without the Oompa Loompas, it was an incredible experience, but that could be the free samples talking. Anyway, when you walk in the door of the Ghirardelli store, you are handed a chocolate square to savor while winding your way through deep shelves, large tables, and colorful displays of company products, and I have to admit that with or without the sample, I knew I was not leaving without making a purchase.   Daniel and I are champion chocolate eaters and one little chocolate square was not going to satisfy our sweet teeth that day, so we hurried next door to Ghirardelli's Soda Fountain where we waited in a long line for a special San Francisco treat: a hot fudge sundae. Minutes later, we were on our way back into the Square where we stood in front of Mermaid Fountain and tossed coins over our shoulders while making a wish or two.   Thomas and I made a deal that neither of us would wish to go home...not yet, anyway.

We took a little time to check out a t-shirt place where we picked up a few souvenirs before returning to the piers.   As we passed Boudin Bakery, we couldn't resist stopping to smell the daily bread and decided that we just had to take home some fresh sourdough for dinner. Yum. Sourdough bread can be found at nearly every restaurant in town and is usually served as a bread bowl with a heaping helping of clam chowder nestled inside.   If this sounds good to you, don't think you have to hit a restaurant to get this treat; almost any food cart on the wharf offers bread bowls with chowder and the price is unbelievable for the size and quality of the food.   Of course, you will have to fend off the gulls if you sit somewhere outside.   (You've been warned.)

Besides the local food carts, there are many places to eat, including a great gourmet store in The Cannery at Del Monte Square called Oakville Grocery.   Foodies will love this place with its fresh offerings and high quality, eclectic-flavored pizzas, sandwiches, and salads. You can also get a great cup of coffee at Oakville as well as wine and interesting sodas.   Don't worry about eating too much because you will have more than enough opportunity to walk off any superfluous calories on the streets and hills of Fisherman's Wharf.

I suppose if you don't want to walk, you can take advantage of the many motorized alternatives like the famous cable cars, but be prepared for a long wait.   The old streetcars are one of the busiest tourist spots in the city and while there, we saw the line at least 70 people deep at all times of the day with the exception of dusk.   At only $5.00, the ride is a bargain and a great way to enjoy a sense of history and see some of the most beautiful buildings in San Francisco, including the section of Lombard Street dubbed one of the most crooked and unique streets in

America. Between Hyde and Leavenworth, Lombard takes a dive down a 27-degree slope requiring several sharp switchbacks. Most visitors take the Hyde-Powell cable car so they can stop and see this crazy design, but Daniel and I decided to test the brakes in the Infiniti and drive it.

There are also pedestrian walks for anyone desiring a slow descent down a beautiful street lined with some of the most fabulous homes in the city. To travel like a local, jump onboard the brightly colored MUNI cars for a mere $1.50 per ride, but keep in mind that these cars travel more of a perimeter route of the city and don't include any sort of narration. Whatever way you get around Fisherman's Wharf, don't leave before you visit Pier 39, where you can take in a great show starring several hundred sea lions who made their home on the pier in 1990, shortly after the earthquake of 1989. Watching these animals is like watching a reality television show that's a cross between *Jerry Springer*, *The Osbournes*, and *The Jeff Corwin Experience*. They bark, fight, and push each other off the floating docks like a huge dysfunctional family. Even if you have seen sea lions at an aquarium, you need to see *these* sea lions. They are not trained, captive, or friendly, so have your camera ready and whatever you do, don't feed them, provoke them, or harass them. They take care of all those things themselves.

Over the course of the week, we visited a few places for Thomas and a few for us. Thomas enjoyed Six Flags Marineworld, an amusement park similar to Busch Gardens, just north of San Francisco in Vallejo. The crowds were light and we were able to take in some great thrill rides, eat some greasy food, and see a fun show with extreme water skiers. We were also able to enjoy some interesting animal exhibits including the obligatory dolphin, whale, and sea lion shows. After a few hours of filling our stomachs and then testing our ability to keep it all down, Thomas was ready to leave. Another great Thomas destination was an adventure museum called the Exploratorium, "the museum of science, art and human perception." It's a fabulous place to spend several hours with a child or husband who has the "Peter Pan" syndrome. The museum's home is the Palace of Fine Arts built in 1915 for the Panama-Pacific International Exposition and is one of the most beautiful buildings in downtown San Francisco, looking like a golden dome shining brightly in the California sun.

Inside the museum are hundreds of hands-on, interactive stations where demonstrations and experiments are fun and easy. It took Thomas three hours to make it through the various exhibits and still he wasn't quite ready to go when I dragged him out the door. If you have children and you take them to San Francisco, the Exploratorium is a must. Just remember to take your hand sanitizer. Hands-on activities used by hundreds of children a day? Oh yeah, you'll need hand sanitizer.

Thomas had a couple of days enjoying kid stuff, so Daniel and I felt no guilt taking him out to wine country. Napa Valley was a short, 45-minute drive from our campground and was just as wonderful as I dreamed it would be. Since we were limited on time and were dragging along Thomas, we chose a couple of places that we really wanted to visit. Most of the area wineries require reservations for tastings and tours; so plan ahead if you want to take advantage of these opportunities. Unfortunately, we couldn't tour because of Thomas's age, but believe it or not, they had no problem letting us buy as much as we wanted. Shocking, I know. The two wineries we visited were Mondavi and Cakebread—sort of the elephant and ant comparison here.

The Robert Mondavi Winery was founded in 1966 and includes 1400 acres of vineyards in three regions. The mission-style establishment is stunning with landscaping that begs to be photographed, and wine...well, that begs to be tasted. We walked around Mondavi for a while before deciding on our purchases and heading out to our next stop: Cakebread Cellars. A good friend said that if we made it to Napa, we had to go to Cakebread, so we did our best to find it. Even though we had the address and were somewhat familiar with the road, it took several attempts to find this small business. One of the employees told us that even after a year of working at Cakebread, she still has to look for landmarks in order to get to work. Cakebread was founded over 30 years ago by a photographer who visited the valley and shared with friends how he'd like to own a winery. The next day, Jack Cakebread's dream came true as he finalized the purchase of a piece of property in Rutherford, California. Cakebread is a family business that has become one of the most successful vineyards in Napa. Another important thing to know about visiting wine country involves timing—meaning that the wineries close around 4:30 or 5:00 p.m., so if you want to visit several, plan your day carefully. Also, make sure you eat before, during, and after tastings. There's a great Dean & Deluca where yummy food can be boxed up for a romantic picnic with California's lush and lovely wine country as the backdrop.

Although I was eager to visit Napa Valley, I was concerned that the area and the people might be a bit too "uppity" for me. I'm not a connoisseur, just an occasional wine drinker. Fortunately, the area was very inviting and the people could not have been friendlier. As we drove away, you can bet that Daniel and I talked about the next time we would visit this special part of California and do our very best to notice the subtle taste of honey in the Chardonnay and chocolate in the Merlot.

You didn't think we'd leave a city without hugging some trees, did you? We couldn't drive five or six hours north to see California's glorious redwoods, so we opted for the quiet respite of Muir Woods National Monument where we found a redwood forest—one that dates back perhaps thousands of years. In 1905, the forest was threatened by loggers, and a conservationist by the name of William Kent bought the land and donated it to the government under the Antiquities Act. At the request of Mr. Kent, President Roosevelt named the land after John Muir, one of America's earliest environmental activists. In 1908, Muir Woods became a national monument. Stepping onto the first trailhead, we knew that we had never hiked in a place like this. Lush ferns act as a carpet on the forest floor while fir, maple and oak trees provide a secondary canopy in the shadow of old redwoods standing guard in a forest that smells so pure and fresh, we wanted to bottle it and take it home. Thomas kept commenting on the fragrance and the intense color and multitude of trees.

John Muir said of his namesake forest, "This is the best tree-lover's monument that could possibly be found in all the forests of the world." Now, I'm not a passionate tree hugger and Daniel does twist my arm at times to make me recycle and do the environmentally responsible thing; however, after spending the afternoon in Muir Woods, I had a much greater appreciation for the need to protect these undisturbed places where ancient trees can continue to act as guardians to seeds, saplings, and wildlife. Spring in Muir Woods brings wildflowers, nesting birds, and spotted fawns. Each time we crossed one of the several bridges along the trails, the three of us would stop and take a look around, trying to imprint the peace and beauty of that particular spot in our minds. Redwood Creek was bubbling and rumbling across the rocks, woodpeckers were drumming on bark, and we were completely silent. It was a beautiful way to spend an afternoon and yes, we hugged some trees...some very big trees.

Our last night in San Francisco was spent taking a boat to an island, an island with a view. Affectionately known as "the Rock," Alcatraz Island is another hot tourist destination in San Francisco, and for good reason. Alcatraz Island first operated as a fort shortly after the Gold Rush took San Francisco from a sleepy town of 300 to a crowded home for 20,000. Alcatraz was the home of over 400 soldiers during the Civil War and it was a small group of these men who became the very first prisoners. Their crime? Drunk and disorderly conduct—what else? In time, Native American prisoners were brought to Alcatraz followed by other military convicts during the Spanish-American War. Alcatraz was destined to serve as a prison. When the Army abandoned the fort in the 1930s, the Bureau of Prisons quickly recognized the island's value as a secure facility and in 1934, it officially opened as a federal penitentiary.

Of the more than 1500 prisoners who served time at Alcatraz, only a handful were high profile; but 100 percent of them were deemed problematic at other facilities, which earned them a trip to the Rock. We were concerned that the tour would be slightly creepy, especially in the evening, but it was no different than touring any other old building...except for all of the bars on the windows.

After leaving the boat, we were guided up the hill to the prison where we each received headphones for the self-guided audio tour. The only bad thing was that everyone moved at a snail's pace, which made each of the stopping points on the tour quite crowded. We did like that the narrators were either one-time inmates of the prison or guards, and we learned that if you visit Alcatraz on the second Sunday in August, actual prison alumni will be available to lead tours and answer questions. Now, before you get freaked out about an ex-con leading you around one of the most feared prisons in the country, keep in mind that this isn't a work-release program; these guys are in their seventies and eighties and their "glory" years on the island are well behind them. Ever the enthusiastic tourist, Daniel took his turn not only on the A-Block, but also in "the hole," or solitary confinement.

Of course, the inmates weren't the only people living on the island. The guards and their families lived on the Rock, too, which meant that to attend school in the city, the children had to take the prison boat across the bay. This was the most fascinating fact for me. Can you imagine being a kid who might normally get picked on at school, but then your classmates find out that you live on the Rock and get transported to and from school by prison boat? I doubt many of them suffered at the hands of bullies.

As our tour wrapped up, we listened to the ex-inmates talking about what they remember as the hardest part of their confinement at Alcatraz and it wasn't what I expected. The hardest part: freedom was just a mile away. They could hear the street cars and smell the chocolate wafting over the water from Ghirardelli. On New Year's Eve, prisoners would huddle by the windows to listen as people celebrated the holiday on their boats in the bay, laughing and enjoying good food, drink, and company. Maybe they should have behaved before becoming a resident there.

For us, it felt great to leave because freedom is something so highly valued that we can't imagine ever losing it. Maybe that is reason enough to visit Alcatraz...it leaves you with a definite impression and perspective of what it would be like to take a boat to that island, walk up that hill, enter the cell block, and hear the clanging of that heavy metal door behind you. Imagine yourself in your cell for 22 hours a day listening to easy laughter across the bay, cable cars taking people where they want to go, and that smell...the smell of fresh chocolate escaping the factory and riding the bay breeze over to the island where it only serves to remind you that you can't possibly visit that store and get your own free sample.   Freedom...it's a sweet thing.

Vicariously Yours,
Traci

Leaving San Francisco was a turning point in the trip for us, emotionally and literally, because it was the official start of our eastward trip back home. It was exciting to pass over the California state line and bid a very fond farewell to a state that provided us with weeks of memories...my first camel ride and sighting of a Joshua tree, church at Saddleback with Rick Warren, getting lost in the desert and nearly falling down a mountain, catching sight of that huge Hollywood sign high up on a hill, watching Mickey Mouse climb Matterhorn Peak in celebration of Disneyland's Golden Anniversary, and crossing the Golden Gate Bridge for the first time.

The drive from San Francisco to Salt Lake City took an entire weekend with over 12 hours of total drive time. On Saturday night we stopped in Winnemucca, Nevada, a place that was much more a rest stop than a destination. Only one night, that's what Daniel and I told ourselves as we pulled into our campground. With nothing to do, we decided not to leave the bus for any reason until we beat it out of town the following morning. As we hooked up the bus to the various outlets, we noticed a green fuzzy layer of bug carnage covering the windshield, side mirrors, and front facade. Examining the bug remains was one thing, but fending off their brethren was too much for me and I sought refuge inside, only to discover that a select group of them had somehow infiltrated the walls and windows of the motorhome and were congregating in the shower. We awoke the next morning to a shower full of dead, green, fuzzy bugs looking like a cult that had followed their Jim Jones insect leader into a place destined to be their end. I guess drinking that day-old shower water was a bad idea for all of them.

The three of us ate breakfast and began another day of driving through parts of Nevada that didn't even make the map. Hours ticked by as miles and miles of pristine nothingness caused us to grasp for anything at all to discuss. The most provocative topic remained our return to Indianapolis and our indecision about where to live and what school was right for Thomas. We had prayed about this stuff for several months now with no answers in sight. We put in offers on three different houses that seemed like slam dunks to me but fell apart for varying reasons. Patience was not my strength and each day tested my willingness to wait on God to show us a "sign." Should we buy the house on Covington? Or Wentz? Or Windermere? Doesn't He know that I'm losing sleep over this stuff? I needed direction.

These were the things that Daniel and I talked about while driving from Winnemucca to Salt Lake City and in the midst of that conversation, something amazing happened. I glanced out my window and there it was...a giant yellow sign with big, bold black letters that read "WENTZ." Did that really say what I thought it said? When I prayed for a sign from God, I didn't think He would be so literal. I didn't say anything to Daniel or Thomas; I didn't want to sound crazy. The next day, in Salt Lake, we were having another discussion about where to live because we felt like we were running out of time. If we didn't choose something soon, we'd have to spend the summer in the bus—not something any of us wanted to do. I finally told my boys about the billboard and within 24 hours, two people we trust implicitly had seen the house and agreed that we should make an offer. On Tuesday, as Thomas and I waded in the Great Salt Lake, the house on Wentz became ours. Unbelievable? Crazy? I know. But, since deciding on the house, all of the details of our return home worked out in a perfect design just for us and our new future in Indiana. When we shared this story with friends and family, some laughed while others nodded with a quiet understanding. Maybe I am a bit crazy. Maybe it was just a sign. But I firmly believe that when you pray earnestly for direction, guidance, and wisdom, you need to allow Him to work in His own ways, and besides...it wasn't like the sign was on fire or had a rainbow over it. It was just a sign—whether I recognized or dismissed it was entirely up to me, but if there's one thing I had learned time and time again on this trip around the country, it's this: don't ask God for something if you aren't willing to accept it. I asked for a sign and I got one. It just so happened to be a big yellow one with black letters standing along the side of I-80 between Winnemucca, Nevada and Salt Lake City, Utah.

We went to see the movie *RV* so we could spend a couple of hours watching another family, albeit a fictional one, struggle through the daily idiosyncrasies of traveling in a motorhome. Of course, the movie capitalizes on only the most dramatic of problems that a motorhome and its users could have, but the comedic antics were a great release for us. I know that we laughed louder and more often than anyone else in the theater, but afterward, being the seasoned travelers that we are, spent upwards of an hour discussing the improbability of the RV catastrophes. Come on, who has crazy things like that happen in real life? One scene in particular includes an explosion of sewage resembling "Old Faithful," where Robin Williams' character gets doused in the wretched stuff. That would never happen.

While Daniel made a service appointment for the bus at Camping World near Salt Lake City on Wednesday afternoon, I took care of all the necessary tear-down and, in my pajamas, went outside to empty the black sewage tank. Keep in mind that I had done this several times and felt comfortable with my ability to handle the job. I turned on the black water flush hose, opened the valve, and stood back waiting for the sewage to empty into the campground's holding tank. That isn't what happened. As I stood there in pink fuzzy slippers watching the sewage begin to drain into the sewer hookup buried in the ground, I heard what sounded like pressure building in the hose. I had a fleeting thought that this was not a good thing followed by a loud "pop" and the surprising sight of raw sewage blowing up out of the ground and into the air, spraying poop all over the place. I was so shocked and horrified that it took me a minute to remember that I needed to shut off the valve in order to stop the flow. Yelling for Daniel, I ran for the door to the bus because the extreme odor outside began filling the air, causing me to dry heave. Daniel threw down his phone, leaving the caller wondering what had happened, and ran outside to find the remnants of my movie moment. Daniel has a strong stomach, but even he struggled through picking up as much of the excrement as possible. In his thickest gloves, he combed the area for a few minutes while I stood 10 feet away watching him. A misfortunate man happened to be walking by, and as he caught a whiff of the issue, Daniel smiled and said, "Well, this is certainly the first time this has ever happened." Taking a closer look, the elderly man sprinted past our site and went inside his own rig, thanking his lucky stars that he wasn't parked next to us.

We went inside the bus and tried to go about business as usual, but I was mortified that our campsite was still littered with foul stuff and smelled like a long-neglected port-o-potty. Daniel called the front office to notify them of the incident while I began packing so we could leave the state of Utah. Surely this offense was something that earned a picture on a wall somewhere where fellow campers and curious onlookers could mock me. How would I ever be able to look anyone in the eye again after having my toilet sludge spray over the surrounding landscape like ogre Miracle Gro?

After the necessary phone call to the office, an unlucky and highly underpaid woman came to the site to notify us that our sewer was backed up. No kidding! She would need to snake and rake our campsite. Thomas thought this sounded like great fun and wanted to watch the entire event. I still wanted to leave town. It took a couple of hours and more than one staff person with rake in hand to fix the malfunction and clean up the remainder of the mess, but by the time we returned from Camping World and the local RV wash, all traces of the episode were washed away, so we didn't need to leave the state after all.

When you visit Salt Lake City, there are a few almost obligatory stops: the Great Salt Lake, doing something Mormon, and touring the Utah Olympic Park. Did it. Did it. Did it. The Great Salt Lake? It was salty...so much that when I waded in with Thomas, the skin on my freshly shaven legs burned and caused me to wonder if an infection might be in my future. Thomas thought it was gross and couldn't imagine that people swim in that water; after all, no marine life, other than brine shrimp, brine flies, and algae can tolerate the high salinity levels. We visited the lake from Antelope Island, the largest landmass in the Great Salt Lake, and home to a large herd of American bison. We saw many bison on the side of the road, crossing the road, and stopping to block the road. Although we had to turn around and head the other direction because of the herd, we did get some great close-up photos of these incredible animals that have lived on that island since 1893.

You might be familiar with Mormons because of the famous Tabernacle Choir or, the Osmond family, but did you know that more than half of the state of Utah professes to be Mormon? No wonder Temple Square was built to hold so many people. As the center of the faith, it encompasses 35 acres in downtown Salt Lake City. It was raining the evening we ventured out to see the many majestic buildings in the square, but we grabbed our umbrellas and braved soaking-wet shoes in order to hear the choir rehearse. The ensemble, a small group of settlers, first performed in 1847 at a church conference just days after arriving in Utah. With 360 members, this world renowned choir performs weekly and recently celebrated its 4,000th broadcast of *Music and the Spoken Word*, a program that began on July 15, 1929. Over the years, they have received Grammy and Emmy Awards, as well as produced both gold and platinum albums, so to visit Salt Lake City and *not* go hear the choir would be like living in Indianapolis without ever seeing the Indy 500.

The Conference Center where the group was rehearsing was one of the largest and grandest venues I had ever entered. It had a 21,000-seat auditorium that was large enough to comfortably park a Boeing 747. There was also an additional 900-seat theater for overflow. Beneath the building was a four-story parking garage able to accommodate 1,300 cars. Within the Conference Center was state-of-the-art everything including a translation facility capable of simultaneously translating 60 different languages. There were 50,000 miles of electrical wiring, 13 passenger elevators and 12 escalators, and a custom built organ with over 7,600 individual pipes. The roof was a landscaped four-acre park setting with fountains, waterfalls, trees, gardens and an irrigated meadow. That was just one building. Membership must be strong.

Back inside, Daniel commented that he was uncomfortable with all of the smiling "ushers" dressed in suits, opening doors, shaking hands, and eagerly guiding us to a seat...like an Amway meeting. Thomas was bored by the entire event and wanted nothing more than to read his book or go outside and play in the fast-moving streams being fed by the rainstorm. I just wanted to hear the choir sing a couple of songs. Was that too much to ask? Thirty minutes later, we scooted out the door and back into the torrential downpour. If the weather would have cooperated, we might have strolled through the gardens, stopping to photograph the thousands of tulips filling the raised flowerbeds. But, I did what I came for. I walked in the Great Salt Lake and heard the Mormon Tabernacle Choir. It was time to see where the 2002 Winter Olympics took place.

The highlight of our trip to Salt Lake City was the tour of the Utah Olympic Park in Park City. Our guide was generous with both his time and knowledge of all things relating to the winter sports. With a group size of only seven, we were able to ask lots of questions and spend extra time at each site, including the K120 and K90 Ski Jumps, Freestyle Training Pool, Men's Luge Track, and Bobsleigh and Skeleton Track. We arrived too late in the winter or too early in the summer to see any athletes training, but we learned an incredible amount about each sport and gathered a new appreciation for what these young men and women do. We also learned that the 2002 Salt Lake City Winter Games were so profitable that an endowment was set up with an amount exceeding 70 million dollars, enabling the facility to operate year-round, maintaining the highest level training resources available in North America.

If you watched the 2006 Winter Olympics in Torino, you saw many athletes who trained in Park City at this facility. One of the gold medalists, Ted Ligety, was a graduate of the on-premise school offered to a select group of athletes, giving them the chance to study core subjects between training runs. Our guide, Carl, said that children as young as six practiced on the K120 Ski Jump—that's the *big* one. Could you imagine sending your young child who still believes in the Easter Bunny and Tooth Fairy flying down a hill at 60 mph? We watched a bobsleigh hit the track and reach the bottom in just over one minute, at speeds of up to 80 mph. I would have loved to try that, but Daniel reminded me how much our necks hurt after Lake Placid and I changed my mind. The Olympic Park offered several intense ride experiences including the steepest zip line in America, where riders exceed 50 mph while gliding alongside the K120 Jump Hill. Guests can also feel the exhilaration of the luge or skeleton by taking a trip down a steel track called Quicksilver, a narrow, curving course. If you'd rather watch other people get extreme, visit the park on Saturday when the Freestyle Training Pool becomes the site of a high-thrills show complete with Olympic athletes showing their stuff in front of hundreds of people.

Whatever you do at the park, don't miss the second floor of the Olympic Museum. We had the opportunity to relive some of the highlights of the 2002 Games including Jimmy Shea's emotional gold medal victory in Men's Skeleton. There were fabulous displays featuring medals, photographs, and athlete's gear. Thomas loved the Curling exhibit where he was able to pick up a curling stone only to discover that it was heavy—45 pounds heavy. The athletes made it look so easy. Honestly, it didn't look like much of a sport to me; like bowling on ice. As we left Park City, we chattered about how much fun we had had and how awesome it would be to come back when the athletes were there. Our first trip to this remarkable city in Utah was successful. We walked in the Great Salt Lake and heard the Mormons sing. We toured the Olympic facility and learned about the dedication of the people there. And, we bought a house. My "to do" list was done.

Vicariously Yours,
Traci

Southern Utah is home to five national parks and more wide open spaces than even the most aggressive developer could fill with coffee shops, big box stores, and lifestyle centers. When driving south from Salt Lake City, you not only leave behind most of the developed land in the state, but also 80 percent of its people. This environment of canyons, lakes, and mountains was an outdoor enthusiast's dream. We knew that the national parks would be stunning (several specials on the Travel Channel prepared us for that), but we had no idea how much we would fall in love with this part of the country. Our days spent hiking in Zion, Bryce, and Arches were far and above the best yet on this trip.

Arriving at our KOA home for the week, we had just enough time to visit Kolob Canyons, a small national park located just south of Cedar City, Utah, and a place that most tourists miss because it sits in the shadow of Zion National Park. Kolob—which means "star closest to heaven"—consisted of towering cliffs of red Navajo sandstone peppered with lush green trees and shrubs. As we drove through the entrance to the park, we noticed a marked delineation in the road. When we asked the park ranger about the materials used to create the roads, he laughed and said it had much more to do with financial reasoning than an aesthetic appeal. The red roads were made of what they called "Utah gravel," a red volcanic rock, an abundant material in the state. Kolob was unusual in that a visitor could see all of the highlights from the comfort of an automobile in 15 minutes. There were a few hiking trails including a strenuous 14-mile one ending at Kolob Arch, but we didn't have time for that. Instead, we opted for a shorter walk to the Timber Creek Overlook where we gazed upon trees, trees, and more trees. Not that we didn't enjoy the scenery, but after spending several months on this trip looking at trees, they began to lose that "treeish" appeal.

The day we drove to Zion, the temperature soared to over 80 degrees. We were prepared though with lots of water, sunscreen, snacks and a collective enthusiasm for spending the entire day climbing and sweating. We discovered that the best way to see the park was to leave our vehicle at the Visitor Center and ride the shuttle. As we approached our trail-head, I looked up to see creamy white sandstone cliffs accented with splashes of copper and mauve. Our driver shared the history and high-lights of the park before we hopped out and began walking. Zion, meaning place of refuge or sanctuary, covers 229 square miles. The ecosystem is pristine. We crossed a bridge over the Virgin River, the waterway responsible for carving the deep canyon *and* the reason the landscape continues to change. The area has both great geological and archaeological value and evidence of human existence in the canyon dates back over 7,000 years. There are active digs in the park that vis-itors can walk through in order to gain a better understanding of the work involved in piecing together the past, but we came to hike.

The Emerald Pools trail system has refreshing waterfalls and basins, especially toward the top of the path where a few hikers had gathered to rest and cool off. After a little persuasion and toe dipping around the edge, Daniel agreed to wade into the water with Thomas, only to dis-cover that the center was far deeper and colder than expected. Others soon joined them and one family climbed a large rock and jumped into the water below. It looked refreshing, but it was obvious that the pond wasn't quite deep enough for that kind of activity because as each of the jumpers emerged, a surprised look covered their faces and their hands rubbed their backsides. We stayed for a while longer to watch the water tumble over the side of a high cliff, creating a mist that fell gen-tly on us below. Large colorful rocks, sweet-smelling trees, and cool refreshing water; this was an oasis in the middle of an organized wilder-ness.

We rested and ate lunch at the Zion Lodge which was designed in the 1920s and destroyed by fire in 1966. Although it was rebuilt shortly after the tragedy, it wasn't until the 1990s that it was restored to its orig-inal form. Accommodations consist of either well-appointed rustic cabins, complete with fireplaces and porches, or standard rooms in the main building. The views from there were breathtaking and I could only imagine how memorable it would be waking up to sunrise over those sandstone cliffs and, at dusk, watching wild turkeys lounging in the trees near the main road. Maybe next time…. For now, it was time to take a short ride on the shuttle, and a long hike into Hidden Canyon. The switchbacks were tough, without a hint of shade and, although the change in elevation was only 850 feet, the footpath was no wider than my hips with an imposing rock face on one side and drop-off on the other. This trail was Thomas's favorite because it required rock scrambling and had a certain air of danger to it. I was glad when it was over.

Our last stop in Zion was a short, but steep, incline to Weeping Rock, a rock formation containing ancient spring water that seeps out, causing the appearance of rain or weeping. On a hot day, it was a splendid place to stand and get soaked. When it was time to leave, we didn't want to. If we could have stayed for another week or month, we would have.

Nature boy, Daniel, wanted to go to Bryce Canyon while we were in southern Utah. Thomas and I did not. It was a two-hour drive from our campground and a large mountain was only one of the obstacles. I couldn't imagine riding in a car for two hours, hiking for several hours, and then getting back in the car. Thomas and I were persuaded to go when Daniel offered up the mighty self-sacrifice of taking a vacation day from work. Yikes! He must really want to see this place. We loaded in the car and headed over the river and through the woods, mountain and all, to get to one of the most unique places I had ever seen. Bryce was similar to the Grand Canyon in that guests entered at the top and hiked down. It instantly charmed me and I fell in love.

The landscape in Bryce is made up of thousands of red rock pillars called "hoodoos," which means "to cast a spell." Shaped like spires, windows, and fins, the hoodoos made me feel as if I had stepped onto another planet, one where angry gods might have changed men into rock, or so the local Paiute legend goes. At the Visitor Center, Thomas asked the ranger which hike was the most challenging and she told us her favorite was one called the Peekaboo Loop. This hike would bring us very close to the park's well known "Thor's Hammer," a tall spire resembling the Viking god's famous weapon, as well as other interesting formations such as the "Wall of Windows" and "Three Wisemen." The day we visited Bryce, the weather was cool, which made our hard work on the paths bearable. After hiking for almost five miles, the last thing we wanted to do was climb the multiple switchbacks from the bottom of the canyon floor to the rim. Thomas and Daniel were miserable. Thomas whined the entire time that he was going to die and

Daniel was not talking at all, which in the "world of Daniel" meant something was wrong. It wasn't that I enjoyed the climbing, but I figured that since there was no elevator and we couldn't change our address to "The Bottom of Bryce Canyon, Utah," it was best to keep on grinding out steps.

During one of our rest stops, I tried to gather my family together and create a game of counting 50 steps before stopping again. Finally, we made it to the top and dragged ourselves back to the car in hopes of finding something to eat. We found the restaurant, but it was closed and our only option was a convenience store. Hmmm...should we opt for the frozen burritos or bagel bites? Not what we needed after a grueling hike. After much deliberation, we each found a snack we could live with and walked back to the rim for our next hike. I checked the park guide and found one described as the "least difficult trail into the canyon." Once again, we began descending, realizing with each step down that the return trip was going to be agonizing. Many hikers passed us going in the opposite direction, each of them looking spent. And then we saw them...two rather beefy gals wearing nothing more than shoes, pants, and bras. We were speechless. When they were out of earshot, Daniel couldn't help commenting on the "wildlife" in Bryce. I imagined that the two of them found climbing out of the canyon taxing on their bodies and removed their shirts to cool off. Then again, maybe the change in elevation just got to them and they lost their minds along with their shirts and sense of modesty. Whatever the reason, it was the sort of fauna that we hadn't seen in a national park before. Mule deer, wild turkeys, and prairie dogs, sure, but half-naked women? I thought they were nocturnal.

The next day we left Cedar City and began a three-day drive to Colorado. The first stop was in Richfield, Utah, and I remember absolutely nothing about it. Nothing. Not the campground, not the drive, nothing. However, the next drive from Richfield to Green River, Utah...now *that* I remember. After setting up camp and wrapping up work and school, we took off for Arches National Park, home to over 2,000 cataloged sandstone curvatures ranging in size from three feet to over 300. The most famous, Delicate Arch, sits near a canyon with the La Sal Mountains as a backdrop and is *the* most photographed landmark in all of Utah. We couldn't wait to hike to it.

The trail was only three miles round trip, but the 87-degree temperature that day, coupled with the complete lack of shade, made this journey much more difficult than those in Camelback, Zion, and Bryce. As we climbed the rock face, we saw our first snake and I didn't even scream. It was so small it was cute, and Daniel was quick to photograph the little guy. When a curious passerby stopped to pick it up, it slithered away as quickly as it had arrived.

After much grumbling, complaining, and whining from Thomas, we made it to the top and saw for the first time the sandstone arch that brings the world to Moab, Utah, and graces countless of postcards and calendars. The arch was stunning, but I was perplexed at the number of hikers sitting around its base, watching as if something unusual might happen at any minute. Maybe they were trying to catch their breath or cool down from the climb. Whatever the reason, I found it interesting that people will sit for several minutes in front of natural beauty like Delicate Arch and yet race through their own lives like it's a sprint instead of a marathon. On this trip, we had the pleasure of taking our time to enjoy both, appreciating not only the beauty of this world, but also of our family.

Daniel flew out of Denver, Colorado, on May 15 and spent an entire week in Indianapolis while Thomas and I hung out at the KOA in Strasburg. We did some touristy things in town, but without Daniel, it just wasn't the same. We couldn't wait to pick him up at the airport and surprise him with an afternoon escape to an amusement park in the heart of downtown Denver. After as many thrill rides as we could stand, the three of us returned to the KOA to get ready for the last leg of the journey. I couldn't believe it was almost over and yet, I felt like a lifetime had passed since we left home. Only a few more places to read about and then you are on your own. You'll have to plan your own adventures, see your own natural beauties, and make your own special memories.

Vicariously Yours,
Traci

Sent: Saturday, June 3, 2006
Subject: Why Wyoming?

Wyoming is a state we knew little about other than its reputation for drawing conservationists, naturalists, and outdoor enthusiasts. We had no idea that within those wide open spaces and mountainous peaks lived cowboys with bigger belt buckles than any we had seen in Texas. There were champion bull-riders and writers, too. These artists see the great state of Wyoming as a tangible encyclopedia of inspiration, fetching and peaceful. What do you get when you take one writer, a couple of cowboys, and those wide open spaces? How about a hint...a large, imposing piece of land with broken vertebrae...any guesses? Of course, the answer is Ang Lee's Oscar losing film, *Brokeback Mountain,* inspired by Annie Proulx's short story.

I read that Ang Lee spent several days exploring the landscape in Wyoming before shooting the movie in Canada; consequently, when comparing the Canadian mountains to those he'd seen here, Lee called our northern neighbor's peaks "a cheap imitation." If he had in mind Grand Teton when he made that statement, then he was absolutely correct in that comparison because, in my opinion, there are no mountains more photogenic than those in Grand Teton National Park. Before we could gaze upon that picturesque beauty, we first had to drive through the not-so-beautiful and forgettable areas of the state better known as the "land between Cheyenne and Rock Springs."

As we passed through Cheyenne and turned west, the landscape changed into what the tourism literature called "stark." I called it barren. There were few trees, few mountains, and few landmarks. Over the next several hours, there was nothing to look at except millions of brownish-green scrub bushes bearing a remarkable resemblance to dirty toilet brushes. After many miles of watching toilet brush farms pass, we found our sanctuary from the boredom, the KOA in Rock Springs, Wyoming, a town more suited for a rest stop than a long-term commitment. Thankfully, it was only one night. We were up early the next morning, driving north toward Jackson and that was when the scenery became something out of a travel magazine.

The winding road followed the Hoback River, allowing us to watch kayakers and rafters weave in and out of the white water. While trees and mammoth rock faces presented a captivating backdrop for the river, herds of horses, antelope, and cows provided animation to a landscape too perfect to be real. Although the speed limit was somewhere between 45 and 55 mph, Daniel slowed down as much as traffic would allow so we could take in the majesty of this part of Wyoming. We stopped for lunch at a large turn-out by the river and, if a film crew had been on hand, the consummate "Go RV'ing" commercial could have been made. Our windows were open so that we could hear the sound of the rushing river, there was a light, cool breeze passing through the bus, and as we ate our turkey sandwiches it dawned on us that these moments were the reason we bought a motorhome and left Indiana last June. It was during that drive that we discovered why people from far away come to a place void of merchandised mega-marts or manufactured family fun.

The town of Jackson is in a lush valley just outside of the Grand Teton National Park along with several other small communities including Teton Village, Moose, Kelly, Moran Junction, Wilson, and Hoback. Often a point of confusion, it is this valley—named for an early trapper—that bears the name of Jackson Hole, not the town itself. As we drove into Jackson, we noticed that most of the buildings are seamless with the surrounding landscape. There are charming log buildings accented with stone and each, whether the large grocery store, local outfitter or cinema, was designed with nature in mind and a clear desire to blend with it rather than compete.

Turning toward our campground, we passed two large pastures on either side of the road, each full of horses and cows. Spring brought with it many young ones and we enjoyed watching the foals test four gangly legs while the calves raced after their mothers to nurse. The grass was emerald green and even the fields of dandelions demanded an appreciative glance. Blue sky hung overhead with only a few puffs of cloud. If I had heard beautiful orchestral music begin to soar in the background, I wouldn't have been surprised. This was a scene out of a film, perhaps *The Sound of Music* or *A River Runs Through It*. The town of Jackson and the surrounding area couldn't be more beautiful if

Claude Monet had painted it. Activities in Jackson Hole were endless, whether you prefer fly fishing, river rafting, skiing, biking, or shopping and lounging at a cozy lodge. It had been our experience that in towns where nature was the main attraction and outdoor exercises ruled, retail and resort activities were limited, yet there we found everything from rustic cabins to luxurious resorts, souvenir shops to fine boutiques, and home-style cooking to "nouveau French cuisine."

After a few hours' work, we built a campfire, the highlight of the day. The mountains served as a marvelous backdrop to the star-filled sky and, other than our flickering logs and a far-away moon, the night was completely black. We cooked hot dogs, toasted marshmallows, and talked about the places we had been: the wonderful and not-so-wonderful, the places we couldn't wait to see again and those that we hoped to avoid. As we drifted off to sleep that night, I thought that place must be the most peaceful one on the planet...no wonder the animals loved it there.

Wildlife in Jackson Hole was as easy to see as a cactus in Tucson or raindrop in Seattle; it took little effort. Having already seen countless animals on our drive into Jackson Hole, we were not at all surprised to encounter scores of small creatures called marmots crossing our path as we hiked around Jenny Lake in Grand Teton National Park. We saw no bears there, but what we did see was equally breathtaking and not at all scary: a roaring waterfall hidden deep in the landscape. We had hiked for at least an hour when we came upon the rumbling sound of a river and, as we climbed closer, talking to each other became nearly impossible. Although the temperature neared 65 degrees, under our feet was 12 inches of hard-packed snow. As we crossed a small footbridge and slid our way around some trees, Hidden Falls came into view. We had seen several waterfalls on this trip, but the glory of this one stood above the rest. It isn't just another cascade; it is surrounded by blankets of pure white snow and fragrant pine trees, and it is powered by a raging river. Standing there, it was easy to imagine bears visiting this place for a meal and a drink.

As we left the water's edge, we hiked further up a rocky path to a place called Inspiration Point where it was easy to understand the name. Far beneath our feet sat Jenny Lake, a crystal clear body of water named for the wife of an early trapper. After three hours of hiking, we found our way back to the car, taking with us an understanding of why the Grand Teton National Park holds such an allure for locals and tourists alike. The mountains are said to be the most perfectly formed in the world and so photogenic that even the most amateur of photographers can take home high quality pictures. From the mountains to the pastures, marmots and horses, log cabins and lovely lodges, everything about Jackson and Jackson Hole was breathtaking.

We were excited about our next destination, Yellowstone National Park. As the oldest national park in the country and first reserve of its kind in the world, it has enamored millions of people for more than 130 years. We were fortunate to drive through much of it on our way from Jackson, Wyoming, to West Yellowstone, Montana, where we would camp for the next few days. I would love to tell you that as we drove through the park, I was struck by the natural beauty, but I can't. Yellowstone has suffered over the years from insect infestation and organized burns, meaning that many parts of it are in a state of regrowth.

We stopped at a turn-out to have lunch and then made our way toward the West Entrance when something stopped us: bison, and lots of them. There must have been 20 or more adults and calves walking in the middle of the street stopping traffic both ways. It was not something Hoosiers see every day. Daniel grabbed his camera and took several pictures of them as they walked toward the bus, moved aside, and ambled past. As we neared the entrance gate, we saw more and more bison milling about a large pasture and realized that there would be no difficulty in getting pictures of these animals.

Our campground was six miles from the park's entrance in a small town called West Yellowstone. It reminded us of Lone Pine, California, with its diminutive tourist square complete with boardwalks, souvenir shops, diners, and a mall boasting 10 stores. After setting up camp, we spent the evening swimming in the indoor pool and roasting marshmallows by the fire. Days and nights like that were part of our lives right now, at least for the next few weeks. Would we have those experiences when we get back home and re-entered "normal" lives? I hoped that we had learned enough out on the road that could be translated into meaningful and unique backyard memories. This trip taught us many things and I prayed that our memories and lessons wouldn't go away easily.

Friday brought with it beautiful weather, perfect for exploring Yellowstone and we began visiting the many hydrothermal features. Everyone has heard of "Old Faithful," but the park has more than 300 geothermals in its 28,000 square miles of preserve. We stopped at a few larger areas in the Lower and Midway Geyser Basins where walkways allow visitors to get close to these pools of hot, stinky water. Most of them smelled like rotten eggs, however the fascination of how they exist and the often intense coloration helped us get past the stench and enjoy them. I was amazed to see some pools emitting red and blue steam. Although I thought they had been treated with festive dye for the impending Memorial Day weekend celebration, I was wrong. The patriotic steam was caused by the assorted bacteria living in the water. The hottest geothermals had no color at all.

Having our fill of bubbling pools, we made our way to the famous geyser, "Old Faithful." As of March 2006, the eruptions occurred approximately every 90 minutes. We arrived in just enough time to grab a seat. There were a hundred people gathered to watch the flare-up, all poised with cameras ready, and, when the show began, a collective cheer sounded from the crowd. It lasted only a minute or so and when it was done, you could hear several people whispering, "Was that it?" I, too, was expecting more than what looked like a spurt. However, the complaints of the spectators became overwhelming and I wanted to scream, "Come on people, this isn't The Bellagio." Have we become so accustomed to man-made showmanship with all of its colorful laser lights and Elton John soundtracks that we can't appreciate the greatness of something as magnificent as Old Faithful? I pondered these thoughts as I made my way to the ladies' restroom where a long line had formed following the underwhelming geyser performance. The water must have made more of an impression than I thought.

It was early afternoon, so we had lunch and drove around the park to see some wildlife. Unbeknownst to me, Daniel had a mental checklist complete with large animals needing to be found and photographed and, since we had only found bison, it looked like it was going to be a long day. I was shocked that other people came here with similar checklists. Do you know how to find animals in Yellowstone? You drive around the park, look for lots of cars pulled off the side of the road and assume that this crowd has gathered to view something on "the checklist." Following this process, we found elk, moose, wolves, coyotes, bald eagles, and a bear—not all in one day, but over several hours and the course of two days. It was an exhaustible commitment.

What I found most disturbing by all of this was the blatant disregard for safety, park rules, and common sense. People were climbing over fences, fallen trees, embankments and each other to get closer to these wild animals just to get a picture. For example, when we saw the wolves, they were eating a dead bison. Not the best time to approach a wolf (if there is a "best time")—and yet a man decided to see how near he could get to the animal before it either attacked him or ran off. Another time, Daniel was photographing a coyote and her pups when an adorable and adventurous Asian family climbed over the protective rail and down into the gorge where the mother coyote was frantically trying to move her babies to safety. Do people just not listen? I believed these folks thought that because the animals lived in a national park, they were somehow "tamer" than those living in the wild. It wasn't true. Yellowstone is not a zoo, it *is* the wild.

One local told us about a family that tried to get their toddler to sit on top of a bison for the perfect Yellowstone photo. And I thought I had placed my kid in danger. Bison weigh nearly 2,000 pounds and can run 30 mph. If you think you can outrun one of these animals, please understand this: not even a doped-up Olympic sprinter could do it. Hundreds of visitors each year are gored by these docile brutes. Especially in the spring when all of the species have their young to protect, they will tolerate no threat, be it from a predator or an idiot with a camera. I pitied the rangers whose job it was to maintain order. On the northeast side of the park, a black bear and her cubs were housed not far off the main road and there were so many people, you would have thought it was a sporting event. We were told that at one point, the ranger warned the crowd that if they didn't step back, the cubs would become very interested in them and if that happened, he would not be responsible for what the mother bear might do. No one budged.

Visitors are responsible for their own safety and, upon entering the park, are told two numbers to remember in case of a bear sighting, 100 and 911. The idea is that if you see a bear, it is best to keep at least 100 yards between you and it...and if something goes wrong, call 911. It would have been good advice if the cellular service in Yellowstone hadn't been so spotty. It would be better to keep your distance. After driving around Yellowstone on Saturday for seven hours through rain, snow, and crowds of people, I had had my fill of creatures. I told Daniel that unless a bison, elk, or moose was either attacking a visitor or being attacked by a bear, I wasn't stopping for a picture—nature girl had reached her limit.

When we woke up the next morning, it was 90 degrees in Indianapolis and it was snowing at our campground in West Yellowstone. It was beautiful, but after being on the road for almost 12 months, I didn't want snow on Memorial Day weekend...so we left. We packed up our hoses and drove north through Big Sky and Bozeman, Montana, before settling in at the country's oldest KOA in Billings where the weather was a bonny 65 degrees. Having spent 10 days in the northwestern and southeastern parts of Wyoming, we learned many things about this prairie state. We learned that the first "dude ranches" were opened in Jackson Hole when wealthy easterners came to visit this unbroken land and the settlers discovered that wrangling tourists—or "dudes"—was easier than wrangling cattle. Tourism flourished and today, it is the primary industry in Jackson Hole. Smart businessmen, huh? Who could have guessed that tourists would bring in more money than cows? Another interesting fact about the Jackson Hole area was told to us by the local sheriff. Did you know that the domestic violence rate in Teton County is higher than in New York City? I can't quite understand why that statistic would be true, but it must be, or they wouldn't advertise it on the big screen at the local theater. It doesn't exactly beckon visitors to sell their homes in Indiana and relocate, now does it?

Vicariously Yours,
Traci

Our last two nights in Wyoming were spent in Buffalo. They painted a large billboard on the side of a building in the historic downtown district to say, "Buffalo...more than a one-horse town." We weren't convinced. What they lacked in horses, they more than made up for in bison, or bison meat to be more specific, which was the one thing we loved about the place. After seeing thousands of them in Yellowstone, we decided to go native and start eating them. You might not dream of making a meal on one of these wild creatures, but you really should consider this "other red meat." Though the small town couldn't claim a tourist attraction closer than 200 miles away, we felt that our stay in Buffalo was worthwhile if only for the custom "cuttery," Big Horn Meat, where we stocked up on buffalo burgers, steaks, and jerky. My dad told me that in Indianapolis, buffalo was advertised at $16.00/pound. Maybe I should sell my steaks on eBay.

The morning we left Buffalo was melodramatic for us. It was June, the month we would return home. Only two weeks left until the leap back into reality. As we crossed the state line into South Dakota, we stopped at the Visitors' Center and gathered additional information about interesting things to do and see other than the obligatory visits to Mount Rushmore, Wall Drug Store, Crazy Horse, and the Corn Palace. The cutest elderly lady was working and boy, did she share her information with us. She talked and talked and loaded us up with several inches of brochures, magazines, and maps until Daniel could take no more. He walked over to the window, acted like he saw someone outside, and left me with her. Shame on him.

We did get great information about "The Mount Rushmore State," most of which we used during our stays in Rapid City, Interior, and Mitchell. However, no tourism collateral prepared us for the spirit and history we found there, where dancing with wolves was perfectly acceptable, little houses on the prairie still inspired, and forefathers, both red and white, were memorialized in mountainous stone. I never would have believed South Dakota would make the short list of favorite stops on this trip. How could the prairie state compete with the likes of Disney's Florida, historical Virginia, or scenic Arizona? But guess what: it would have been true. There was something unexpected in South Dakota—something summed up in the state's tourism slogan, "Real. America. Up close." Yep, that just about says it all.

Our first stop was Rapid City, a hub for tourists visiting Mount Rushmore, the Black Hills, and Badlands National Park, and home to more than 60,000 residents including 22 former presidents. Of course, they are full-size bronze sculptures, but they reside in downtown Rapid City, nonetheless. The people there intend on immortalizing each one in bronze, giving locals and visitors alike an opportunity to spend time with our country's chief executives. While I found the statues to be nice, the only presidents I wanted to see were those carved in stone, so we drove the short distance to the historic mining town of Keystone where we saw for the first time a carving so monumental that it took more than a decade, hundreds of crew members, and every penny of the $900,000 allocated to the project.

When Mount Rushmore was proposed, it was to be a tourist attraction honoring western heroes like Lewis and Clark; however, the sculptor, Gutzon Borglum, convinced the decision-makers that subjects of *national* focus should instead be memorialized. Four presidents were chosen—George Washington, father of our nation, Thomas Jefferson, expander of America's territory, Abraham Lincoln, protector of our union, and Theodore Roosevelt...friend of Gutzon Borglum. It wasn't that I questioned Roosevelt's contributions to our nation or his strength of character, but when looking for a president of equal caliber to Washington, Jefferson, and Lincoln, Roosevelt doesn't really come to my mind. As a "Ranger Talk" began at the monument, I assumed others felt the same way because our narrator spent several minutes listing Roosevelt's hardships and accomplishments as if he were justifying the man's presence on the mountain. Okay, so he had a part in the Panama Canal and he was an ardent conservationist, but don't you think it interesting that he was chosen? Then again, he doesn't have his face in the most visible spot of the foursome; he's sort of nestled between Jefferson and Lincoln in the shadow of two great noses.

Besides discussing Roosevelt's secondary positioning, the three of us shared another impression: Mount Rushmore was a lot smaller than we expected. As we walked on the Presidential Trail and gazed upon various views of the mammoth sculpture, it wasn't the faces of the four men that we enjoyed the most, but rather the fantastic landscape surrounding the artwork. The setting was gorgeous and serene with statuesque and fragrant fir trees, filtered sunlight and soothing singing birds. Benches were placed at points along the trail, allowing visitors to sit under this enchanting canopy and gaze up at a few great men forever immortalized in stone.

While visiting the monument during the day was good, it wasn't until our return trip later that evening that we discovered the true beauty of what Borglum created. At 9:00 p.m., the park service held a lighting ceremony and more than 1000 people were seated in the amphitheater. It began with a narrative of the history of Mount Rushmore and the four presidents. As the ranger spoke about each man, he made special note of their birth and death as well as the "—dash—" in between. He challenged each of us in attendance to consider this: will your time between birth and death be spent doing something worthwhile and lasting? Will it be something worth remembering? The sun set, leaving us to ponder his words under the night sky and in the darkness, a film called *Freedom* began playing, highlighting all that our country struggled through and how each man carved high above our seats had affected the history of our young nation. As the movie came to a close, lights began to shine on the monument and soon the only thing we could see was that incredible sculpture of four brave leaders looking out into the evening.

The ranger again took to the stage and requested that all members of our country's armed forces, past and present, join him for a flag ceremony. Thirty-five men made their way down the stairs to take their place on the stage. As four of the men took the flag down for the day, the ranger read a patriotic poem while the other servicemen stood at attention. When Old Glory had been properly folded, it was passed from the first serviceman to the next until each of the 35 had touched it. I watched them carefully and noticed that each and every passing of the flag was done with great care. As each one took the flag from his "brother in arms," he held it just a little longer than was necessary, straightening it when needed so that it was as perfect at the end of the line as it had begun. Their reverence for that piece of fabric was palpable.

Each man was then asked to say his name, branch of service and what theater he had served in. The group represented past conflicts including World War II, Korea, and Vietnam, but also current conflicts in Afghanistan and Iraq. It was humbling to stand and sing "God Bless America" in the shadow of Mount Rushmore while those 35 men stood in front of all of us. Tears came easily to many in the audience. These men, all of them, had served our country in whatever way they could and regardless of their politics, were still proud enough as American servicemen to get up out of their seats and be identified as one who fought for freedom. Though we won't all have the opportunity to do that, we can all certainly honor those who have and those who continue to do so each and every day. Walking away from Mount Rushmore that night, I realized that although I have had many "mountaintop" experiences on this trip, this night was extraordinary because it was spent at the base of a mountain—one that symbolized dedication, commitment, and freedom…a mountain symbolizing America.

On a much lighter note, Thomas and I had ridden elephants and camels, but never a horse. I promised him back in Kentucky that we would give it a try and the day had come. Daniel hadn't saddled up since he was a young boy, but he was game for planning an afternoon ride in the hills of South Dakota. We arrived at the Holy Smoke Stables and, after signing waivers, were assigned our steeds. Thomas rode a beautiful black quarter horse named Mirage, Daniel rode a draft horse named CLC, and I was given Dollar...a smoky gray quarter horse with an attitude. The manager of the stable told me my horse was the smoothest one available. She lied. I climbed up in the saddle and was led to the front of the line where my new friend and I waited for the others in our group to get their mounts. Dollar wanted to stand somewhere else—anywhere other than the place he was supposed to be. He crowded two other riders, pinning my leg between his body and another animal. He turned around and trotted back toward the corral, something that was not at all acceptable to the employees and the manager scolded me for not controlling her horse. Was she kidding? I pulled on his reins and he ignored me. I pulled again and kicked him lightly, hoping he would respond. Several swift kicks later, he relented and returned to the front of the line. He then backed up for no apparent reason. Daniel was busy clicking away with his camera, enjoying my inept horsemanship when one of the guides came up and took hold of my naughty steed, forcing him to conform. "I thought Dollar was the smoothest one in the bunch," I mumbled. The guide laughed and said, "Well he is, he's just high maintenance." Great.

Thomas loved his horse and everything about the hour-long ride through the hills. Since he was in front of me, I could watch and listen to him as he talked to the guide and I had to smile as he told her about the trip and his experiences over the past year. I guess he had been having fun after all. My horse was still not happy with me as a rider and tried several times to knock me off by scraping along tree trunks. When he wasn't trying to unload me, he trotted and galloped, which became quite uncomfortable on my back side later that day. Climbing back into the car, Thomas commented that he would have loved to ride twice as long, while Daniel and I were thankful the hour was over. Our horseback experience was pretty good, considering the fact that my mine was ornery and Daniel's was lazy. I did develop a deeper appreciation for horses and those who ride well. I also developed a funny walk for a couple of days.

Keystone began in the 1890s as a mining town, rich with gold. Today, it welcomes visitors from all over the world with attractions from Mount Rushmore to the boardwalk, Big Thunder Gold Mine to the Presidential Slide. Thomas wanted to skip over those amusements in favor of a competitive round at Holy Terror Miniature Golf, a course named for the local Holy Terror Mine and one that left us "screamin' for Mulligans." Why the moniker Holy Terror? Many of the men who mined in Keystone long ago dedicated their claims to their wives, so when William Franklin honored his better half by naming his mine "Holy Terror," I'm sure he meant it in the nicest way.

Sure, the golfing was fun, but it was our visit to Bear Country that blew me away. As we were visiting Mount Rushmore, I overheard a woman talking on her cell phone about a certain animal sticking its head inside her window and eating potato chips. Wherever it was, I knew we had to go. Bear Country was a drive-thru zoo where large and small animals roamed free within their assigned areas, allowing visitors to get up close and personal with only a car window separating them. This was wonderful in the elk and goat area, but an entirely different emotional experience with the black bears.

As we approached the entrance to the bear exhibit, three large black animals were frantically pacing back and forth just beyond the cow grate, preventing us from entering. Hmmm...I didn't feel a strong sense of hospitality there. Daniel saw an opening and drove between them and then stopped to take a picture. These were big bears staring us in the eyes. Hadn't he seen the commercial on television where the bear breaks the window to get a box of donuts? I frantically looked around the car to make sure we had no foodstuff of any kind.

Did you know that black bears aren't all black? Their coloration varies by geographical area, meaning that black-black bears most often live in Maine, while blonde-black bears reside in California. We were amazed at the incredible size, number, and diversity of these creatures walking no more than 10 feet or so from our car. We saw them swimming, wrestling, and even some scratching their backs on a tree...just like Baloo in *The Jungle Book*. If they weren't too close, we would roll down the windows to get a better look, which was very much against the rules of the park. One time, as Daniel had his window down, a big bear took notice of us and began walking across the road to investigate. Thomas and I didn't like this. Daniel calmly sat and clicked his camera while Thomas yelled, "Close your window!" As Daniel rolled up the glass, the animal could have fogged it up with his breath—that's how close he was.

Another mandatory South Dakota destination was Crazy Horse, even though we had no idea what it was. We drove into the Black Hills and found a mountain that left us speechless. A sculptor by the name of Korczak Ziolkowski was asked years ago by a Lakota Chief, Henry Standing Bear, to carve a likeness of Crazy Horse in a mountain in the sacred Black Hills, to show that the Red Man had heroes, too. In 1948, Korczak chipped away at the first bit of granite and began what would become his life's work.   For years he worked alone with used equipment, blasting and drilling, climbing 741 steps each day. He dedicated himself to the project and spent the final 36 years of his life toiling among the massive stones with second-rate tools.

In time, Korczak's children joined him in his work and upon his death in 1982, seven of them, along with his widow, committed to seeing the monument through to the end.   The artist made an intense commitment to this piece, knowing he would never see it completed.   Before his death, the sculptor made drawings, calculations, and revisions to allow someone else to follow his dream. It has been almost 60 years and the project continues.   It wasn't the enormity of the monument that surprised me, even though when complete, Crazy Horse will dwarf many times over Mount Rushmore.   It was the self-sacrifice that Korczak made. Why would he do it? Why would this man live in near poverty, taking no money for his work, all for the sake of creating a monument for the Native American?

As I thought about this man and his life, I realized that he had decided to be significant, to do something worth remembering.   He spent 36 years toiling on that mountain, all the while making certain that upon his death, his "dash" between those two dates of birth and death would represent something so big that it was carved in stone.   In his dash, he created something in South Dakota...something in the Black Hills...something wondrous.

Our next destination after Rapid City was a pit stop at Wall, South Dakota, a town famous for its drug store which began as a family business in December, 1931.   The story goes that this husband and wife, the Husteads, bought the store and after years of struggling, Mrs. Hustead came up with the idea of posting a sign offering "free ice water" to travelers, to wrangle more business.   The idea worked and many years later, the Wall Drug Store continues to thrive as a tourist destination, rest stop, and general roadside attraction.   We stopped, drank our ice water, and got a t-shirt. Next.

To reach our campground near the Badlands, we had to drive through the park and it was then that we discovered something.   We wouldn't need three days to explore this place. Maybe we should have stopped here *before* seeing Utah. We thought we would just hang out in Interior, South Dakota, and enjoy the 90-degree weather, but the community was significantly smaller than any other place we had been. With only 67 residents and one two-story house, owned by a park ranger, it wasn't a town tourists hung out in. We ventured into "town" to get a couple of necessities (water and bread) and found that what was advertised as the "uptown shopping district" included nothing more than three run-down buildings—the local grocery that inventoried less than a vacant convenience store, the post office, and an abandoned Native American craft store. I wanted to leave. Daniel didn't.

The next day we drove for 30 miles through the Badlands National Park to see a prairie dog town which was home to 6,000 of the cutesy creatures. These animals, too, were on Daniel's list to be found and photographed. (I wanted to see this list.) As we surveyed the thousands of holes, all I could think of was what might happen if the prairie dogs decided to take over the town of Interior. The humans wouldn't stand a chance—they would be outnumbered by almost 100 to one. I think it would be great for Interior; an animal uprising would add a fantastic amount of excitement and bring people from all over the world to see it.

We tackled both of the hikes labeled as the most difficult in the park because they were short and we had grown accustomed to the heat and exertion by now. We came upon a mountain goat and watched him scurry away, climbing steep inclines and exhibiting his incredible agility. It reminded me of those fitness freaks at Camelback Mountain in Phoenix. I had a sudden pang to leave South Dakota and drive back to Arizona. Couldn't we start the trip over again? At the very least, could we re-live the last few months?

Instead, we ate lunch at Cedar Pass Lodge, a famous and historic place that has existed since 1928, pre-dating the establishment of the national park. The dance hall and entertainment used to draw large crowds who had to walk to the venue because there were no roads yet. Regardless of those interesting facts and the mountain goats, we couldn't stay in a place we considered the interior of the middle of nowhere. To put the location of Interior, South Dakota in perspective, when Daniel asked a resident working at the park where he shopped, he said Rapid City, which is approximately 90 minutes west of Interior. With gas prices the way they were, I would have to go "pioneer"—buy a cow, learn to bake my own bread, hunt and fish. On second thought, I'd rather go home.

Mitchell was our last stop in the great state of South Dakota and thankfully, it was a one night stand. When we checked into the campground, the owner said, "Well, you're just in time for severe weather. When we knock three times on your door, it's time to take cover." Suddenly all of those jokes about mobile homes in a tornado became less funny to me. Daniel decided that we should just grab our valuables and leave the bus to its fate. Wouldn't that have been a great ending to the story of our adventure? I thought so, but the tornadoes avoided our area and we were able to visit the Corn Palace and still go home on the bus.

The Corn Palace was interesting to me and possibly Daniel, but Thomas was weary of quirky venues. We stayed long enough to get the grand tour from a boy who must have been a Scout because he looked all of 13 years old. If you haven't seen or been to the Corn Palace, it really is a good roadside attraction. Built in 1892, the original Corn Palace was a structure representing the fertility of the surrounding farmland and an open invitation to all settlers to come and develop it. Lewis and Clark had deemed the soil to be desert where nothing would ever grow, so the idea of the Corn Palace was to prove how wrong they had been. The building was covered with local crops and was so popular that a second Corn Palace was built in 1905 to accommodate the enormous crowds and possibly sway the state of South Dakota to choose Mitchell as its capital.

The capital was not placed there, though, and the second Corn Palace was condemned for safety reasons, so in 1921, a third and final Corn Palace was built. It is this building that receives a new design theme each summer. The structure operates as a tourist attraction between Memorial Day and Labor Day, while the rest of the year it serves as a community center and gymnasium where the local high school basketball team, the Kernels, play. Because Thomas was somewhat bored here, we looked through historical photos, bought a package of Corn

Palace popcorn, and left. No, it wasn't the most incredible tourist attraction, but there was something quintessentially "South Dakotan" about it; the building represented commitment and dedication to land and community, something still found in that beautiful, fertile prairie today.

As we left Mitchell and entered Minnesota, we noticed right away that the land was different. Sure, there were many farms, but the tall blowing grass of the prairie was left behind...along with a little bit of my heart. Would I ever have guessed that South Dakota would come to mean so much to me? As a girl who grew up watching "Little House on the Prairie," I should have known.

Vicariously Yours,
Traci

Sent: Thursday, July 13, 2006
Subject: The End of the Story

My heart ached at the thought of acknowledging the end of what was the most incredible experience of my life. A year couldn't possibly be over...the trip couldn't possibly be over...and yet it was. As Thomas's excitement grew about getting closer and closer to Indiana, Daniel and I silently mourned the conclusion of our dream. Our year of discovery, not only of this beautiful country, but of us was coming to an end.

I've never been the type of person who could walk away from some-thing without finishing—except for the Atkins and the South Beach diets, but a girl has to eat some bread, right? Anyway, here we go...a story picking up in Minnesota, carrying you through Wisconsin, stopping briefly in Illinois, and ending on the north side of Indianapolis with three exhausted people looking to re-enter the fast-paced lifestyle of social, occupational, and community commitments. It was what most people call daily life.

We lingered in Minneapolis for four days and yet saw nothing of Minnesota's famous artistic city. What we did see from top to bottom and every point in between was the Mall of America—a monument every bit as inspiring as Washington's or Lincoln's, if only to those who enjoy retail therapy. For those who have never been to the Mall, it was huge, with more than 500 stores, an indoor amusement park, and more Asian fast-food joints than necessary. The place was so big that many retailers leased additional spaces in order to catch shoppers on multiple floors. Starbucks, for example, had at least three locations that I frequented to "caffeine load" for my shopping marathon...and I do mean marathon.

For three days, Daniel took me to the mall in the morning and picked me up in the evening. It was the first time in several months that I had been alone and I enjoyed every minute of my "girly" experience. On the first day, I got my hair done and spent several hours combing through store after store on the first floor shopping for shoes, accessories, and non-campground clothes. Since we were close to home, I no longer had to restrict my souvenir shopping (shoes could be souvenirs, you know), and with no sales tax, I stocked up on the necessary, unnecessary and frivolous. By the time Daniel and Thomas arrived to help me with my bags, I had already rented a large locker for my first collection of goods and was quickly becoming overwhelmed with the second.

The second day was very much like the first, with the exception of my payload. Though I had covered the second and third floors, I didn't have much to show for it other than a new face. Yes, I gathered enough courage to have a makeover at one of those cosmetic places that separates the chapstick women from the painted girls. I had worn makeup before, but after living in the bus for a year and not caring what I looked like at any given moment, the idea of coming home with a polished look appealed to me. I braved the aisles of lipstick, end caps of mascara, and rounders of unrecognizable products just to feel feminine again. And do you know what? Thomas hated it. He told me I looked weird. I didn't care. I learned on this trip that 10-year-old boys did not affect my self image. See? Personal discovery and growth without therapy...it could happen.

Day three at the Mall of America involved very little shopping. The three of us took in the rides at the amusement park, watched a movie at the theater, and had dinner at Bubba Gump's. No amount of Starbucks could coax my body into shopping for more than a couple of days. As we returned to the KOA for our last night in Minnesota, I shared with Daniel and Thomas what I had learned about the fourth floor at the mall: in less than a year, it had gone from a thriving nightspot to a deserted cavern. Local residents didn't flock to the comedy club or piano bar. The once-bustling eateries now sat empty. Why? The town of Bloomington, Minnesota, passed an ordinance prohibiting smoking in public restaurants and bars, which in a short time, brought about the closing of all establishments on the fourth floor. I was shocked.

The entire state of Florida had the same ordinance; so did New York. Two of America's most popular tourist destinations continued to thrive despite the ban, and yet the fourth floor of the Mall of America imploded without the smokers. One of the employees told me that after the ordinance began, the entire mall saw a drop in sales of 10 percent. I didn't realize that many people still smoked. How could anyone afford $3.00/gallon for gas, $3.00/pack for smokes, and have any disposable income left to eat or buy new shoes?

While getting my hair done in Minneapolis, two locals listened to the tale of our drive around the country and, when I was finished, tried to give me ideas on what to do while in town. "You could go camping up north...but, you've already been to Canada." "You could go to the amusement park...but, you've already been to several of those." "You could go to the new water park...but, you're on your way to the Wisconsin Dells." The two of them looked at each other somewhat defeated and said, "I guess there's nothing to do because you've already done everything." Had we? Had we done everything? I didn't think so, but sometimes it felt like we had.

We were told by several people that we would love the Wisconsin Dells. Water parks, amusement parks, and entertainment venues...all creating an abundance of family fun in a charming town set along the river. The campground was conveniently located to the main attractions so, as soon as camp was set up, we ventured out in search of something to do. Thomas was in charge of our three days and his first choice of touristy fun was something called Wizard Quest, a treasure hunt "Harry Potter" style with clues, riddles, and a maze. I begged off and sent Daniel on the crusade to save the four magical creatures. While I walked down main street and visited the local book store, candy maker, and knickknack establishments—which all sold the same stuff at the same price—Daniel and Thomas thwarted evil, crawled through tight spaces, and saved the damsel in distress.

Ninety minutes later, they emerged and wanted to do something where solving riddles was not necessary. I bought tickets for a tour via the Original Wisconsin Ducks, so off we went. The tour operator was much more interested in telling bad jokes and pointing out deer than giving us any real history of the area. Deer weren't too exciting anymore, and the three of us walked away feeling disappointed.

Over the next couple of days, we invested our time in other family activities including miniature golf, horseback riding, and a magic show featuring Rick Wilcox. He was the highlight of our stay there. Thomas loved it and said that the next time we go to Vegas he would like to see a big-name magician like Lance Burton. Oh, *now* he wanted to do that. We didn't go to the water or theme parks. Thomas didn't want to. He had had enough amusements, attractions, and adventure. The only thing on his mind was home.

Home…only two more stops before we would be there. The Wisconsin Dells was not a bad place to visit, it just wasn't anything special for us and maybe that was our fault. Was it possible that we had seen too much of the United States and done too many incredible things? After spending time in San Antonio, Lake George, and San Francisco, how could the Wisconsin Dells even hope to compete? Would we go there again? I don't know. Thomas would say no. Daniel would say no. I would say maybe, but only if I got a few prized tickets to a Packers game...or at least a big block of real Wisconsin cheese.

As we were packing up to leave the Dells, Daniel and I realized that there was one more campground between us and home. We would unhook all of the cords, hoses, and cables just one more time. Although we were happy to leave the Wisconsin Dells, it was difficult...knowing that we were almost done with our trip...almost done with our beloved bus. We were looking forward to going to Milwaukee where we planned a dinner with Daniel's relatives. It would be nice to see familiar faces and spend time with family. Our campground was at the Wisconsin State Fairground and yes, it was scary. It was nothing more than a parking lot with various hookups and lots of people looking like they were in for the season of carnivals. "It's only for one night," Daniel and I told each other as we set up camp for the last time.

With a few hours before dinner, we ventured downtown to a waterfront park. As we strolled on the path, we talked about Bar Harbor, Boston, and Portsmouth where we watched boats come into the marina for hours while the tide rose and fell. A collective sigh was followed by silence. There were no words any of us could say to brighten the mood.   Sure, we wanted to go home, but it was difficult to accept that our days of combing beaches, smelling salty air, and watching campfire flames were nearing an end. How could we look out over a great lake and feel inspired by its beauty?

As we sat at a downtown brewery where a fog of cigarette smoke hung over the tables, Daniel's brother told us that if Thomas wanted a beer, it was no problem.   Children were allowed to drink alcohol in Wisconsin if they were with family. Did families in the state of cheese and Packers really drink together at public establishments? Aren't there laws in most of the Union regarding underage drinking?   Thomas thought this would be a fine time to try the local lager, but I disagreed. I didn't think my son should be downing any type of liquor at the ripe old age of ten.   He could barely hold his Mountain Dew.

Thursday, June 16, we rolled out of Wisconsin and entered familiar territory in Gurnee, Illinois. Asking for directions, mapping out routes, and following the atlas were no longer necessary. We were almost home.   Since we had no pre-arranged campground for the night, we hung out in Gurnee at Six Flags for a while and then hit the outlet mall. Thomas had grown several inches since our last visit to Great America, which meant he could ride anything he wanted...and he did.   We had a wonderful time for about two hours and then we were done.   Done standing in lines.   Done riding rides. Done amusing ourselves among strangers.   We wanted to go home...all of us.   Trying to avoid the bulk of Chicagoland traffic, we waited until after rush hour to begin the final drive home. At 10:00 p.m., we crossed the Indiana state line.

Daniel felt like driving all the way to Indianapolis instead of boondocking in Merrillville. The miles ticked away through the darkness and soon, as we passed Lebanon, Indiana, familiar sites filled our gaze. We turned on the radio, dialed into our hometown family favorite, and pointed out billboards and buildings, old and new, that lined I-465. We were almost there. It was midnight and for a moment, we considered dropping in on my parents to let them know we had made it, but decided to let them sleep. We pulled into "our" Wal-Mart parking lot at 12:30 a.m. and breathed a sigh of relief and sadness. Exhausted, we began getting ready for bed—sliding out the room extensions and dropping the jacks—and then something happened. Many times on this journey, Daniel and I had joked about how the bus would fall apart as we rolled back into town. When we tried to extend the driver-side slide, it refused to operate. Daniel and I looked at each other and burst out laughing. Thomas didn't think it was funny because it meant he'd be sleeping on the floor.

Friday morning we woke up in our hometown. Part of me was ecstatic and couldn't wait to go to my favorite store and stock up on *our* bread, butter, and yogurt, but the biggest part of me wanted to convince my son to go out for another year. If we hadn't already bought a house, I would have begged him to go again. Deep inside, I knew it was time for us to put Thomas first and return his life to normal with a house, a dog, a school, and some friends. It was time to come down off of the mountain and accept the life that most people have with commitments, schedules, meetings, and responsibilities. My wildest dream had come to an end and it was time to find something new to pursue. Although many of the details of our trip around the country had already become fuzzy, I would never forget how much the past 12 months had come to mean to me. I had grown in many ways personally, but the most marked growth came in the relationships between Daniel, Thomas and me. Through the many miles, big cities, small towns, beautiful scenery, funny stories, and occasional mishaps, Daniel and Thomas filled my heart with such joy and happiness that I couldn't imagine any greater life—on wheels or not—than mine. They say that home is where the heart is...and if that is true, then I suppose I never left mine. My home, my heart, has always been with my family. The journey was over and I knew that I would never again be the same person that left Indiana on June 3, 2005—none of us would ever be the same. And, as all good stories end, we are living happily ever after.

Vicariously Yours until the Next Time,
Traci

Bio: Traci Bray

Traci Bray, a suburban wife and mother, has done many things on her career path including professional meeting planning, interior decorating, and teaching water aerobics. However, nothing could have prepared her for the challenges and mishaps she and her family would encounter while living in a motorhome and traveling the United States. Encouraged and inspired by family and friends, Traci shares stories of life on the road from big cities to small towns and charming camp-grounds to Wal-Mart parking lots. Traci currently resides in Carmel, Indiana, with her husband, Daniel, and son, Thomas.

Acknowledgments

It is a wonderful thing to have many supportive friends and family members; however, it makes thanking them all difficult. What if I forget someone? I inevitably will and then that person will forever feel slighted. It is best then, I think, to apologize in advance for the omission of that one name. I assure you I do appreciate your loving kindness and encouragement. Consider yourself "special." Everyone else was mentioned *after* you.

My thanks go to Dan and Dave of New Century Publishing for convincing me that this story had legs. Without your belief and urging, this book would have remained a heap of emails to a limited audience.

To my editor, "sister" Heidi, I thank you for angering me enough to write something better than "De plane. De plane." Your insistence on making me stretch my ability caused this experience to be both exasperating and exhilarating. *Fortunately, I still think you're a great, beautiful little gal. Unfortunately, the three-headed monster of my literary skill—my habitual passive voice, asinine redundancies, and superfluous adverbial usage—might rear its ugly head again and you, my sister, will have to beat it back.*

I can never thank enough Kelly, Karen, and Gwen for inviting me to attend *The Oprah Winfrey Show.* It was an incredible day for me and the beginning of this wild ride into the unknown.

To Eric and the gang at Innovative, thank you for exceeding my expectations time and time again. Your collective creative abilities make me proud to know you and prouder still that I was smart enough to hire you.

JD, thanks for taking time out from your studying to proof my manu-script in record time. You saved me the horrible embarrassment of countless misspellings and typographical errors.

And finally, to my dearest husband and son...thank you for sharing this life-changing journey with me. Your patience throughout the process was amazing. You will never know how much I appreciated your easy laughter and listening ears. More than anything, I look forward to our next adventure together. But this time, I get to use the kitchen table.